Audience Engagement and the Role of Arts Talk in the Digital Era

Also by Lynne Conner

Pittsburgh in Stages: Two Hundred Years of Theater (2007).

In the Garden of Live Flowers (with Attilio Favorini, 2003).

Spreading the Gospel of the Modern Dance: A History of Newspaper Dance Criticism, 1850–1934 (1997).

Audience Engagement and the Role of Arts Talk in the Digital Era

Lynne Conner

palgrave
macmillan

AUDIENCE ENGAGEMENT AND THE ROLE OF ARTS TALK IN THE DIGITAL ERA

First published in 2013 by
PALGRAVE MACMILLAN®
in the United States—a division of St. Martin's Press LLC,
175 Fifth Avenue, New York, NY 10010.

Where this book is distributed in the UK, Europe and the rest of the world,
this is by Palgrave Macmillan, a division of Macmillan Publishers Limited,
registered in England, company number 785998, of Houndmills,
Basingstoke, Hampshire RG21 6XS.

Palgrave Macmillan is the global academic imprint of the above companies
and has companies and representatives throughout the world.

Palgrave® and Macmillan® are registered trademarks in the United States,
the United Kingdom, Europe and other countries.

ISBN: 978–1–137–02391–9

Library of Congress Cataloging-in-Publication Data

Conner, Lynne.
    Audience engagement and the role of arts talk in the digital era / by
    Lynne Conner.
        pages cm
        ISBN 978–1–137–02391–9 (alk. paper)
        1. Performing arts–Audiences. 2. Performing arts.
    3. Communication and culture. I. Title.
PN1590.A9C66 2013
790.2—dc23   2013023819

A catalogue record of the book is available from the British Library.

Design by Newgen Knowledge Works (P) Ltd., Chennai, India.

First edition: December 2013

10 9 8 7 6 5 4 3 2 1

For my sons, Miles and Roy de Klerk,
who make all my days meaningful.

CONTENTS

ACKNOWLEDGMENTS

This book would not have been possible without the support (intellectual, emotional, and financial) of Janet Sarbaugh and The Heinz Endowments Arts & Culture Program. I am particularly grateful to Janet Sarbaugh for her vision and sense of risk taking—two qualities that allowed us to be leaders in building grants-based laboratories for testing audience engagement practices. I am also grateful to the 12 Pittsburgh-based arts organizations (identified in the body of the book) that took part in the Endowments' Arts Experience Initiative and allowed me to test the original iteration of my Arts Talk hypothesis. Thank you.

Early on my ideas for this project were encouraged by Steven J. Tepper; I am grateful for his continued advice and support, including his insightful commentary on aspects of the book's structure and thesis articulation. I am also grateful to Andrew Taylor and Alan Brown for their interest in this work and for the opportunities they provided to present my research at various conferences and convenings.

Over the past decade, I have had fruitful conversations with many colleagues, students, friends, and family members willing to talk about the nature of talking with me, to share their reactions to my theorizing about the role of social interpretation in audience engagement, and to put some good ideas into my head. They include Ella Baff, James Barrett, Karla Boos, Abigail Colella, Miles de Klerk, Malik Gillani, Jessica Gogan, Lucas Held, Sali Ann Kriegsman, Tavia La Follette, Stephanie McConachie, Dan Mills, Allison Reader, Cyd Roach, Greg Sandow, Nat Shed, Louise Sicuro, Andrew Taylor, and Sarah Wilkes. Colby College provided research funds supporting the second phase of work on this project. My editors at Palgrave Macmillan have been welcoming and supportive. And the members of IFC (Catherine Besteman, Jill Gordon, Margaret McFadden, Mary Beth Mills, Andrea Tilden, and Ankeney Weitz) were generous with both intellectual sustenance and valuable housekeeping tips. I offer a special nod to comrade Margaret McFadden, whose challenge to write first and answer e-mails later helped me to turn the corner.

Finally, as ever, as always, my love and gratitude to Peter: day in, day out.

PREAMBLE: WE THE AUDIENCE

To have great poets there must be great audiences too.

—Walt Whitman

In twenty-first-century America, should the audience get to say what a work of art means, or why it holds value? Do audiences who have access to the public construction of meaning experience the arts in a richer, more satisfying way? And are they, as a result, more engaged? Yes.

This book is based on the theory that an audience member's pleasure is deeply tied with the opportunity to interpret the meaning and value of an arts event or arts object. Before the twentieth century, most arts environments were open to public interpretation because the arts event itself was a form of community property. The function of interpretation was understood as both a cultural duty and a cultural right; that is to say, the arts event's meaning could only be discerned through a thorough interpretive process, which, by definition, included the audience's perspective. This does not imply that there was regular, or even much, consensus in the process or protocol of interpretation; the history of arts reception is full of vivid examples of the violent ways in which artists, producers, and audiences disagreed. But that is just the point—art did not arrive with a fixed meaning. Rather, it was received by the audience as an inherently flexible commodity yielding ever-changing interpretations. Past cultures took as an article of faith what contemporary reception theory has argued at least since Gadamer: meaning does not exist in the arts event/object itself, or in the intentions of the artist, but rather in the perceiver's historically and culturally constituted horizons of understanding.[1] In ancient Athens, Elizabethan England, Renaissance Italy, Golden Age Spain, eighteenth-century Paris, and nineteenth-century America, a wide array of discursive practices facilitated the hermeneutic process and empowered the audience with various levels of sovereignty over the meaning and value of the art they consumed. These audiences enjoyed a culturally constructed understanding that their part in the interpretive function—their role as decoders of meaning—was central to the way in which the arts functioned in society. An arts *experience*, including witnessing an arts event/object and having the opportunity to participate in the articulation of its meaning and value, was a form of cultural capital negotiated largely through a wide array of public, internal, and backchannel discourses.

Today there are plenty of signals that we are once again moving into an era of renewed cultural vitality defined by the sheer pleasure of making meaning and ascribing value. Powered by a postmodern, postanalog ethos that challenges the twentieth-century notions of hierarchical mediation (in which experts interpret the art work and offer its meaning to a largely passive public), the twenty-first-century audience is retrieving its historical position as the centerpiece of the arts apparatus. This cultural turn is spurred on by a new wave of do-it-yourself social energy and the wide array of digitally powered engines that have helped to engender a sense of ownership in cultural practices ranging from science to politics to journalism to creative expression. The live | digital transformation has delivered us into a world where we expect to be able to participate in meaningful ways in a wide range of activities that analog generations received passively. Importantly for the purposes of this study, our participatory nation is, by nature and increasingly by practice, also an opinion nation; all of these participatory structures are in essence vehicles for the formation and dissemination of opinion.

Participation as a concept and a practice is of course pervasive within the US arts industry as well; found in major research reports, a host of web-based interfaces, products offered by arts consultants, and increasingly in the day-to-day work of arts organizations and individual artists. (An analysis of recent and current cultural participation practices in the arts sector is included in Chapter 6.) As an industry concept, participation was perhaps most visibly introduced in a widely discussed 2001 RAND report, *The Performing Arts in a New Era*, in which the definition of the term was broadened beyond simple attendance at an arts event to include involvement in related activities such as playing an instrument or belonging to a community theater group. The report's main message was based on its finding that participation in the arts as a social activity increased interest in attending professional arts events. The connotation of participation has since broadened to include the concept of audience engagement, which for most users signifies some type of emotional or affective relationship between consumer and arts event and/or arts organization. As I write this introduction in the fall of 2013, this more active definition of participation as engagement accounts for an ever-increasing number of initiatives, projects, and mission statements directed at helping arts organizations and arts workers reconnect with their audiences.

So what's the problem? Evidence suggests that the arts industry in the United States isn't fully prepared for this so-called redemocratization of the audience's position in the power structure of arts creation, delivery, and valuation. Some arts workers—my term for artists, presenters, producers, educators, and commentators—simply don't want the audience to take over the meaning-making process, since control over meaning (and thus value) is central to their vision of what it means to be an arts industry professional. Other arts workers, though energized by rising audience-centered hermeneutic practices, don't know how to facilitate those practices, how to participate in them, or even when to get out of the way of them. But the problem goes deeper than power struggles and ego positions among arts professionals. The evidence also suggests that twenty-first-century audience members, silenced by more than a hundred years of "audience etiquette" and a surrounding culture of hierarchical interpretive gatekeeping, are decidedly unprepared to take full advantage of this potential renaissance in the meaning-making process. They lack data; they lack analytical skills; and, perhaps most significantly, they lack the will/desire and the agency to enter the interpretive process with a level of preparedness and energy appropriate to the level of the art work itself. In short, they aren't that good at interpreting meaning and ascribing value.

I like to use the sports industry (from production to consumption) as a way to demonstrate my thesis. Imagine the Super Bowl culturally situated and institutionally produced in the same way as, say, an opera or a production of a Shakespeare play. In the weeks leading up to the game, instead of scores of pages of pregame analysis, data, and discourse in your local newspaper and online, you get one 800-word preview article (maybe). Instead of prolific radio and television coverage, you get silence on the broadcast bands. Instead of social interaction constructed around the upcoming game—social interaction filled with sports talk of all manner and open to a wide variety of people—you get small talk about anything but sports. On game day, you sit in a dark room, quiet and still. And, after the game is over? Instead of yet more free-flowing conversation about the event, again filled with sports talk of all manner and open to a wide variety of people, you get more silence (except for the one review that appears in the lone remaining local newspaper).

As I have written elsewhere, sports fans are constantly being invited to participate in publically structured processes of interpretation; in our society, opportunities for the analysis of and debate about sporting events abound. The distinction here is obvious—we don't have the same attitude or approach to being an arts fan as we do to being a sports fan. We rarely carry the energy of an art-experience into our work environment, and we rarely (if ever) feel knowledgeable or empowered enough to debate the meaning or value of an arts event (unless we are arts professionals and then we feel perhaps too empowered). Why is it that sports fans don't hesitate to analyze and debate? I firmly believe it is because they have been given the cultural permission to express their opinions openly and the tools they need to back up their opinions.[2]

If sports were culturally packaged the way the arts are in the United States, would that industry be facing the same issues with engagement that the arts face right now? *Arts Talk* argues that over the course of the twentieth century arts audiences in the United States lost access to the interpretive process, resulting in a lack of real, committed interest in the serious arts. The book does *not* argue that audiences don't currently engage in the act of interpretation (this happens as an embodied response—the brain is busy making meaning of everything it encounters), but rather that without public opportunities to articulate our individual decoding processes, the pleasure of the interpretive function is cut short and thus engagement is limited. The ruling idea of *Arts Talk* is a simple one: The pleasure inherent in the interpretative function is enhanced significantly when meaning making is made social.

This does not mean that meaning making on an individual, personal level is not important or valued. The quiet and private contemplation of an arts experience is a critical form of authoring meaning, and it is of course a part of every receptor's experience. By stressing the importance of social interpretation I am not creating a hierarchy of value about how meaning should be made. I am instead attempting to acknowledge the fact that participatory activities can also include meaning making around the arts. Art (expression through metaphor) is inherently a learning system. It is not inherently a delivery system, as it became under capitalism. Rather than seeing "us" as producers and "them" as consumers, I posit that arts workers join their patrons to gather and share opinions and, importantly, to learn from each other through the exchange of information and ideas; in short, to form a new kind of audience-centered learning community engaged in a collective effort to decode the layers of information that constitute the value of great art.

To that end, this book operates using three terms with very specific definitions: (1) *social interpretation*: audience-produced meaning making that occurs in/through public settings and mechanisms; (2) *arts experience*: the total phenomenon of arts-going, including not just the moment of reception but also the ongoing phenomenology of pre- and postspectatorship; and (3) *Arts Talk*, a new modality for arts-centered conversations that reframes the critical roles that both dialogue (consensus building and the creation of something new out of group exchange) and discussion (analysis and debate over competing points of view) can play in the organization of a healthy and productive arts ecology. In this volume, Arts Talk connotes not just literal talk, but also a spirit of vibrancy and engagement among and between people who share an interest in the arts. Arts Talk connects us in the profoundest of human ways—as hearts and minds looking to make the world mean something.

The Arts Experience

This book is the result of many years of thinking about audiences and the arts experience in American culture. In my professional life as a theater and dance historian and a playwright, I've both studied historical audiences and been judged by contemporary audiences. In my personal life as a steady consumer of the arts, I have been engaged and disengaged, empowered and disempowered, loyal and removed. But only in the past ten years or so, as a consultant working closely with foundations and arts organizations on the issue of audience engagement, have I come to understand the way in which access to the interpretive process and the power structure that controls it informs the health and ultimate sustainability of the arts in American life.

Between 2004 and 2008, I was the principal investigator for the Arts Experience Initiative (AEI), an innovative grants-based project organized and funded by The Heinz Endowments' Arts and Culture Program under the direction of Janet Sarbaugh. Designed as a laboratory, the project goals were based on the argument that what contemporary arts audiences most want—and most lack—is the opportunity to formulate responsible opinions about their experiences with the "serious arts," the term I employ here to designate art forms that are primarily concerned with serving aesthetic inquiry rather than commercial forces. Over the course of two grant cycles, established arts organizations in the Pittsburgh area were invited to test new practices dedicated to enhancing the audience's satisfaction with an arts event through experiences that support and expand the event itself. A total of twelve arts organizations engaged in a two-year effort to create and facilitate enrichment programming designed to encourage an audience-centered exchange around the meaning of the arts.[3] As part of the laboratory structure, each participating organization was required to assemble a project team made up of executive and program-level staff and at least one board member. Team members designed and implemented the project together. In addition, team members were required to attend periodic peer convenings, hosted by the Endowments, in which they shared findings and sought/offered advice. Most unusually, success was *not* measured by numbers of audience participants in these programs, but rather by the level of expressed engagement among both the organization team members and the audience participants. The grantees were encouraged to rigorously evaluate their projects on a regular basis and, if warranted, to change their program design at any point in the two-year cycle. Traditional metrics, such as survey tools, were used by some organizations, but with permission to look beyond quantitative measurements the AEI teams began to experiment with a variety of qualitative tools. Anecdotal exchanges between team members and audience participants, for example, were seen as valuable indicators of whether an enrichment experience was in fact influencing a person's level of engagement.

While outcomes varied among the participating organizations, the Heinz findings support the working hypothesis I brought in to the experiment: Most people need to talk in order to fully process their opinions, and, given effective facilitation and the right physical environment, most audience members are willing to share their opinions in a public setting and to openly engage in social interpretation. Several themes emerged from the Heinz experiment that continue to influence my thinking about how contemporary audiences construct meaning and derive pleasure: (1) The key role that talking plays in the interpretive function; (2) The necessity of effective facilitation to launch productive talk about the arts; and (3) The impact of the physical environment on the vitality and effectiveness of arts talk. The Heinz findings also demonstrate just how fluid the context, style, and point of departure for talking can be, from creative activity in the gallery to hands-on technique workshops at the ballet barre to social gatherings after the play to digital conversation on an organization's website to patron-organized dialogue in restaurants and living rooms. All of these varied Arts Talk activities produce the kind of social interpretation this book is focused on defining and promoting.

Another significant outcome of the Arts Experience Initiative was the realization that, over the course of the twentieth century, arts workers have generally forgotten the democratic impulse behind the ideal of a citizen audience. By buying a ticket, the audience elects us to represent them as curators of an arts experience. They do not, however, elect us to prescribe or control its meaning. In order to create a more perfect union of arts workers and arts audiences for the twenty-first century, we need to acknowledge that when it comes to making meaning and ascribing value, our audiences want to have a voice, and they want that voice to matter. All of us—arts workers and audiences alike—want the opportunity to formulate and exchange opinions about the arts events we see, hear, and feel.

WHOSE AUDIENCE?

In English-speaking contexts, the term audience (from the Latin *auditorium*, or hearing place) is generally interchangeable with spectator (from the Latin *specere*, to look), though the shift of emphasis between hearing and viewing implied by each word's etymology has some implications in American culture, where the word spectator is more frequently associated with sports going than arts going.[4]

The idea of a temporarily assembled group known as the "audience" has been discussed and interrogated in Western culture throughout recorded history. As a situated phenomenon, the audience's live presence has no permanent status; what constitutes *the* audience on one night will have no relevance the next night and so on. But despite its temporary status, *the* audience has consistently been understood as a monolith. In sociological terms, *the* audience is sometimes a "crowd" and sometimes a "public," the latter defined as gatherings of people (physical or virtual) that "exhibit a dimension of debate or discussion absent in crowds or mass."[5] In political terms, *the* audience has often been construed as dangerous: feared for its ability to incite civil disobedience, to become violent, and to spread prurience and disease. In aesthetic terms, *the* audience can be friend or foe: not just capable of lifting the arts experience through the power of a positive reception but also alarmingly susceptible to making the "wrong" choices about what constitutes "good" art.

There is of course no monolithic definition of what an audience is. I can use it here as a collective term, but I cannot, in fact, speak of an essential American audience any more than I can speak of an essential American. Obviously, social constructions of age, gender, ethnicity, and class impact what an audience is and how it functions in a given place, time, and community, and just as obviously no study of this size can assess all of those variables. Further, critical constructions of audience types are so numerous in the literature (from sociology, media studies, performance history, psychology, etc.) that I cannot comprehensively survey them here.[6] I can, however, acknowledge as transparently as possible the self-imposed limitations of my analysis. To begin, *Arts Talk* is focused on the United States and specifically on arts-going protocols derived largely from the Central European tradition. To that end, the review and discussion of hermeneutical scholarship in Chapter 1 and the survey of historical audiences in Chapter 2 focuses on data collected from primary sources produced by Europeans. Many of the issues associated with Western arts reception are not shared by non-Western cultural traditions as they exist in twenty-first-century America, however. It is clear, for example, that African American and Hispanic audiences have constructed and maintain an active interpretive ethos inside and outside the concert hall and playhouse, an ethos that illustrates a different modality for engagement. It is also clear that, as formerly traditional boundaries are crossed in both live and mediated settings, alternate American modalities for spectating are increasingly influencing mainstream audience experience and expectations. As I explore in Part II, studying and analyzing culturally determined differences in styles of talk as well as in audience protocol and etiquette are critical to an understanding of contemporary audiences.

Another self-imposed limitation in my definition has to do with my decision not to address in detail the assumed differences among theater audiences, dance audiences, museum visitors, etc. This is because I believe that the central concern of this book—how to engender a productive interpretive environment—can be applied to any participatory community. I acknowledge that for most audience members it is harder to talk about nonnarrative dance forms than, say, traditional theater, and that the operation of spectating in a museum is phenomenologically different from spectating in a darkened auditorium. The nature of a performance event positions the audience inside a single space and thus renders them a collective, while the visual arts, in galleries and exhibit halls, process individuals. Clearly the impact and effect of a collective audience as opposed to individual visitors is significant. That acknowledged, both audience cultures have been encouraged to understand their roles as interpreters to be private, and both have undergone a century of etiquette-as-arts-appreciation conditioning that has all but silenced social interpretation. Because of that shared history of silencing, I believe that the fundamental aspects of the Arts Talk model laid out in this book are fully operational in both settings.

Arts Talk argues that regardless of how the art form operates, arts workers have to learn how to tap into embodied and socially constructed hermeneutic protocols and to carry them forward into a productive audience learning community where multiple forms (live and digital) of Arts Talk take place. By regularly citing examples from a range of performing and visual arts forms I acknowledge a wide spectrum of audience experience without essentializing audiences in terms of the type of art work they consume. The idea here is to investigate how the interpretive process happens beneath the hood; to grasp the embodied as well as the socially constructed natures of making meaning in order to apply them to a variety of contexts and environments.

Arts Talk also investigates the impact of the digital turn. The merging of live and digital constructs in everything from theater to classrooms to healthcare has been and continues to be under considerable scrutiny within the academy and among cultural critics writing in the public realm. And for good reason. To call the emergence of a live | digital realm a paradigm shift is perhaps the understatement of the millennium. That a screening of contemporary American lives has been accomplished is undeniable. There is hardly a person in the United States, regardless of class, whose everyday behavior is not impacted and influenced by screens. That a merging of live and digital that defies the old binary between a live performance and a recorded one is underway is also, I believe, undeniable. From museums to orchestra halls, screens, and their attendant digital idioms, now impact and influence audiences of all types, and in many circumstances. Red-level anxiety over this shift is evidenced in a range of books, articles and editorials, from Andrew Keen's *The Cult of the Amateur: How Today's Internet Is Killing Our Culture and Assaulting Our Economy* to every third op-ed piece in *The New York Times* and *Wall Street Journal*. It reminds me of political theorist Antonio Gramsci's famous observation from his *Prison Notebooks*: "The crisis consists precisely in the fact that the old is dying and the new cannot be born; in this interregnum a great variety of morbid symptoms appear."[7]

Perhaps this high anxiety is also because the very concept of liveness is actually relatively new. According to performance theorist Philip Auslander, the word "live" as a qualifier for the word "performance" first made an appearance in the 1930s when recording technology was ubiquitous enough for society to conceive of the difference between a live event (stage) and a recorded event (film, recording, etc.). Auslander notes that audio recording technology "brought the live into being" in such a way that the difference between the original live event (a pianist playing a sonata) and its recording (the gramophone disk) were clearly distinguishable. The advent of the radio, however, blurred that distinction because listeners could not be sure whether what they were hearing was being broadcast live or from a recording, subverting the "formerly complementary relationship between live and recorded modes of performance" and thus reconceiving the relationship between them "as one of binary opposition rather than complementarity."[8] Now, 120 years later, the complementarity of the live and the digital realms (in ways unimaginable to Gugliegmo Marconi) is firmly at the nexus of the live | digital construct. The question for the arts industry is whether there is a productive interplay between the live performance experience and digital expressions of emotion, inquiry, and insight that flow from that experience. Could, for example, the use of Twitter, Facebook, or texting actually inform and advance social interpretation not just on line but also in physically copresent environments? The serious arts industry is under real pressure to acknowledge and answer these questions. As the Google Chrome commercial says, "The web is what you make of it."

STRUCTURE AND METHODOLOGY

Arts Talk is a journey from theory to practice. It is designed to be read and used by a wide range of arts workers: arts administrators who want to nurture their audience's capacity to explore the art work they produce and present; artists who want to be in dialogue with their communities; arts educators looking for additional tools for launching authentic conversations about the arts; arts students seeking their own tools for participating in meaningful conversations; and arts funders who want to expand their understanding of the meaning and value of the work they support. It is also a book that is, I hope, of value to the general public—to the members of the citizen audience who long for the chance to talk about their experiences with the arts as a part of everyday discourse.

Arts Talk is, then, quite deliberately a work of public scholarship. Traditional academic epistemologies often idealize the distance between inquiry and application. Public scholarship pursues active engagement with a community of users and holds as a central value the direct connection between the work and specific public groups; its best work contributes to the public good by integrating discovery, learning, and public engagement.[9] As a public scholar, I am interested in the intersection between history, theory, and practice as it is applied, thus the determined movement from history/theory to practice over the course of this book's two parts.

In **Part I: Defining Arts Talk**, I explore the fundamentals of social interpretation by laying out a road map of the meaning-making operation marked by five signposts: an experience (combined with) taste (produces) talk (which arouses) pleasure (thus engendering) engagement. **Chapter 1: Road Map to Pleasure** begins with a review of the thinking around the hermeneutic process geared toward providing definitions and intellectual context for these five signposts before focusing on what I have termed the taste-talk-pleasure Arts Talk calculus. The chapter includes a discussion of the audience experience as a broader construct in which a full measure of the interpretive process/journey is considered—not just in the moment of reception but also what happens when the spectator leaves the arts venue. (This is in contract to most of the critical writing on the subject of audiences and interpretation, which is concerned with physical behavior and cognition *while* spectating.)[10] **Chapter 2: Eras of Social Interpretation** is a diachronic investigation of historical arts events (what I call eras) that demonstrate an authorized audience. Historically, how did audience groups debate the meaning and value of a work of art? What role did taste, talk, and pleasure play in those public constructs? How did public processes impact the autonomy of individuals to make meaning? I argue that there is a clear historical link between a given community's interest in attending an arts event and the opportunity to inform its meaning. Similarly, the quest of **Chapter 3: Geographies of Social Interpretation** is to better understand the mechanics of Arts Talk through a synchronic analysis of contemporary practices in popular culture (what I call geographies) that demonstrate an authorized audience. What aspects of the Arts Talk calculus are currently in use in other cultural industries such as sports, gaming, and various new media practices? What role do taste, talk, and pleasure play in these public constructs? As I illustrate, there is a clear contemporary relationship between a given community's interest in attending a sporting event or playing an online game, for instance, and the opportunity to participate in the social construction of its meaning.

In **Part II: Facilitating Arts Talk**, I analyze the role and function of dialogue building and effective learning environments before offering ideas on how to design and implement a culture of Arts Talk. My goal is to provide the critical resources for arts workers and audiences to connect through a rich and complex conversation about the arts in their lives. **Chapter 4: Audience Learning Communities** offers an analysis of adult learning from both a biological and cultural perspective, identifies a set of values associated with effective learning environments, and explores those values as structures for implementing a culture of Arts Talk. **Chapter 5: Fundamentals of Productive Talk** is an analysis of the role and function of productive talk—what it is, how it operates, and what it takes to get it going. From this review I glean techniques for listening, argumentation, and debate as well as articulation of ideas, feelings, emotions—all elements of Arts Talk. I also identify methodologies for sustaining complexities in our dialogues about the arts: How do we live with the colliding truths of great art and how can a mindful tolerance of complexity lead to insight (both individually and collectively)? **Chapter 6: Arts Talk** concludes the book's journey with an analysis of the role of cultural participation and power within the contemporary arts industry before exploring five values for building the kinds of audience learning communities capable of supporting meaningful and productive social interpretation. All three chapters in Part II offer a new modality for arts appreciation in the twenty-first century. By understanding how taste, talk, and pleasure impact our experience with the arts we are better able to explore the environmental, social, philosophical, and psychological conditions that *allow* us to talk, productively and pleasurably, about the meaning and value of the arts.

Blessings of Liberty

Arts Talk provides historical background and a review of current thinking about the interpretive process in order to offer ideas and insights into building audience-centered and audience-powered conversations about the arts. My goal is to help arts workers and audience members think their way through to the best approach for their specific situations and for their specific organizational capacities. By looking outside of the arts industry and academic fields devoted to audience studies and hermeneutics, I mine the wider world of inquiry and experience for ideas, data, and modalities of practice. *Arts Talk* is not, however, a formula. I offer no monolithic solutions here, no single approach or set of step-by-step instructions, and no definitive list of best practices. Instead, I ask my readers to process the book's material in such a way as to produce methodologies appropriate for their own needs. What I am offering is information, a point of view, a set of values and, I hope, a measure of inspiration. One last lofty goal. I hope this book will provide the motivation for arts workers to take the time to ponder and wonder about their own relationship with the arts and with the process of meaning making. Even more, I hope that the book will encourage all of its readers to examine their search for personal and shared experience in and through the arts.

Ultimately, *Arts Talk* is intended to help arts workers *and* arts audiences to engage in a productive interpretative process and thus to reclaim the deeper pleasures associated with attending the arts. In a time of significant crisis for the not-for-profit arts industry (in both economic and social capital terms), this purpose ought to have traction with both constituencies. Do we need the arts in American society? Obviously. I won't waste anyone's time here by defending the place of the arts in human happiness. The real question for all of us, arts workers and audience members alike, is how to make sure that the future of the arts in American society includes the audience in an authentic way. For if Great Art is great because it yields itself up to a variety of interpretations over time and across cultures, it follows that a great audience has the capacity to meaningfully interpret that work for its own place and time. Our goal should be to empower audiences to engage in constructive and pleasurable dialogue about the arts and to celebrate those audiences who, by virtue of their vital and engaged presence, can turn any arts space into a site of public assembly ripe for intellectual and emotional connection. Our vision should be to provide twenty-first-century audiences with a bill of rights assuring that every member of the audience has by definition not only the right to interpret but also the right to be heard as a viable interpreter.

I will have succeeded with my project if, by the end of the book, arts workers understand why using the increasingly popular expression "audience-centered cultural institution" ought to be deemed unnecessarily repetitive. The audience *is* us.

PART I

DEFINING ARTS TALK

MESSENGERS OF THE GODS

When Hermes, the messenger god, discovered language and writing and gave it to humans, he invited us to engage in the process of translating our experience and perception into words; in short, he gave us the gift of interpretation. In homage to Hermes, the Greek word for interpret (*hermeneu*) focuses on the role of language: how we use it to organize our sense of the world by linking words into structures of thought; how those structures express, intend, and signify other structures of thought until, at last, we have meaning—meaning that can be communicated to others. But do we interpret in order to understand, or is understanding a function of a reflexive, elemental need to make sense of our worlds? Is this desire to make meaning for ourselves and then to share our thoughts with others what makes us human? As cognitive psychologist Paul Bloom notes in *How Pleasure Works*, developmental psychologists have "long marveled at how children naturally point, wave, and grunt to draw attention to interesting things in their environment. This might seem like the simplest skill until you realize that no other species does this. By some accounts, this desire to share our thoughts is responsible for much of what makes us human, including language and our sophisticated culture."[1]

When it comes to the interpretive process, we are all messengers of the gods. We find real pleasure in making meaning and, importantly, in sharing our understandings with others. By pleasure I do not mean comfort or ease, but rather the deep satisfaction that comes from working something through. It is satisfying to work at processing an opinion about the interesting things that surround us. Especially art. What can be more pleasurable for me as an audience member than experiencing a work of art not as a product with a fixed meaning but rather as a process of meaning making dependent on my participation? And what can be more satisfying than sharing that process with other audience members? The psychological reality and subsequent emotional value of this basic human desire to make meaning and then to share one's findings with others is the underlying tenet of this book.

But what, precisely, is meaning making? Analyzing and articulating the nature of meaning—the message that is intended or expressed or signified—is fundamental to the history of thinking, of course; in the Western tradition, this work extends back to Plato's *Dialogues* and Aristotle's *On Interpretation* and continues to this day in a range of disciplines that includes semiotics, philosophy, aesthetics, anthropology, sociology, phenomenology, media studies, performance theory, reception theory, cognitive science, and learning science. For Plato, thinking (and its attendant meaning making) is a dialogue of the soul with itself. For Aristotle, meaning making arises from the relationship between two kinds of things: signs and the things they intend, express, or signify. When words are spoken, they become symbols or signs of the affections of the soul.[2] In Aristotle's view, the logical structure of language is the way in which the "facts" of the world are worked through and conveyed to oneself and to others. Language, then, becomes the representation of meaning—the machine that allows the soul's dialogue to emerge and to transmit "what is meant." Once that communication is launched, meaning making begins its journey into the realm of interpretation. The Latin word *translatio*, meaning "to carry over on the other side," conveys the essential idea of this journey, the "translation, or 'interpretation', of thought into language."[3] It's worth noting here the interchangeability of the nouns "translator" and "interpreter" in contemporary usage. Implicit in this definition of translation is the key idea that interpretation is both a practice (transforming something into another idiom for the purpose of understanding) and, more generally, a way of knowing, or understanding, a phenomenon. The human mind is always busy "translating" symbols (whether language-based, corporeal, or natural) in the external world. The human mind is also always looking for opportunities to integrate those symbols into a higher-order unity, in the same way that letters integrate into words, words into sentences, sentences into poems and novels and essays and plays, etc. Indeed, it is in these examples of higher-order unity that meaning not only takes concrete shape but also takes on its deep, satisfying, life-determining quality.

In Western thought, theories on how the interpretative function operates both culturally and cognitively were first systematized under the label "hermeneutics," a term traceable to early nineteenth-century philosopher Friedrich Schleiermacher.[4] Critical to Schleiermacher's thinking (and others of that era) is the idea of hermeneutics as a science organized around the project of systematizing human knowledge: Can we locate a set of rules, a group of interpretive techniques, that will help us to understand texts and thus to make meaningful any set of data regardless of its disciplinary focus or cultural situation? "Prior to Schleiermacher, the task of textual interpretation was thought to require different methods as determined by the type of text to be interpreted. Thus, legal texts gave rise to a juridical hermeneutic, sacred scripture to a biblical hermeneutic, literary texts to a philological hermeneutic, and so on."[5] Wilhelm Dilthey, a transitional figure writing in the mid-nineteenth century, extended the discourse by arguing for hermeneutics to be categorized along with the fields of epistemology and logic so as to become an "essential connecting link between philosophy and the historical disciplines, an essential component in the foundation of the human studies themselves."[6] Both Schleiermacher and Dilthey wanted to find a theory for their concept of "'understanding', an intellectual activity seen as different both in object and in form from explaining."[7]

The field of modern philosophical hermeneutics, influenced by Martin Heidegger, repositions hermeneutics as "structures of Being," that is, activities of understanding *and* interpretation.[8] From Heidegger, German philosopher Hans-Georg Gadamer articulates the idea of the *hermeneutic circle*, or the acknowledgment that our approach to understanding a historical phenomenon (a text, a work of art) is necessarily conditioned by the series of interpreters (and interpretations) that precede us. In *Truth and Method*, Gadamer proposes that the job of interpreting can be understood as the fusing of two horizons: that of the interpreter and that of the object being interpreted. (A horizon is the context of interpretation.) "A person who is trying to understand a text is always projecting," argues Gadamer. "He projects a meaning for the text as a whole as soon as some initial meaning emerges in the text. Again, the initial meaning emerges only because he is reading the text with particular expectations in regard to a certain meaning. Working out this fore-projection, which is constantly revised in terms of what emerges as he penetrates into the meaning, is understanding what is there."[9]

Of particular resonance here is Gadamer's acknowledgment that our personal horizons, which include our biases and limited/situated historical understandings, are an essential component of any interpretive act. And even more resonant is his understanding, from Heidegger, of the implications of what he calls the hermeneutic circle:

> Just as we cannot continually misunderstand the use of a word without its affecting the meaning of the whole, so we cannot stick blindly to our own fore-meaning about the thing if we want to understand the meaning of another. Of course this does not mean that when we listen to someone or read a book we must forget all our fore-meanings concerning the content and all our own ideas. All that is asked is that we remain open to the meaning of the other person or text. But this openness always includes our situating the other meaning in relation to the whole of our own meanings or ourselves in relation to it... This places hermeneutical work on a firm basis. A person trying to understand something will not resign himself from the start to relying on his own accidental fore-meanings, ignoring as consistently and stubbornly as possible the actual meaning of the text through what the interpreter imagines it to be. Rather, a person trying to understand a text is prepared for it to tell him something."[10]

For Gadamer, this fusion of horizons, the ideal state wherein the tensions between the lineage of the interpreter's historical horizon or range of vision (the fore-meanings referred to in the above quotation) and another interpreter or interpretation's horizon, is resolved through meaningful conversation, a belief we will return to in Part II in the discussion about how to launch an Arts Talk ethos.

Another well-known use of the horizon metaphor comes from Hans Robert Jauss, whose "horizon of expectations" refers to the shared set of criteria that a reader (or an audience member) uses to judge a text (or arts event/object) in any given period. For Jauss, these criteria are situated, which is to say that the values used to interpret (and judge) a work are formed through social structures, like education, and, as such, are not stable from one generation to another. Jauss's work is part of the reader-response critical tradition, which posits that in order to understand the meaning of a text it is necessary to acknowledge the historical horizons by which a reader creates meaning. As he famously said in his 1965 essay, "Literary History as a Challenge to Literary Theory," "A literary work is not an object which stands by itself and which offers the same face to each reader in each period. It is not a monument which reveals its timeless essence in a monologue."[11] The important idea here, for our purposes, is his insistence that in order to make meaning we must understand the difference between an art event's interpretive position in the past and its potential meaning in the present. This, as performance theorist Susan Bennett puts it, "dispels the notion of objective and timeless meaning contained independently within a text."[12] A particularly resonant explication of this phenomenon is contained in literary critic Terence Hawkes's essay, "A Sea Shell," in which he likens the process of reading *Hamlet* to picking up a conch shell at the shore. What we say we are doing is listening to the ocean (reading Shakespeare's intentions). But what we are actually doing is listening to our heart muscle pump blood through our own vascular system (rereading our own foremeanings).[13] In other words, we are conditioned to understand what we already understand and to find new "truths" in the rediscovery of our already established "truths." We are limited by our cultural and social horizons.

More recent work on the problem of meaning construction encompasses not only verbal and nonverbal communication, but also other aspects of understanding and cultural learning that happen before formal language takes over. Contemporary theorists, working from disciplinary points of view as disparate as cognitive psychology, anthropology and reception theory, routinely acknowledge interpretation as both a function of social constructions *and* an embodied process arising out of the *mind/brain*, term employed by cognitive scientists to underscore the fact that soft phenomena such as emotions, which are often ascribed to "the mind" (as a metaphorical container), are, in fact, hardwired physiological realities locatable as neural activity in the brain. For cognitive psychologist Jerome Bruner, meaning and meaning making are intertwined with our conceptions of "the real." As he argues in *Culture in Mind*, people "live out the details of their daily lives in terms of what they conceive to be real: not just rocks and mountains and storms at sea, but friendship, love, respect are known as false or real...This is the domain of meaning making, without which human beings in every culture fall into terror."[14] Cognitive anthropologist Bradd Shore stresses that meaning making "involves the perpetual encounter of a meaning-seeking subject and a historically and culturally orchestrated world of artifacts."[15] Cultural models, he argues, "render certain kinds of experience perpetually significant and readily communicable within a community."[16] For Shore, as with other cognitive-based theorists, the first point of meaning making, the perceptual encounter, is an aspect of the mind/brain—again, an embodied process of the physical mind/brain rather than of the metaphorical mind. The field of neuroaesthetics takes the mind/brain concept a step further by testing the relationship between the physical brain and the contemplation and creation of a work of art.[17] By looking for the neural correlates of artistic judgment, these researchers are in the process of identifying the physiology of aesthetics: what areas of the brain produce what types of artistic activity (both creative and interpretive acts).

This is interesting in juxtaposition to a number of emerging concepts about the evolution of human cognition and its relationship to meaning making in an arts context. In evolutionary anthropologist Ellen Dissanayake's recent study of the relationship between art making and the "infancy of the human species," she notes that meaning was first located in "what 'felt right'—a full stomach, a safe environment, nearness of familiar others, or ways to acquire these" and that, over a millennia of human evolution,

> the mind increasingly became a "making-sense organ": interrelated powers of memory, foresight, and imagination gradually developed and allowed humans to stabilize and confine the stream of life by making connections between past, present, and future, or among experiences and observations. Rather than taking the world on its own terms of significance and value (the basic survival needs, sought and recognized by instinct), people came more and more to systemize or order it and act upon it. Eventually this powerful and deep-rooted desire to make sense of the world became part of what it meant to be human—to *impose* sense or order and thereby give the world additional (what we now call "cultural") meaning.[18]

In *Engaging Audiences: A Cognitive Approach to Spectating in the Theatre*, performance theorist Bruce McConachie extends the argument to audience behavior, asserting that the "primary assumption of social constructivism—that social and cultural learning (nurture) operate separately from genetics and 'hard-wired' cognition (nature)—is no longer tenable."[19] For McConachie, the hardwired thesis at the core of cognitive theory puts into question the subjectivity and relativism of past hermeneutics, since there is "no culture without cognition and no cognition without nature"[20] and, therefore, "social constructions of class, age, gender, and so on, though not unimportant, constrict audience imagination less than we have generally supposed."[21] In terms of meaning construction, then, the suggestion here is that audiences arrive at the moment of interpretation with a set of embodied tools at their disposal that they may use in conjunction with the social constructions that model interpretation in particular circumstances. McConachie's investigation of the mind/brain offers some interesting insights into the underlying functions of perception and meaning making and opens up new ways of thinking about the role of social interpretation.

I end this brief introductory survey of the hermeneutic landscape by acknowledging the fact that the scope of this book cannot possibly interrogate the vast literature surrounding the theory and practice of interpretation. Nor can I realistically offer a comprehensive summary—a project that would constitute a volume of its own due to the way in which definitions and conceptualizations have been parceled out across disciplinary silos over the centuries. Rather, my project in Chapter 1 is to identify some basic cognitive and social structures of interpretation that surface in theories and definitions from a range of disciplines. The goal is to help arts workers grapple with these siloed understandings and, inevitably, with colliding truths associated with discipline-specific theories on the nature and function of interpretation.

CHAPTER 1

ROAD MAP TO PLEASURE

*The meaning of life is whatever you ascribe it to be. Being alive is
the meaning.*

—Joseph Campbell[1]

Chapter 1 is organized as a kind of road map of the meaning-making
operation marked by five signposts: **an experience** (combined with)
taste (produces) **talk** (which arouses) **pleasure** (thus engendering)
engagement. It is important to underline here that I am not positing
these signposts as *the* essential components of the meaning-making
process, but rather as useful markers for the journey that most audience members take in their urge to participate in the construction of
meaning. These terms are useful in this context because they arise
in disciplinary theories *and* are also well used (indeed, perhaps over-
used) in the arts industry at large. By starting with an examination of
their etymology, social usage, and historical position within theories
of meaning making, I hope to produce a useful calculus for the Arts
Talk model: **taste** plus **talk** equals **pleasure**. The reader is probably
noticing at this juncture that my proposed calculus does not adhere
to the normative assumption that talk is a product of engagement
(we're excited about something so we want to talk about it). In fact,
both the historical record and what we know about how embodied
learning operates support the notion that it is the other way around,
as I explore below and in the following chapters.

AN EXPERIENCE

The *Oxford English Dictionary* gives the following definition for the
word experience: "The fact of being consciously the subject of a state

or condition, or of being consciously affected by an event; personal knowledge; to feel; to undergo."[2] To be consciously affected is to undergo a change in condition. This is the sine qua non of human meaning making—a movement toward knowledge. The "impulse to make meaning from experience," according to Bradd Shore, "exploits analog rather than digital processing and distinguishes human from machine-intelligence."[3]

Experience alone, however, is not the subject of the Arts Talk model. I refer here to educational theorist John Dewey's distinction between *experience* ("the constant interaction between live creature and environment") and *an experience* ("when the material experienced runs its course to fulfillment").[4] For Dewey, an experience is characterized by unity ("a single quality that pervades the entire experience in spite of the variation of its constituent parts")[5] and a sense of satisfaction through consummation. Experiences alone are often inchoate, a kind of drifting without "genuine initiations or concludings. One thing replaces another, but does not absorb it and carry it on. There is experience, but so slack and discursive that it is not an experience. Needless to say, such experiences are anesthetic."[6] This is an important distinction, because an "aesthetic" experience implies, for Dewey, that the person undergoing it brings a consciousness toward it and is able to demark it for analysis and understanding. An anesthetic experience, by contrast, lacks the kind of intellectual and emotional engagement necessary to create a sense of satisfaction through interpretive agency.

An arts experience is also defined by the level of consciousness the subject brings to the process. In previously published work on the contemporary arts ecology, I argued that audiences don't want "the arts," they want an arts experience—the opportunity to participate, in an intelligent and responsible way, in telling the meaning of an arts event.[7] This aligns with Dewey's analysis by underlining the idea of satisfaction; audiences want to engage in social interpretation because this is, for most of us, how we identify and subsequently narrate to ourselves and to others a "real experience."

But why do people pursue an arts experience in the first place? What draws us to the world of art making and art makers? According to philosopher Dennis Dutton, human psychology includes what he labels the "the art instinct," an innate aspect of human nature that is evolutionary and can be applied cross-culturally. For Dutton, the urge to experience an arts event is bound up in his belief that a work of art is "another human mind incarnate: not in flesh and blood but in sounds, words, colors...I believe that this intense interest in art as emotional expression derives from wanting to see through art into another human personality: it springs from a desire for knowledge of another person."[8]

This human desire for knowledge, whether of another person or of a set of ideas, is fundamental to the metaphorical concepts that form human cognition and the mind/brain. As linguist George Lakoff and philosopher Mark Johnson famously describe it in *Metaphors We Live By*, the metaphorical concepts that govern our thoughts "are not just matters of the intellect. They also govern our everyday functioning, down to the most mundane details. Our concepts structure what we perceive, how we get around in the world, and how we relate to other people."[9] Lakoff and Johnson's theory disrupts the assumption that metaphor is the child of language; in fact, it is the other way around, with language adopting metaphor only because our pre-linguistic concepts are metaphorically structured.[10] This suggests strongly that art making and thus the art instinct are hardwired into us: We need metaphor in our lives because, in a very real sense, we are made of metaphor. The act of taking the metaphors we live by and narrating them into solid meaning structures to be shared with others we care about is fundamental to human biopsychology and thus to human society; it is the spark that ignites the very idea of art as a social opera-tion. Why else would we make art except to experience it in this way? Seeking out an arts experience in which the audience member reaches a state of fulfillment based on her capacity to sort out metaphors and to feel a sense of consummation in narrating the meaning of those metaphors is elemental to human psychology—indeed to being human. Acknowledging the metaphorical nature of our ordinary conceptual system is helpful in understanding the embodied (neural) nature of meaning making as it applies to human experience.

TASTE

"Did you ever taste beer?" "I had a sip of it once," said the small servant. "Here's a state of things!" cried Mr. Swiveller... "She never tasted it—it can't be tasted in a sip!"
—Charles Dickens, *The Old Curiosity Shop*

As Dickens playfully indicates, it is not by accident that the English word taste refers both to the gustatory sense and to a sociocultural process—both usages have their roots in the Latin *taxare*, meaning to evaluate or to handle. Defining one's aesthetic taste is a compli-cated process that cannot be reduced to immediate sensation, whether physiological or emotional. You can't sip *Hamlet*, for example, and expect to come away with a legitimate sense of taste about tragic drama. Personal taste in everything from beer to Shakespeare comes about through a combination of biology, past experience, cultural norms, individual predilections, and, importantly, a drive to know and a willingness to engage one's cognitive attention.

On a biopsychological level, taste is associated with the affective realm, one of the ABCs of psychology (along with cognition and behavior). Paul Bloom notes that gustatory taste is derived from bio-logically sourced cultural learning rooted in special neural systems that "ward us away" from bad foods. But this kind of learning is also social: "Perhaps, like rat pups, we figure out what foods are safe to eat—and hence which foods we should get pleasure from—by moni-toring what our parents give us to eat and observing what they eat themselves. One can explain these facts by taking seriously the idea that food learning is in part a form of cultural learning. It is more than ascertaining what is nutritious and nonlethal. It is part of being socialized into a human group."[11] As Bloom points out, babies and young children cannot be disgusted (the word's literal meaning is "away or apart from taste"); that reflex emerges at about age three as an aspect of neural development.[12] In a related fashion, preference, an aspect of taste that also has biological roots, is clearly affected by knowledge. Knowledge "doesn't change the experience itself but instead the value that we give to the experience," states Bloom, "and this alters how we talk about it and think about it."[13] The major point here is that belief affects experience itself and, by extension, as we will see in Part II, how we make meaning.

This leads us to the long-standing habit of interrogating the con-cept of taste in the Western philosophical tradition. The most reso-nant voices arguably belong to David Hume and Immanuel Kant. Hume's 1757 essay "Of the Standard of Taste" posits that despite the obvious differences of taste even in small circles of acquaintance, its principles are "uniform in human nature" and, furthermore, that it is "natural for us to seek a Standard of Taste; a rule, by which the various sentiments of men may be reconciled; at least, a decision, afforded, confirming one sentiment, and condemning another."[14] He bases his argument on the "Test of Time" theory ("the same Homer, who pleased at Athens and Rome two thousand years ago, is still admired at Paris and at London") and on his assertion that success-ful artists have tended to "inculcate the same moral precepts, and to bestow their applause and blame on the same virtues and vices."[15] As Denis Dutton understands it, for Hume, individual judgment of aesthetic taste fails only when it is "insufficiently practiced in actively experiencing and criticizing works of art. This fault goes along with unfamiliarity with a wide comparison base on which to make a judgement (the man who has only seen two operas in his life is not in a position to be an opera critic) and prejudice against an artist or, perhaps, the work's cultural background."[16]

Kant's *Critique of Judgment* argues that while it is not possible to identify a socially determined standard for good taste, it is possible to recognize a *sensus communis* (Latin for common sense) or a pure aesthetic state "shared by us all." For Kant, this pure aesthetic state is an idealized condition wherein the community shares a harmonic view of beauty that is united with individual taste; we see a painting, for example, and we declare it "beautiful" and expect others to feel similarly. This subjective universality is rooted in "a subjective principle, which determines only by feeling rather than concepts, though nonetheless with universal validity, what is liked or disliked."[17] This is Kant's explanation for why human beings tend to assume that our individual taste, particularly when it comes to recognizing aesthetic beauty, will be automatically shared by other people. Importantly, however, Kant is not defending the limitations of individual taste (as determined by sociocultural constructs); instead, he is arguing that *sensus communis* is "an operation of reflection which enables us to free ourselves from our own prejudices by comparing 'our own judgment with human reason in general'."[18]

More recent theorists and cultural critics have been considerably less concerned with universalist or idealized notions of taste. In *Distinction: A Social Critique of the Judgement of Taste*, for example, philosopher Pierre Bourdieu corrects both Hume and Kant by arguing that taste is a sociocultural construction based on class structure and on attendant status competition and social emulation. His well-known theory of habitus (those aspects of culture that are anchored in the body or daily practices of individuals, groups, societies, and nations and that produce and reproduce the practices of an economic class) helps to illustrate how the ruling and intellectual classes preserve their social privileges through the acquisition and control of taste. As Bourdieu understands it, any given habitus not only informs but also controls cultural capital, his by-now well-worn term for the accumulated knowledge necessary to make cultural distinctions (and thus to operationalize taste making).[19] In this view, taste is less an ontological or epistemological problem and more a behavioral phenomenon—we acquire our good taste by emulating those with good taste. We in turn also regulate social mobility by using taste as a weapon of social stratification, because, as Bourdieu argues, the "most intolerable thing for those who regard themselves as the possessors of legitimate culture is the sacrilegious reuniting of tastes which taste dictates shall be separated. This means that the games of artists and aesthetes and their struggles for the monopoly of artistic legitimacy are less innocent than they seem."[20]

This view of the sociocultural construction of taste is supported by contemporary economists who study consumption patterns and by cultural sociologists who identify the ways in which both individuals and groups willfully construct identity through their taste in everything from food and clothes to fine art and music.[21] It is important to note, however, that some recent theorists disrupt the high/low configuration of Bourdieu's critique by pointing to the many instances in contemporary life when taste is not determined by traditional up–down notions of social mobility but rather by other forms of status marking. An intriguing example is Richard Peterson's theory of the cultural omnivore. In a widely cited article from 1992, Peterson and his coauthors presented evidence of a historical shift in which highbrow status was in transition from strictly enforced affiliations with traditionally elite cultural activities to "omnivorousness," or the quality of being equally open to and appreciative of both elite and popular forms of entertainment.[22] At first, this shift suggested to Peterson and his colleagues the emergence of a new form of cultural democracy indicating a move away from the kind of snobbishness that defined the early twentieth-century sacralization of the arts in which the artist and arts object/event were placed in a sacred position removed from the audience's direct reach. But in subsequent writing in response to a lively debate among cultural sociologists questioning this ostensible relationship, Peterson began contextualizing omnivorousness as "the formulation of new rules governing symbolic status boundaries."[23] His revised thesis suggested that elite cultural consumers previously understood to be self-restricted in terms of taste were actually embracing a variety of popular culture forms *as part of* their elite identity. (Ostentatious openness as a new form of cultural capital, or, as we used to say, slumming it.)[24]

As students of cultural history know, anxieties about the personal and collective tastes of any given cultural moment are as constant as the Northern Star. The elite of the Western tradition has always told the public what to value when it comes to the arts, and gatekeepers have always been concerned with identifying appropriate taste makers. Plato famously complains in his *Laws* (700a–701b) that the "once silent audiences have found a voice, in the persuasion that they understand what is good and bad in art."[25] In analyzing this passage, most historians point to the real source of Plato's concern: He didn't trust the demos (general public) to discern the truth and thus to collectively weigh judgment on the arts, or anything much else.[26] Bourdieu argues that the relationship between class and taste making is so embedded in our sociocultural constructions that judgments of taste are themselves acts of social positioning: We are what we like; we like what we are. For Plato, the people of fourth-century BCE Athens had somehow been reduced to a low-brow, crowd-pleasing state in which making "judgment by uproar" had replaced the interpretive authority previously granted to (for Plato) more appropriate gatekeepers.

In the United States, anxiety over the relationship between aesthetic taste and social class was famously expressed by Van Wyck Brooks in a 1915 essay in which he popularized the terms "highbrow" and "lowbrow" while disparaging both: The highbrow was a "superior person whose virtue is admitted but felt to be an inept unpalatable virtue" and the lowbrow a "good fellow one readily takes to, but with a certain scorn for him and all his works."[27] Brooks longed for a "genial middle ground," but could not locate it in what he saw as the Puritan American legacy—a people caught between high ideals and everyday practical needs. By mid-century, social critic Russell Lynes saw the situation in somewhat different terms: "In recent years a new social structure has emerged in which taste and intellectual pretension and accomplishment play a major role. What we see growing around us is a sort of social stratification in which the highbrows are the elite, the middlebrows are the bourgeoisie, and the lowbrows are hoi polloi."[28] For Lynes, the acquisition of taste was not inherently based on class, as most postwar arts workers and their audiences had been socialized to believe, but instead was made up of three common aspects of American life: "One is education, which includes not only formal but informal education and environment. Another is sensibility, which Webster's defines as 'the ability to perceive or receive sensation'. And the third is morality—the kinds of beliefs and principles which direct one's behavior and set a pattern for judging the behavior of others."[29] Lynes' postwar version of cultural egalitarianism posited that Americans of all classes had the right to express their taste (opinions), as long as they agreed to properly prepare themselves for the task. Nonetheless, he never questioned the hegemonic bias inherent in his positivist concept of morality; the source for his "kinds of beliefs and principles" went unexamined, as did the assumption that education would lead all classes and cultural types of arts consumers to normative conclusions about what constitutes a good work of art.

Today, the most common articulation of the morality of taste within the arts industry, I would argue, is the concept of "artistic excellence." We see and hear it at every turn: on mission statements and grant proposals, at arts conferences, in board rooms, in the classroom, at talkback sessions, and in advertising. Like Lyne's postwar version of aesthetic morality, normative standards couched in words such as "excellence" and "quality" feel good to say, and they protect the gatekeepers who have somehow earned the right to label with authority. But what do they actually mean? (There is not a reader for this volume who hasn't struggled with the issue of clashing evaluation—one person's "great" is another person's "hated it.") I am not interested here in talking about "artistic excellence" as either an aesthetic concept or an ethos for production and performance. Even if it exists in some objective way (which I challenge later in the book), it isn't the point and it obfuscates a more critical dialogue about the audience's right to interpret the art they consume (of whatever type, in whatever manner).

I *am* interested, however, in exploring the concept of cultural rights as they relate to the idea of taste and taste making. This is, in my view, related to the ways in which Americans access (or don't) the expression of individual and public interest in what cultural policy expert Bill Ivey calls the *expressive life*: "The interior space where heritage and free expression operate simultaneously."[30] Ivey's thesis is based on his argument that a legacy of governmental disinterest, media manipulation, and corporate control over cultural production in the United States has undermined our capacity to lead an expressive life. The arts industry's habit of hiding behind a concept such as "artistic excellence" is, I think, related to Ivey's critique; it is at best a simplistic method of operation that makes it easier for dominant individuals to set the agenda and, at worst, a willful practice of social separation and segmentation. In other words, despite the apparent freedom of choice in arts-going in American culture, our own class-based concept of taste and the gatekeepers who maintain it ultimately restrict access to the arts.

Regardless of its ontological, biological, and/or cultural status, taste is an undeniable factor in the meaning-making process and in this book's road map to engagement. In the end, we cannot really separate aesthetic taste (however it is acquired) from pleasure or from the overall meaning-making process—they all operate on a cognitive/neural level and they all run together as forms of cultural learning. But there is more to engagement than just taste—if my theory of working through meaning is true. As the book explores in later chapters, we can derive pleasure from understanding a work of art even if we do not particularly like it.

TALK

People like to talk. Especially contemporary Americans. We talk all day long, in person, through a wire, digitally, in groups, alone, online. Most people like to talk out of the urge to share their feelings, ideas, and reactions to something they've recently undergone; talking is a way of processing experience. It is also a mechanism for formulating an opinion about that experience; talking facilitates the human need (and desire) to make meaning.

Where does this need to talk come from? According to psychologist and cognitive neuroscientist Merlin Donald, a biocultural explanation of language acquisition asserts that language proceeds from outside to inside: "The evolutionary origins of language are tied to the early emergence of knowledge networks, feeling networks, and memory networks, all of which form the cognitive heart of culture."[31] For Donald, symbolic thought (metaphor) and language are inherently network phenomenon, with modern culture running "on languages and symbols, the way our economies run on money or computers on Boolean algebra."[32] Language cannot, however, explain thought (as Donald points out, primates "can obviously think, but they have no natural language"), but language can "improve the quality of thought."[33] In other words, we can make meaning with improved capacity when we develop and use a shared system of language.

The linguistic nature of meaning making has long been argued in philosophical discourse, from Augustine, who first establishes a connection between language and interpretation, to Friedrich Schleiermacher, whose "linguisticality hypothesis" argues that humans understand the world best through its linguistic context (regardless of the nature of the "text" being interpreted), to Gadamer, who, as noted earlier, points to conversation as the mechanism by which the fusion of horizons is reached. For Gadamer, language is at the core of our ability not only to know the world but also to know another. "Language is the medium in which substantive understanding and agreement take place between two people,"[34] he writes, stressing that in participating in the act of conversation we have to put our own prejudices (fore-meanings) and understandings to the test.[35]

Because language and verbal communication are so important to the interpretive process and because they constitute the core strategy for the Arts Talk model, it is useful to devote some space here to my use of the term "talk" as opposed to "dialogue," "discussion," or "discourse." By employing the phrase Arts Talk I am purposefully constructing an attitude (and an attendant methodology) that signals open access and cultural availability. The English word *talk* operates as both a noun and a verb, derived from "tale" and "tell," respectively, and signaling casual and topical conversation often associated with a public context. *The Oxford Universal Dictionary* defines talk as "the familiar speech of ordinary intercourse" and "to speak in a familiar language" and also "to speak trivially" and "to indulge in idle or censorious gossip."[36] In contemporary American culture, we continue to use talk in both of these connotations—"let's sit down and have a good talk" and "that's just talk" are common usages. It is this sense of accessibility and ease, even to the point of gossip, that I find most useful about the word "talk." Arts Talk *should* be as common and as democratic as sports talk, for example. Our societal goal *should* be to construct an interpretive culture about arts-going that feels familiar and ordinary and whose boundaries are permeable and expansive.

But my formulation of the Arts Talk construct is also intended to go beyond the casual. I am deeply interested in uncovering ways in which we can facilitate our audiences' capacities to engage in more intentional discourse and to explore the role that both authentic dialogue and rigorous discussion can play in strengthening our pleasure as audience members. To be clear, dialogue and discussion are not synonymous but rather two distinct discursive modalities. The object of a dialogue, as David Bohm, author of the widely admired *On Dialogue*, explains it,

> is not to analyze things, or to win an argument, or to exchange opinions. Rather, it is to suspend your opinions and to look at the opinions—to listen to everybody's opinions, to suspend them, and to see what all of that means. If we can see what all of our opinions mean, then we are sharing a common content, even if we don't agree entirely. It may turn out that the opinions are not really very important—they are all assumptions. And if we can see them all, we may then move more creatively in a different direction. We can just simply share the appreciation of the meanings; and out of this whole thing, truth emerges unannounced—not that we have chosen it.[37]

This definition of truth—one that arrives from listening and observing—is extremely appealing in an arts context, since it serves the idea and ideal of multivalence. With the fluidity of meaning that defines great art, it *does* turn out that the opinions are not really very important—they are indeed all assumptions. And, if we can share in an appreciation of various meanings, we may indeed move in more creative directions as arts goers (not to mention as citizens).

The object of discussion (from the Latin *discutere*: to break up), on the other hand, is not to suspend opinions but rather to engage in an analytical process (break up) constructed through a spirited, though ideally civil and structured, exchange. The underlying goal of a discussion is to convince or persuade others. In the Arts Talk model, I envision arts experiences where discussion (and debate, from the Old French *debatre*, meaning to beat down) are as at home as they are in the sports experience and its attendant sports talk. The kind of experience where people disagree with gusto and walk away from exchanges about the arts fueled by the adrenaline released when things matter. Contemporary Americans generally do not equate the arts-going experience with this kind of pleasure, but our European forebears did, if the eighteenth-century French critic and historian Denis Diderot is to be believed:

> Fifteen years ago our theatres were tumultuous places. The coolest heads got overheated on entering and reasonable men more or less shared the transports of the mad...People became agitated, moved about, pushed one another, spirits went wild. What mood could be more favorable to a poet? The play commenced with difficulty and was interrupted often, but when a good part was reached...the enthusiasm went from the parterre to the loges, and from the loges to the boxes. The people had arrived flush with excitement; they left the theatre intoxicated...It was like a storm that would dissipate far in the distance, a storm whose rumbling would last long after it had moved on. *That was pleasure* [author's emphasis].[38]

As Diderot vividly narrates, the value of discussion and debate lies in the stakes—when we care about something we are more willing to enlist our critical thinking skills in order to support the process of argumentation. But, alas, in twenty-first-century America, this is not likely to occur without help. For a variety of cultural reasons, most Americans are not particularly good at discussion or debate, even when engaged. We shy away from difficult face-to-face conversations, instead resorting to back-channel methods of asserting our points of view and our differences. This is particularly true when discussing the arts, where the "games of artists and aesthetes and their struggles for the monopoly of artistic legitimacy" have left contemporary audiences speechless. This book's central notion, that arts workers should be enlisted to help in the creation of an audience that knows how to engage in productive meaning making (including a good argument), challenges both the power of interpretive gatekeepers and the audience's tendency to relinquish the fundamental responsibility to make meaning.

PLEASURE

Theories of pleasure abound in Western culture (as in all cultural traditions), produced by aestheticians, moral philosophers, neurobiologists, psychoanalysts, cultural critics, cognitive psychologists, modern-day hedonists, and more. This should come as no surprise—theorizing on the nature of pleasure is a daily habit for all of us, whether we acknowledge it consciously or not. As Epicurus, the Greek philosopher who gave us the concept of hedonism, noted, we are by nature and by culture pleasure-seeking creatures.

That humans seek out the sensation of pleasure is axiomatic; that we agree one to the other on what gives pleasure is not. For, and despite the prevailing use of the term in contemporary culture, "pleasure" is not reducible to feeling good. Quite to the contrary, pleasure is a very complex human response with myriad sensory and intellectual possibilities all rooted in a biological foundation. In *How Pleasure Works*, Paul Bloom asserts, for example, that many pleasures are shared by all humans, regardless of their sociocultural positioning.[39] Bloom also points, however, to the often mysterious cognitive and affective nature of human pleasures: "Some teenage girls enjoy cutting themselves with razors...people slow their cars to look at gory accidents, and go to movies that make them cry."[40] Recent studies from affective neuroscience on the biology of pleasure point to multiple, intra-serving neurobiological mechanisms. Biologically speaking, the sensation of pleasure comes from what brain scientists now identify as a distributed system of the cortical and subcortical regions whose major components include liking, wanting, and learning, with learning defined as "associations, representations, and predictions about future rewards based on past experiences."[41] While most understandings of pleasure place it in the affective (as opposed to cognitive) realm, some researchers argue that pleasure "clearly influences cognition, and cognition influences pleasure."[42]

There is less agreement about the phenomenology of pleasure, however. Is it an experience in and of itself, or a feature of that experience? A signal of what we value and desire? An indicator of the quality of goodness? A flash of momentary consciousness? A short-term neural activity? The ultimate aim of human consciousness (with pain the ultimate thing to avoid)? For Epicurus, pleasure was "freedom from pain in the body and freedom from turmoil in the soul."⁴³ Plato theorized pleasure as a sensing or awareness of the improvement in one's condition that comes from restoring the body to balance (even if we were unaware of being imbalanced). Aristotle claims that pleasure is necessary to a happy life and asserts that there are pleasures other than those of the body, such as the pleasure associated with thinking theoretically and the pleasure associated with the aesthetic imagination (as I discuss in more detail later).

Understanding the nature of aesthetic pleasure is its own difficult and complex territory. Experiential pleasure as an affective response can come from the direct consumption of an arts event (without consciously analyzing or even understanding it), and it can come from the consciously constructed appreciation of that arts event. There can be tremendous pleasure from the rush of feeling that comes from experiencing a work of art that is familiar in form and/or content; there can also be tremendous pleasure in working through the sensations brought about by experiencing difficult works of art—whether difficult because they are unfamiliar as forms or because the content is troubling, distressing, or painful. Indeed, the association between pain and pleasure is a long-standing problem in aesthetics. Aristotle talks of the "proper pleasure of tragedy," apparently referring to the aesthetic pleasure one gets from feeling and then purging the pity and fear aroused through a well-wrought tragic drama.⁴⁴ Modern expressions of the pleasure/pain continuum include Edmund Burke's formulation of the sublime—pleasure evoked through terror and pain.⁴⁵

Pleasure need not be confined to a particular feeling (comfort, happiness, terror), however, or to playing to the opposite in the pleasure/pain binary. In this volume, the concept of pleasure is defined not as an endpoint but, instead, as a process leading to gratification. Gratification (related to the idea of pleasing or being pleased—from the Latin *placere*) refers to a sense of satisfaction of the senses or of the mind. Pleasure in this sense is derived both from the act of working and from the deep satisfaction when the goal of the work is obtained. This definition aligns with the motivational effect theory of pleasure, which focuses on pre-goal attainment pleasure (attention, readiness, and motivation) and post-goal attainment pleasure. It also aligns, happily, with Aristotle, who notes in chapter 4 of the *Poetics* the essential pleasure we human beings find in "contemplating" mimesis (art), which he refers to as the pleasure of learning and inference. Aristotle observes that we "delight in contemplating most exact likenesses of things which are in themselves painful to see" because "learning is most pleasant, not only to philosophers, but to others as well." All people, when contemplating a work of art, delight in "learning and reasoning out what each thing is."[46] Recent findings in brain science support the biological validity of Aristotle's thesis. As biologist and educational theorist James Zull notes, humans are born with the "capacity for fear and pleasure, but not necessarily with knowledge of what to fear or what gives pleasure. We learn most of those things…We enjoy real learning, and we want to learn. In order to survive we had to want to learn."[47]

Working toward meaning, then, is a form of pleasure. Pleasure is related to intellectual challenge and the use of our cognitive powers. And, perhaps most importantly for our purposes, pleasure of this kind is where value is located—an experience is deemed important because it yielded the pleasure of learning and reasoning out the arts event. This type of pleasure is not reflexive; rather, it has to be cultivated, since, as Paul Bloom points out, "when you first experience something, it's hard to process and not enjoyable."[48] We gain familiarity (and thus the pleasure of knowing something) through work—cognitive and affective work—based on the human desire to understand. This, then, is how I employ the term pleasure in this road map to engagement. Pleasure is gained from the satisfaction of working toward meaning. Once the pleasure associated with learning, reasoning, and theorizing has been activated, an audience member is not merely attending an arts event; she is having an arts experience. It is this question of how we learn to "appreciate" an arts event that interests me (and comprises an underlying theme of Part II of this volume).

ENGAGEMENT

Perhaps the best way to explain engagement with an arts event is to describe when it doesn't happen, a task I leave to playwright Bertolt Brecht and his description of the German bourgeois theater: "Let us go into one of these houses and observe the effect which it has on the spectators. Looking about us, we see somewhat motionless figures in a peculiar condition…They scarcely communicate with each other; their relations are those of a lot of sleepers…True, their eyes are open, but they stare rather than see, just as they listen rather than hear…Seeing and hearing are activities, and can be pleasant ones, but these people seem relieved of activity and like men to whom something is being done."[49] Brecht was describing Berlin's boulevard theaters of the 1920s, but nearly 100 years later, this description is uncomfortably familiar. For many audience members, attending an arts event never becomes an arts experience because engagement does not occur, either during the event or afterward.

The word engagement is derived from the action of gears built into a mechanism: When the gears *engage*, the mechanism gets to work. Emotionally and intellectually, people engage when they involve themselves in a process of some sort—when they have the sense that they, too, are an element in what makes the gears work. An engaged classroom, for example, is one in which the students are authentic learners; that is, they have been charged with and accept responsibility for their own learning process. Emerging research on the nature of knowing in general and specifically about how people process new information is unveiling the key cognitive preconditions for engagement, two of which are particularly resonant in the arts context: (1) Prior knowledge is the axiomatic beginning of new knowledge (there is no such thing as a tabula rasa brain) and (2) Understanding the theory behind a given point of knowledge is essential; that is, we have to be provided with some information about a process before we can embark on actually learning to do it. On the first point, neuroscience is providing evidence to show that learning literally changes the physical structure of the brain; activity in the nervous system associated with learning experiences somehow causes nerve cells to create new synapses.[50] On the second point, as cognitive learning theorist Tim Van Gelder writes, "Knowledge of theory allows you to perceive more of what is going on . . . The better you can 'see' what is going on, the more effectively you can understand what you are doing and how you can do it better."[51] These cognitive preconditions for engagement have real and significant impact on audience experience and on the successful launching of an Arts Talk environment, as I explore in Part II.

I want to end the discussion on engagement by pointing out an important distinction in my analysis. The term "audience engagement" is often deployed in arts industry literature in reference to what happens to the audience *while in the act* of consuming a work of art.[52] What I mean when I talk about engagement is not focused on what happens in the moment of reception, however. The Arts Talk construct is predicated on the idea that the most significant opportunities for engagement come before and after the arts event *when audiences are invited to formulate and express an opinion in a social context*. Returning to the sports analogy is useful here. Sports fans, unlike their arts counterparts, have been given societal permission to express their opinions openly and, importantly, can readily find the tools they need to organize and back up those opinions. The experiences that surround the sporting event—from talk shows to 10 pages of sports writing in the daily newspaper—help the audience to prepare, to process, to analyze, and thus to feel the sense of satisfaction that comes from learning and inference. Throughout the twentieth century, the sports industry has understood the benefits of promoting opportunities for public debate and civic discourse. The arts industry, on the other hand, has largely rejected involvement in any form of social interpretation. And we are paying for it now. If we think of our jobs as being restricted to providing (producing and/or creating) the arts event, then this whole discussion on "engagement" will seem extraneous (or worse, the product of yet another cynical incarnation of marketing science). But, if we see ourselves as part of a larger cultural operation in which the quality of the audience's arts experience is as important as the quality of the arts event we deliver, then we can have a more meaningful discussion about the role and function of "engagement."

The road map outlined here is intended to offer a way to identify and thus to contain some essential components of the meaning-making process so that we can apply them diachronically and synchronically, cognitively and culturally, across the following chapters. My distillation does not reduce the varying disciplinary perspectives to a hierarchy or formulate yet another theory about *how* we interpret. Rather, the five signposts described and defined earlier—**an experience** (combined with) **taste** (produces) **talk** (which arouses) **pleasure** (thus engendering) **engagement**—emerge through a process of identifying common concerns arising in various disciplinary definitions of the meaning-making process. My goal in rendering the interpretive process down to these elements is to help readers isolate and explore the environmental, social, philosophical, and psychological conditions that *allow* arts audiences to successfully engage in the interpretive process. A solid understanding of those elements is essential to creating an Arts Talk ethos and environment.

CHAPTER 2

ERAS OF SOCIAL INTERPRETATION

> *With more than pow'r of parliament you sit,*
> *Despotic representatives of wit!*
> *For in a moment, and without much pother,*
> *You can dissolve this piece, and call another!*
> *As 'tis no treason, let us frankly see,*
> *In what they differ, and in what agree,*
> *The said supreme assembly of the nation,*
> *With this our great Dramatic Convocation!*
> *Business in both oft meets with interruption:*
> *In both, we trust, no brib'ry or corruption;*
> *Both proud of freedom, have a turn to riot,*
> *And the best Speaker cannot keep you quiet.*[1]

English playwright John Burgoyne was not being entirely facetious when he wrote this prologue comparing the audience's authority to that of Parliament. By most accounts, eighteenth-century English audiences had remarkable sovereignty over their arts experiences—from determining the actual flow of content during the event to making public judgment on its value, efficacy, and meaning afterward. They did indeed hold the power, in the manner of Parliament, to "dissolve this piece, and call another!" Part of that power came from the fertile nature of the venue–audience exchange[2]; audience to performer, performer to audience, and intra-audience discourse all included a variety of approbative and disapprobative gestures that constituted an acceptable (indeed expected) standard of active behavior while inside eighteenth-century playhouses. But importantly, a significant part of the audience's power arose from what I will call the audience–community exchange; the audiences' participation, as individuals and as members of various subcultures, in a variety of activities centered on public meaning making and evaluation taking place outside of the playhouse or concert hall or gallery. As I illustrate later, prior to the twentieth-century acts of social interpretation were commonplace in Western society, taking the form of competitions, querelles, pamphlet wars, audience leagues, arts appreciation societies, and other public forums for discussion and debate over the meaning and value of a work of art. This aspect of our arts going past, while not nearly so well known as more sensational forms of social interpretation (the riots and outcries that greeted *Hernani, Rite of Spring,* and *The Fountain,* for example), is fertile territory for understanding the relationship between interpretive agency and engagement. Where there is an audience engaged in some form of social interpretation, there is inevitably evidence of how meaning making is constructed and how specific cultures enable it to flourish or to fail.

The quest of Chapter 2, then, is to better understand the mechanics of Arts Talk through a diachronic investigation of historical arts events (what I call eras) that demonstrate an authorized audience. There is a clear historical link between a given community's interest in attending an arts event and the opportunity to inform its meaning; it is a reciprocal status that reflects a healthy balance between the needs of artists, producers, and audiences. Historically, how did audience groups debate the meaning and value of a work of art? What role did taste, talk, and pleasure play in those public constructs? How did that public process impact the autonomy of individuals to make meaning?

A Brief History of Social Interpretation
in the Arts

The Western audience's "right" to determine both the structure of an arts event and its meaning and value can be traced at least to the Greeks and to the range of artistic pursuits associated with annual civic festivals such as the City (sometimes translated as Greater) Dionysia held annually in March. Our knowledge of the culture inside Athen's Theater of Dionysus (the festival venue) illustrates the kind of active behavior that continued up through the end of the nineteenth century, when the process of sacralization began to disenfranchise audience sovereignty. In this section, I examine a number of historical cultural behaviors defined by the opportunity given audiences to engage in social interpretation, an opportunity that engenders what I defined in Chapter 1 as an arts experience. In all of these

arts experiences I find evidence of a deep audience connection to
the arts event's aesthetic value and place in shaping community life.
Importantly, this engagement is often intellectually critical: Audience
participation is demonstrated through conceptualizing, analyzing,
synthesizing, and evaluating information gathered from observation,
communication, and reflection.

Before moving forward, this is a useful place to refer back to the
earlier discussion on defining the term "audience." As the introduction asserts, the singular construction ("the audience") I employ later
is a consequence of necessity, since it would be impossible to uncover
and to explore the variety of social, economic, ethnic, and gender differences that constitute any one of the historical audience sets used
as evidence in this overview. Further, as many recent studies on audiences have shown, cultural systems and horizons of understanding
inform the nature of an individual audience member's reaction to
an arts event; as such, there can be no essentializing of what "the
audience," whether historical or contemporary, thinks and feels. With
these qualifications in mind, however, there are some basic patterns
about the demographic makeup of Western audiences that operate
here. First, in the commercial arts arena (basically all work produced
outside of court and church settings), audience members were predominantly (though certainly not exclusively) male until the nineteenth century, when attendance patterns began to shift as families
and single women gained greater access to popular-priced venues and
social restrictions on women began to ease. And though women did
attend public performances during the classical, Renaissance, and
early modern periods in Europe and during the colonial period in
the United States, they were often (although, again, not exclusively)
silenced by convention if not decree. As a consequence, we have less
historical evidence of how women may have participated in the active
behavior and social interpretation described in this chapter.

Second, in the commercial arts sphere, most venues catered to
economically mixed audiences. Slaves and citizens alike attended the
Theater of Dionysus, manual laborers filled the pits of the Globe and
the Comédie Française in full sight of kings and queens, the *mosqueteros* (literally mosquitos) of Spanish Golden Age *corrales* controlled the
patio section located just below the private rooms reserved for aris-
tocrats and clergy, upwardly mobile merchants attended eighteenth-
century musical consorts in wealthy private homes, nineteenth-century
robber barons owned their own boxes high above the hoi polloi in
New York's nouveau riche venues such as the Metropolitan Opera
House, and by the tail end of the nineteenth century, the working

class visited privately held fine arts collections (on Sunday, the "public" day).[3] Whether audience members were always physically segregated by class once inside the venue is a point of contention among historians, but it seems logical that in ticketed venues (including the Theater of Dionysus), a person's ability to pay would have dictated where they sat. As illustrated later in the chapter, the results of class mixing and class segregation are major themes in period accounts of the historical audience, and clearly they have a great deal to do with how audience cohorts worked, separately and together, to make meaning. Still, as cultural sociologist Richard Butsch warns, "Discourses on audiences, whether academic, elite, intellectual, journalistic, or popular, are neither innocent description nor private opinion, but are filled with political implications that sustain mainstream conceptions of citizenship and worthiness. Whatever our assertions about audiences, we need to be cognizant that we speak in the context of these long-term discourses and that our claims may be incorporated into and our meaning transformed by them."[4]

VENUE–AUDIENCE EXCHANGE

The most obvious site of social interpretation of the arts is in the active auditoriums of the past, where audience "participation" was prescribed by social convention and the important role that the public sphere has historically played in fashioning opinion in a variety of realms. Borrowing from Jurgen Habermas's *The Structural Transformation of the Public Sphere,* many recent cultural histories have commented on the connection between the flowering of social interpretation of the arts during the early modern period and participation in direct public debate on issues of public concern. Museum historian and theorist Tony Bennett, for example, notes that beginning in the eighteenth century, "as works of culture no longer derived their meaning from their place within an authoritative tradition emanating from the monarch (or church), the process of arriving at a meaning and a value for cultural products was a task which bourgeois consumers had now to undertake for themselves, both individually and, via debate, in collaboration with one another."[5] Much of this debate (though not all, as we will see) occurred inside the arts venue in direct response to the live arts event. Period drawings, civic documents, newspaper commentary, memoirs, police records, and sometimes the arts works themselves illustrate that the atmosphere of the playhouse and concert hall was as much defined by the role played by the spectators as it was by arts workers. Perhaps more so, if period comments like this notice from the *Theatrical Guardian* (1791) are to be believed: "The public is the only jury before who the merits of an actor or actress are to be tried, and when the endeavors of a performer are stampt by them the seal of sanction and applause, from that there should be no appeal."[6] The examples of audience sovereignty cited in this chapter are part of the function of what Richard Butsch calls an "embedded audience": an audience whose main focus is on immediate social interaction and not on the arts event per se. It is useful to be reminded that for thousands of years Western audiences were able to consume, enjoy, process, and understand without the kind of silent and still spectatorship that contemporary arts workers associate with an engaged arts audience. This challenges an industry belief holding that audience members who are physically "quiet" are also cognitively quiet; that is, that physically still audience members are fully attentive and don't have internal/back channel conversations going on in their minds while they are consuming an arts event/object. Understanding the phenomenon of the embedded audience and the qualities of attentiveness has significant ramifications for working with contemporary cultural consumers, as I examine in more detail in Chapter 3 and Part II.

The power of the historical audience was derived from several long-standing protocols of spectatorship. First, an audience member was not expected to sit throughout a performance, but rather came and went at will. From the ancients and up through the end of the nineteenth century, this corporeal freedom allowed spectators to physically curate their own cultural experiences as a normal course of action. And to do so with impunity. In the prologue to a revival of his play *The Mother-in-Law*, the Roman playwright Terence complains that during its first production the audience left in the middle of the performance to go see a rope dancer and to watch the gladiators.[7] We know that Elizabethan theatergoers routinely moved from one playhouse to another over the course of a day—a Shakespeare play at the Globe, a round of bear baiting next door at the sporting ring, a comic dance and a cup of ale at a tavern, topped off with yet another revival of the bloody fifth act of Thomas Kyd's *The Spanish Tragedy* at The Swan.[8] It is a similar story in the early music industry. In her study of Italy's *opera seria* of the mid-eighteenth century, musicologist Martha Feldman notes that wealthy citizens literally owned their opera boxes ("like little landed estates") at the commercial theaters and brought their households with them (including servants, who waited in the hallways) to eat, drink, gamble, visit, and people watch.[9] Feldman goes on to quote a fascinating eyewitness account by a visiting Englishman of the scene inside the Regio Ducal Teatro in Milan in 1773: "There is in the front a very large box, as big as a common London dining-room, set apart for the Duke of Modena, governor of Milan...the noise here during the performance was abominable, except while two or three airs and a duet were singing, with which every one was in raptures: at the end of the duet, the applause continued with unremitting violence till the performers returned to sing it again..."[10] However appalled the English visitor may have been, conditions were not far off in the early concert halls of England, as Susan Wollenberg and Simon McVeigh point out in *Concert Life in Eighteenth-Century Britain*: "An individual would often attend several theaters in an evening, arranging to see favourite scenes, players or singers or meeting with people in different halls and boxes...It was not thought obligatory to sit through it all."[11]

Audiences of the past also made themselves as comfortable as if they were in their own homes. At the Theater of Dionysus, attendees brought picnic baskets (or left mid-performance long enough to go home for a meal, as Aristophanes suggests in *Birds*).[12] Picnic baskets were also common at two distinctly different early nineteenth-century venues: the working-class theaters on the Boulevard du Temple in Paris, where a meal of garlic sausage was "washed down in the course of an excursion to the nearest wineshop"[13] before returning to the theater; and P. T. Barnum's American Museum in lower Manhattan, where neighborhood families brought not only baskets of food but also babies and pets. (A habit many working-class New Yorkers attempted to continue at the Metropolitan Museum of Art in 1891 when the institution finally agreed to open to the public on Sundays. According to a *Boston Herald* article from May 1891, the "good natured crowd" brought "big baskets of lunch" and many also brought "a small baby, which yelled vehemently.")[14] Elite audiences were also accustomed to eating while spectating—at the eighteenth-century "consorts" that marked the beginning of commercial concert performance, attendees routinely ate supper and played card games in their opera boxes, sometimes rigging up a mirror at the rear of the box so they could catch a glimpse of the musical performance on stage while remaining focused on the primary activities: eating and playing card games.[15]

Eating and card playing were not the only indicators of audience comfort in the arts venue, however. The historical record includes descriptions of spectators in the standing areas playing sporting events or singing along (quite loudly) with the performers, prostitutes performing services in the third gallery, and wealthy spectators strategizing their social mobility by buying seats placed literally on the stage floor or by purchasing their own opera boxes. At the Paris Opéra during the early and mid-eighteenth century the most prestigious boxes were placed directly on the stage itself, where poor sightlines for viewing the stage action were trumped by the opportunity to be seen and observed.[16] Indeed, scores of historical illustrations of European performance from the Renaissance through the end of the nineteenth century, all drawn from the perspective of the audience, place the point of focus on elite audience members rather than on the stage action. This is perhaps most famously demonstrated in the widely published period etching of the first public ballet performance (*Comique de la Reine*) from 1581. The viewer's perspective is forced not on the dancers themselves but rather toward the foreground, where the king and his entourage are seated in an area that looks like an early iteration of an opera box.[17]

Three hundred years later, Edith Wharton provides a sardonic take on the evolution of opera box behavior in *The Age of Innocence*, this time among New York City's uppertens. The characters arrive late (*de rigueur*), move about from one private box to another, and actively socialize during the performance. They also freely use opera glasses not to better engage with the stage action but rather to inspect the people in the other boxes. Attention to the arts event (in this case, a production of the operatic version of *Faust*) happens only during a few prescribed moments: "Everyone talked through the Mephistopheles and Martha scenes" though "the boxes always stopped talking during the Daisy Song."[18] There is evidence that the New York elite of that era treated visual arts spaces with similar entitlement, including the Metropolitan Museum of Art, which was established in 1870 by a group of wealthy collectors and artists and operated like a private social club. *Scribner's Monthly* complained at the time, for example, that the institution functioned as a "mere extension of [the trustees] parlor."[19]

Opera boxes at the sides or even those built directly on the stage contained structured boundaries acknowledging the separation between performer and audience member. Individual, temporary seating on the stage floor, on the other hand, allowed for a kind of agency that at times profoundly altered the world of the performance. Not surprisingly, stories about audience "participation" by individual patrons seated on the stage abound in the historical record, including this amusing account of Charles Holland's performance of Hamlet in 1756 in London. After the actor's hat fell off accidentally during the Ghost encounter scene and following scripted dialogue about the cold air ("The air bites shrewdly; it is very cold"), a woman "with infinite composure crossed the stage, took up the hat, and with the greatest care placed it fast on Hamlet's head, who on the occasion was as much alarmed in *reality* as he had just then been feigning."[20]

The question at hand is in what ways these kinds of venue–audience exchanges allowed the historical spectator to engage in social interpretation in a real-time context. The most prominent expression of an audience's critical engagement is in the range of approbative and disapprobative behaviors that are constant throughout Western arts-going history. According to theater historian Dennis Kennedy, "audience gestures" are "part of a larger set of social behaviours related to the reception of performance in the western tradition: cheering, shouting bravo or encore or *bis* and other approbative signs; booing, hissing, catcalls and other diapprobative signs; laughter and weeping."[21] For Kennedy, audience gestures are cultural constructions with their own histories and phenomenologies; as such, they are the "most obvious indicator that miscellaneous spectators have become an audience."[22] They are also powerful mechanisms for galvanizing opinions inside a venue so that they can be organized into a marketable notion of what the public likes or does not like; in other words, these big audience gestures become "public opinion" in the collective construction of taste. This kind of collective feedback marks the point at which a physically active audience becomes an authorized audience ready to engage in the meaning-making process, to assert collectively organized evaluations of the arts event, and, in some cases, to challenge the cultural authority of institutional gatekeepers.

I return to the Theater of Dionysus, where the historical record includes ample evidence of public meaning making and evaluation in the form of *krotos* (applause), *surittein* (hissing), *pternokopein* (stomping or hitting the backs of the seats), and *thorubos*, a term used by ancient chroniclers to describe a collective uproar, verbal and/or physical.[23] There is also anecdotal evidence of the Greek audience throwing stones, nuts, figs, wheat, and other food items on the stage in both protest and homage (and some evidence that performers threw food out to the audience as well). Even more interesting are accounts of "rectors" (beadles or ushers) assigned the job of hitting spectators with sticks in order to get them to sit down and to be silent.[24] Plato complains that by the fourth century BCE the rowdy lower-class audience members had taken control of social interpretation and reduced it to low-brow notions of cheap gratification ("common taste").[25] But contemporary scholars generally note the abundance of evidence supporting the noisy, active nature of the whole Athenian audience, regardless of class. Greek theater scholar Arthur Pickard-Cambridge points out, for example, that at least during the golden era of the fifth century the Theater of Dionysus was a noisy space because "most of the audience took its playgoing seriously," particularly in regard to the moral and political content.[26] Both Plutarch and Seneca chronicle *thorubos* in response to Euripides' plays, claiming that in one instance a new work had so offended the taste of the audience that the playwright himself had to beg them to allow the production to continue. "According to Seneca," notes classicist Robert W. Wallace, "after a character in one of Euripides' plays uttered a scandalous speech praising money above all else, 'the whole audience rose up with one accord to drive out both the actor and the play. But Euripides jumped to his feet and asked them to wait and see what end this grasper after gold would meet'."[27] The moral and political taste of the audience also countered positively at times—apparently the audience demanded that the parabasis (choral address) of Aristophanes' *Frogs* be repeated because of its political wisdom. And aesthetics clearly played a role in the audiences' evaluative process: Aristotle claims that one fifth-century playwright (Agathon) failed to secure a win at the City Dionysia contest because the audience felt he had "crowded too many events into a single plot."[28] He also states (in *Politics*) that the "opinion of the multitude on literary works…is worth more than that of the single critic, which may be one-sided."[29]

After the emergence of the commercial entertainment industry in the sixteenth century, interpretive control shifted to the working-class habitués of the English pit, the French *parterre* (literally "on the ground"), and the Spanish *patio* and *cazuela* (literally "stew pot"). In these standing room spaces the audience functioned as the "public judge" whose collective opinion about the value of a particular arts event was a critical component to its success both in real time and in terms of artistic legacy. In seventeenth-century Madrid, working-class men (known as *mosqueteros*) standing in the *patio* responded to the *comedia* with "applause, catcalls, whistles, barracking and even missiles" while working-class women, segregated in a railed off section of the *corrales*, "rattled keys against the railings" and "never stopped talking and laughing."[30] In seventeenth-century France, according to theater historian Jeffrey Ravel, the process of opinion formation in Parisian parterres was in fact so fundamental that it went beyond aesthetics to "issues basic to French political culture in the seventeenth and eighteenth centuries."[31] Ravel's thesis aligns with the taste-talk-pleasure calculus by demonstrating the ways in which public taste (both aesthetic and moral-political) combined with talk inside France's state theaters to create a fundamental mechanism for the formation of public opinion, thereby encouraging these venues to become among the first forums in France where the subjects of the Bourbon Crown could "express discontent with the monarchy through their cries, gestures, and collective actions."[32] In his view, the autonomous and authorized quality of the parterre environment is evidence of a critical thinking capacity among working-class audience members, a quality so profound that it eventually undermined the authority of the state.

Ravel's examination of police records and fiction from the period provides evidence of the type and quality of social interpretation of arts events taking place in a range of venues, including the Comédie Française, where the audience's interpretive agency was considerable. In one instance from June 1711, a spectator named Matheiu May interrupted the actors on stage to question the classical sources for the play being performed (Racine's *Britannicus*). When the actors refused to engage in a critique of Racine, a brawl broke out on stage. "Three decades after the King had created a privileged space for the presentation of French-language drama also performed at court," Ravel notes, "a commoner attending this theater thought himself authorized to question a text by one of the most revered writers of the French stage, and to query the performances of the actors who received pensions from the King and entertained the court."[33]

Similar demonstrations of audience interpretive agency were regular features of nineteenth-century popular price theaters in England, France, and the United States. At Boulevard du Temple theaters such as the Petit-Lazari, where "audience participation was a recognized feature of the entertainment," the parterre crowd would routinely shout out a comment to the actors on stage, who would routinely reply "using the vilest slang; this would be followed by reciprocal threats and a cross-fire of invective which delighted the assembly, who would often fill the same part as the chorus of antiquity, until the authorities intervened, though always cautiously."[34] London's Victorian-era playhouses were equally notorious for active audiences across a wide spectrum of class-stratified venues. Charles Dickens provides an amusing fictionalized account in *Great Expectations,* in which Pip goes to a London theater to see a production of *Hamlet*: "Whenever that undecided Prince had to ask a question or state a doubt, the public helped him out with it. As for example; on the question whether 'twas nobler in the mind to suffer,' some roared yes and some no, and some inkling to both opinions said 'toss up for it'; and quite a Debating Society arouse."[35]

The existence of an authorized audience throughout the nineteenth century is in keeping with what we know about American concert halls, playhouses, and museums of the period. In the United States, the groundlings began in the pit and over the course of the century were moved upstairs to the gallery, where they exerted considerable control over the way in which an arts event unfolded, from booing performers off the stage to demanding that a song or dance or even a complete scene be repeated at will. Like their European counterparts, they treated the auditorium as an extension of the home, where the "friendly interchange of commodities—apples, pignuts, etc., between the tenants of the upper boxes and pit" was commonplace enough to be commented on in local newspapers accounts.[36] They also took their aesthetics seriously. Concern over the level of the acting at the Pittsburgh Theater in the early 1830s, for example, led the audience to hiss the theater manager off the stage during a curtain speech; he was accused of bringing in third-rate performers while saving his top-tier actors for his other theater in the more cosmopolitan Philadelphia.[37] In New Orleans, a touring Italian opera troupe in 1837 cut the final scene of Rossini's *Semiramide* (presumably for the convenience of the company) without warning the audience. The resulting riot nearly destroyed the theater. The next night the company performed the opera to the "full extent, and every thing passed off without further commotion."[38]

Some of the most vivid examples of social interpretation inside the arts venue are found in the music industry. Musicologist Carlotta Sorba points out that the Italian public was the ultimate judge of an operatic work, so much so that they played a leading role in what she calls the "author/actor/spectator triad." "Indeed, the image of the public as protagonist is found throughout the correspondence of composers, which abounds with references to the audience, or rather to the 'Public', as the arbiters of their work. Composers frequently expressed their full awareness that the public joined them, along with sovereigns, as active participants in the process of production (at least as recipients)."[39] In nineteenth-century Italy, opera audiences routinely separated into factions identifying with one composer, or a particular singer. During the 1843–1844 season at the San Carolino in Palermo, for example, rival fans of the two leading sopranos formed audience claques in the auditorium and competed back and forth through cheers, boos, and other audience gestures. According to music historian John A. Davis, one of the claque ringleaders, Rosolino Pilo, "would later play a leading role in the revolutions of 1848: Whether he learned his skills as a political leader from the San Carolino conflicts remains unclear."[40]

Audience claques have an interesting history, often traced to Nero, who had his soldiers applaud after his speeches in order to assure the proper level of enthusiasm.[41] The habit of forming claques spread to France in the late sixteenth century, when playwrights began buying up tickets to distribute to supportive friends, and then to England and the colonies. Most claques were amateur in the sense that they were relatively ad hoc affairs, often prompted by the self-promotion instincts of an artist or the passionate intensity of an aficionado. The playwright William Popple gives an account of the formation of an ad hoc anti-claque in London in 1734, describing how a group of young men met at a coffee house to discuss their aversion to his play *Lady's Revenge* before heading off to the theater to disrupt the performance. Before the performance that night, the leading actor came on stage and "told them he found the house was divided, and as the majority was for having the play, he hop'd those who were not, would go out. The house on that were unanimous, and cry'd, Turn them out, Turn them out." The claquers left "under the general hiss of every person present."[42]

In France, claques evolved into professional, institutionalized structures. By the eighteenth century, the position of *chef de claque* drew a regular salary at the Opera and the Comédie Française, where duties included attending rehearsals and consulting with the directors and conductors in order to identify the places in the performance where applause and cheering were desired. The most critical aspect of the *chef de claque*'s job description was to recruit a team of *claqueurs* for each performance, mostly unskilled laborers who agreed to follow instructions for the price of admission. Once admitted into the playhouse, the *claqueurs* were coached on which sections to applaud/ cheer, after which they were spread around the auditorium for maximum effect. There was, not surprisingly, consistent opposition to the institutionalization of claques. Writer and critic Théophile Gautier complained bitterly about a claque at the Vaudeville in 1839 that began its business by insulting the regular audience (for hissing a "truly deplorable and highly indecent scene") and ended by beating them up: "A theatre auditorium ought not to be turned into a boxing ring; it's not nice at all to return home with a bloody nose and an eye all the colours of the rainbow; no musical is worth incurring such risks."[43]

While most *claqueurs* did not resort to this kind of violence, there is evidence that several of the most famous riots in performance history were ignited by the presence of a paid claque, perhaps most infamously on the occasion of the so-called Battle of *Hernani* in 1833.

Victor Hugo distributed tickets for the premiere of his new play to supporters of the emerging Romantic genre of drama, hoping to seed appreciation for his dramaturgical innovations among the conservative Comédie Française audience. The move backfired spectacularly, however, when the young men he ticketed proceeded to get drunk and affectively highjack the performance. And while the riot at the premiere of *Le Sacre du Printemps* cannot be directly attributed to preformed claques, there is evidence that Sergei Diaghilev, the impresario of the Ballets Russes who produced the modernist ballet by Igor Stravinsky and Vaslav Nijinski, anticipated a scandal, reportedly telling his collaborators that the opening night riot was "exactly what I wanted."[44] Fascinatingly, it appears that the Russians are still engaged in manipulating audience reaction today. Apparently some of the most prominent Bolshoi dancers have a "mysterious" relationship with a ballet fanatic named Roman Abramov, who runs a claque providing "artists with a guarantee of applause, and in return it receives free passes allocated to artists."[45] Some Russian critics speculate that this reemergence of the historical claque is due to the fact that average Russians have been priced out of the market by the country's economic transformation; today the increasingly expensive tickets go more often to foreign tourists and the country's nouveau riche than to the "well-versed balletomanes of the Soviet era." As a result, the audiences have become timid and less likely to respond without prompting. Russians who approve of the trend "say it transmits the sound of a vanishing generation, ordinary working people raised with a passion for classical ballet."[46]

The stories outlined thus far in the chapter underline the fact that historical audiences felt authorized to comment on aesthetic matters such as word choice, poetic meter, standards of tonality and rhythm, choreographic idioms, etc., and point to how important the free expression of that commentary was to their sense of citizenship. These types of aesthetically informed responses were sourced in the audience's sense of sovereignty over their cultural consumption and the belief that art played a significant role in defining their communities and their social selves within those communities. There is some evidence that as early as the Victorian era this interpretive agency was being threatened, at least according to the author of an article that appeared in *Belgravia: An Illustrated London Magazine* in 1878. According to H. Barton Baker, audiences of his day did not have the "courage to hiss bad pieces or bad actors, but will tolerate and even applaud performances that their grandfathers would not have endured for a single night." For this commentator, the idea of the audience relinquishing its evaluative sovereignty was cause for real alarm. "Art cannot flourish under such laxity," he continued. "If the buyer is indifferent about the article he purchased, depend upon it the seller will not trouble his head about the quality."[47] Baker's assessment of the reciprocity between product and consumption highlights an important fact: the presence of an audience engaged in acts of social interpretation demonstrates just how significant the public judge was to the health and vibrancy of past arts ecologies.

AUDIENCE–COMMUNITY EXCHANGE

This section narrates and analyzes what I refer to as audience–community exchange—the particular manner in which social interpretation made its way out of arts venues and into the fabric of everyday life. In the following examples, the meaning-making process surrounds the arts event rather than occurring simultaneously with the initial reception experience. In general, social interpretation in the form of audience–community exchanges has gone underreported and underexamined in the field of audience studies for two key reasons: (1) the influence of performance semiotics on reception theory, wherein scholarly attention has been concentrated on the moment of reception rather than on the ongoing process of meaning making; and (2) the nature of the archive, which rarely collects descriptions of hermeneutic operations that occur outside of institutional structures. Who, for example, would have been likely to record the reactions of an audience member occurring before or after the arts event itself? Not journalists or civic officials or arts institutions. As a result, locating data about audience–community exchanges is challenging for historians, but, as I will illustrate, not impossible. Some of the examples of audience-generated exchanges cited in this section of the chapter operated quite independently from the gate-keeping authority of court, state, and arts elites, while others were initiated by civic authorities, arts producers, and individual artists as a way to respond to public demands or to engage in promotional strategies. All are institutional in the sense that they help to organize and implement new structures for assembly, debate, and critical analysis of the arts. And all employ the taste-talk-pleasure calculus of social interpretation.

Once again the ancient Greeks provide a useful diachronic entry into the discussion, this time in the form of two institutionalized exchanges occurring as part of the annual City Dionysia festival. The *proagon* (literally "before the contest") was a formal presentation by the competing playwrights given prior to the start of the festival (and thus prior to the productions of the competing tragedies) at the Odeon, a music concert hall adjacent to the Theater of Dionysus. While the exact nature of the *proagon* is speculative (only a few accounts exist), one of the goals seems to have been to allow the playwright to introduce both his creative team—including the actors, who appeared without their masks or costumes—and his creative agenda in the form of describing the major themes of his new tragedy. This preshow information session allowed the playwright to appear before the people "in his own identity, effectively dramatizing the poet's authorship of his work,"[48] thus making transparent the aesthetic qualities of the forthcoming event. By allowing the playwright to address the themes of the play in advance, the *proagon* also served to invite the audience to begin its hermeneutic process well before seeing the production. Since Greek tragedies were primarily based on existing religious narratives (myths) and the *proagon* took place as much as six days before the competing tragedies were presented, the audience would have had time to access their own knowledge base about the storyline before receiving the performance. When it came to enjoyment, Greek audiences had a distinct advantage over contemporary audiences because their a priori knowledge of the storyline allowed them to enter into the spectating experience with a more developed understanding. (Education theorists confirm the importance of this kind of transparency in the learning process, a factor I explore in greater detail in Chapter 4.) At the other end of City Dionysia festival timeline was the *ecclesia*—a term derived from the regular meetings of the Greek assembly—which gathered citizens together the day after the close of the festival in order to "scrutinize the conduct of the officials."[49] Extant records indicate that the preponderance of comments was focused on the behavior of the audience rather than on the content of the tragedies.[50] Still, this invitation to weigh in on the running of the festival serves as a reminder that a sense of ownership in a larger cultural process is often a critical component to engagement.

Beginning with the early modern period, audience-generated social interpretation takes on a variety of new formulations, from animated debates in coffee houses to street-level gossip to arguments waged in querelles and pamphlet wars to arts appreciation-style interpretive activities managed by and for audience members themselves. What is notable about many of the examples that follow is the way in which audience members were able to directly interact with arts workers, particularly artists. This regular intermingling resulted in a rich circular exchange of opinion between artist and spectator, a reciprocal relationship acknowledging the artist/arts event/audience triad at the core of any meaning-making operation within the arts sphere. Audience members were comfortable in discussing their taste and in openly formulating their opinions about a particular arts event through everyday talk. And while cultural gatekeepers certainly existed throughout this period, they did not have the authority to regulate community discourse.

Why? Perhaps because this was an environment where arts talk was a normal commodity of daily cultural commerce. In the coffee houses of eighteenth-century Paris, *parterre* patrons "mingled in the Procope, the Café de l'Opera, the café de la Comedie-Italienne, and other theater cafes with actors, authors, gens de lettres" while arguing, according to Jeffrey Ravel, "the merits of new and old works" and attempting "to organize cabals against certain plays and players."[51] In early nineteenth-century Venice, if a production failed to please the audience it would form the "constant topic of conversation, criticism, and general observation in shops, associations, and private gatherings."[52] So too if it *did* please the audience, as in the successful premiere of Ponchielli's *I Lituani* in Milan in 1874, where according to a period commentator in *L'Opinione*, "in the streets, in cafes, in homes the subject was only one."[53] Like contemporary sports talk in the United States, arts events regularly drew the attention of the public outside of the venue and fueled everyday conversation long after the performance was over.

The arts also fueled audience-led actions designed to affect both organizational and artistic decision making. In the early 1730s, for example, a member of the parterre audience at the Comédie Française sent word to the actors requesting that they perform *Tartuffe* in the next few days. When playbills were posted the next day with no mention of *Tartuffe*, an audience cabal of some 400 men formed at the coffee shop across the street from the theater to organize a strategy, and that evening they set off a riot in the theater.[54] In 1824, Parisian newspapers reported the public's negative response to Rossini's use of a stage band (in addition to the orchestra) in *La Dona del Lago*. It seems the public pressure was so intense that Paris Opéra officials (as the presenters of the opera) formulated an official request to Rossini, in the name of the audience, to remove the offending section of music.[55]

Other means of public discourse on the arts included pamphlet wars in the form of essays written by various factions of the arts community and read with gusto by the arts-going public. The early

English stage was riddled with antitheatrical pamphlets (most infamously the Puritan Jeremy Collier's "A Short View of the Immorality of the English Stage" from 1698), while the French stage was affected by a series of *querelles*, or public quarrels taking shape in the form of essays, newspaper notices, and salon gossip. *Le Querelle des Bouffons* in 1752, for instance, focused on a battle over the relative merits of French and Italian opera and, underlying that, the direction that the state-managed Royal Academy of Music should take. While most of the essays that constituted the texts of the *querelle* were written by France's intellectual elite (Rousseau, among others), they reached a large segment of the reading public, including the rising merchant class. As a result, an aesthetic discourse once confined to a small segment of cultural elites extended to the public sphere—beyond those who held office or had financial power.[56]

The level of the public's influence on the interpretive function is also marked by the formation of audience-centered musical societies, arts appreciation clubs, drama leagues, and other membership-driven organizations gathering to create art, to present professional artists, and to share in a dialogue about the value and meaning of art in the community. Musical and art societies, and, later, drama leagues, existed in many towns and cities to provide outlets for amateur artists to participate in various forms of creative expression. Participation is, of course, the key word here. The cultivation of amateur artistic skills was highly valued, and sharing those skills with other similarly minded citizens was considered a mark of good society in Europe and in nineteenth-century America, where even the smallest towns had an array of music and art appreciation societies hosting regular performances and exhibitions in taverns, court houses, and other community sites of assembly. In Frontier-era Pittsburgh, for example, the Apollonian Society—the city's first community orchestra association—gave performances at Mr. Carr's Tavern, sharing the stage with readings, recitations, and amateur theatricals performed by other local residents.[57]

Aside from self-entertainment, the other role of local arts societies was to foster appreciation for professional-level art through group study, discussion, and curatorship. In early modern Europe, local musical societies were breeding grounds for the professional concert music that emerged in the eighteenth century. At meetings and salon concerts, amateur musicians and nonplaying enthusiasts shared what they knew about the canon and promoted new composers and artists. Those discussions resulted in a network of influence that had a profound impact on public taste, because patrons played a significant role in advancing a musician's career by "encouraging friends to buy tickets for benefits, obtaining positions at public concerts or discovering 'unknowns'."[58] Curatorial activities such as choosing artists and arranging the repertoire are inherently interpretive; a person engaged in them is involved in a critical process.

A particularly interesting curatorial structure in the United States was the audience league. Created and managed by and for serious patrons of the arts, audience leagues encouraged independent thinking about the arts and provided a venue for members to assemble on their own terms in order to voice opinions, debate, and generally take ownership over their cultural experiences. A good example is the Drama League of America, founded in Chicago in 1910 in order to "stimulate interest in the drama."[59] By the mid-1920s, there were 37 chapters around the country sponsoring study groups (called "discussion teas") for "those who like to read and discuss great plays as well as see them in the playhouse." Among the various League activities centered on social interpretation, of particular interest are the "bulletins" written and disseminated by the members; each bulletin reported on a current production playing in a professional theater and included an analysis of theme, plot, acting, and "value." A bulletin issued by the Pittsburgh chapter in January 1914 on *The Blindness of Virtue*, for example, describes the play's theme as "the danger to children of ignorance of the facts of sex" and notes in the value section that though the play is "talky" its worthiness "lies largely in the quiet sincerity of the presentation and in the vitality of the theme." Pittsburghers of this era had access to a dozen daily newspapers and as such to a dozen newspaper reviews; it's telling, then, that the city's most passionate theatergoers felt the need to create their own system for reviewing plays. One clue into understanding this phenomenon is the statement printed at the bottom of all league bulletins: "This official statement of the Drama League is independent of any outside influence."[60] That is to say, independent of the theater producers, newspaper critics, and other industry gatekeepers.

There is one more mechanism for social interpretation that has a long history in the European tradition and is worthy of discussion here: arts competitions. Despite present-day anxieties about the conflation of aesthetics and competition, contests for the best arts works played a significant role in our cultural past; in fact, we derive some of our most revered art from them. Consider *Oedipus Rex*, for example. In 429 BCE, Sophocles entered his version of the well-known House of Thebes myth into the City Dionysia competition for the best tragedy. He was selected as winner by ten judges, one from each tribe, who had themselves been selected by public lot from the names of all Athenian citizens. The public nature of the selection of judges was thought necessary in order to avoid bribery and other forms of payola. (During the first performance of Aristophanes' *Clouds*, the audience reportedly demanded that the famous comic playwright be given first prize, but the judges refused to acquiesce to their fellow citizens.)[61] As hundreds of other examples of arts competitions in the Western tradition illustrate, participation in the decision-making process (even if once removed) is an indicator of the role that the public, as audience members and as citizens, played in evaluating important pieces of institutional art. This type of social interpretation also points to a fundamental desire among cultural consumers to be heard in a way that matters.

FROM SUBJECTS TO OBJECTS

Given this hermeneutically rich history of the Western arts-going tradition, just how did American audiences lose access to the public construction of meaning? Audience sovereignty over the American arts-going experience, beginning with physical sovereignty associated with behavior inside arts venues, began disappearing in the second half of the nineteenth century. Some historians trace the shift to the post–Civil War period, when discrete but complementary factions of intellectuals, artists, wealthy patrons, and religious officials initiated deliberate efforts to create a cultural hierarchy in order to "raise up the masses."[62] In his groundbreaking study, *Highbrow/Lowbrow: The Emergence of Cultural Hierarchy in America*, historian Lawrence Levine calls this shift the "sacralization of culture," tracing a complicated path from audience sovereignty to arts-industry sovereignty organized around socially engineered efforts to control the corporeal presence of American audiences of all classes and in a variety of venues. Around 1880, for example, institutionalized changes in arts-going etiquette began to impact popular-priced theaters such as the Keith-Albee vaudeville "palaces" that sprang up first in Boston and later in other major cities. In these venues, the new standard for audience behavior included enforced seating, the elimination of eating (except easily consumed items sold at the venue's concession stand), new standards for what constituted "applause" (foot stomping was prohibited), active shunning of catcalling and other loud, physicalized audience gestures, and restrictions on clothing (women were asked to remove large hats, for instance). In order to educate Americans in the rules of this emerging protocol, Keith-Albee patrons were handed flyers advising them "not to stamp their feet, smoke, or talk during the acts."[63]

Elite venues soon joined the campaign; in 1891, the management of the Metropolitan Opera House placed notices in the opera boxes (frequented by some of the city's richest families) "requesting" that talking during performances be discontinued.[64] At about the same time, Metropolitan Museum director Luigi Palma de Cesnola told a newspaper reporter that he had ended the display of "offending personal habits" of the working-class visitors to the museum. Under his tight control, he boasted, there was "no more whistling, singing, or calling aloud to people from one gallery to another."[65] A similar storyline comes from the evolution of the symphony orchestra industry. Led by conductors defending both their artistic rights and the "sacred" nature of orchestral music, American symphony orchestras started promoting their "divine appointment" in the mid-nineteenth century.[66] They ended the long-standing practice of mixed programming in which popular music was played along with orchestral scores because, as Levine states, "The urge to deprecate popular musical genres was an important element in the process of sacralization."[67] They also insisted on greater and greater control over the performance environment, culminating in the wholesale invention of etiquette "standards," such as holding applause until the end of a multimovement work. As Greg Sandow has amply documented in his "On the Future of Classical Music" blog, applause between movements and indeed over the music was a standard feature of European concert fare from its inception and into the twentieth century. Clapping was not only normal, it was desirable. Mozart is said to have loved it when his audience burst into spontaneous applause in the middle of a piece. And Beethoven once stated that "silence is not what we artists wish—we want applause."[68]

According to pianist and musicologist Kenneth Hamilton, silent, reverent attention during musical recitals was rare in public concert settings, which were often "packed, noisy, at times almost riotous affairs . . . where the yardstick of success for a pianist was not the silence of the audience, but exactly the opposite."[69] The idealized type of listening that is often associated with concert music, he continues, was "really only expected to be found in private, cultured circles."[70] Only in the early twentieth century, when it became fashionable for conductors such as Leopold Stokowski to assert their divine authority, did the American audience finally begin to sit on its hands. As musicologist Oliver Daniel tells the story, after the Philadelphia audience burst into applause during a performance of Tchaikovsky's Fourth

Symphony in 1929, "Stoki turned, signaled for silence, and explained that his remarks were not intended as a rebuke for their appreciation. 'But,' he added reflectively, 'I have been considering this matter of applause, a relic from the Dark Ages, a survival of customs at some rite or ceremonial dance in primitive times."[71]

It is obvious why artists and presenters would be interested in promoting the protocols of sacralization, particularly the demand for a silent and still audience. An assumption about the reciprocal relationship between silent listening and deeper attention (and thus appreciation) has long informed the way in which cultural history has been narrated and the way in which artists and producers have measured the success of their work ("The audience was rapt with attention."). Beginning in the late eighteenth century, concerns over proper etiquette inside music venues were conflated with the aesthetic theory of "attentive listening," a term used to describe the kind of intellectual effort thought necessary to fully appreciate sophisticated music. As musicologist Matthew Riley notes, this emerging standard was a by-product of Enlightenment notions of "absolute music" and "art religion" that demanded a "reverential attitude on the part of the listener that previously would have been more appropriate in a place of worship."[72] Cognitively, the context and manner in which one listens would seem to be influenced by the aesthetic demands of a given artistic work. In *Listening in Paris*, cultural historian James Johnson offers an elegant argument to that end, equating the "steady expansion in boundaries of possible meaning" signaled by new compositional techniques such as those of Beethoven's, to a shift from "superficial to engaged listening, and, by extension, from talkative to silent audiences" in nineteenth-century Paris.[73] As demonstrated earlier, however, the presence of more sophisticated art is not a complete explanation for quietization in American venues. The growing silence in these spaces does not appear to have been an individual choice, but rather the result of institutional regulations brought on by gatekeepers and maintained by changing habitus. In other words, the evidence supports the fact that audiences quieted down to begin because they were forced to by administrators and artists and then continued to be quiet as it became the normative behavior for a rapidly evolving professional class. And, as Lawrence Levine stresses, "It is important to understand that although sacralization became a cultural fact and shaped twentieth-century cultural attitudes and practices, it never became a cultural reality."[74]

Perhaps the ultimate explanation for the eventual quieting of the audience is less sociocultural than environmental. None of the social restrictions cited above seems in retrospect as critical to the sacralization process as the widespread introduction of electric lighting. The ability to turn the house to black while highlighting the stage action transformed the very nature of performance and was a significant contributor to the advance of stage realism. Controlled lighting also moved the audience, for the first time in history, into complete darkness and thus into a secondary relationship with the arts event. See for evidence the plethora of historical drawings, cartoons, and paintings contained in the archive rendering the inside of theatrical venues. The preponderance of the pre-twentieth-century images includes the audience in one fashion or another (and many are focused on the audience, with the stage action clearly positioned as a secondary feature of the event's phenomenology). But images of theatrical performances from the twentieth and twenty-first centuries almost never reference the audience. Lost in the dark, they became lost from the construct as well.

The other impact of controlled lighting was to move the audience, again for the first time in history, into a newly isolated emotional state, one informed by the physiology of darkness. As recent findings in the field of cognitive science reveal, emotions are not metaphysical, but rather "short term, biologically based patterns of perception, subjective experience, physiology, and action (or action tendencies) that constitute responses to specific physical and social problems posed by the environment."[75] Empathy relies on a person's ability to embody others' emotional states; our empathetic links spread emotions just like germs spread colds, from one body to the next. This emerging understanding of emotion and empathy has significant implications for understanding audience behavior. "When Western audiences could see each other in lighted auditoriums," asserts Bruce McConachie, "the facial expressions and bodily movements of others in their seats—in addition to their audible vocalizations—helped to evoke a more uniform response among spectators than today, when darkened houselights inhibit emotional contagion."[76] In a related theory, film theorist Carl R. Plantinga argues that because "emotions are intimately tied to our cognition, inferences, evaluations, and all of the other mental activities that accompany the viewing experience," they have "implications for ideas" and thus for our interpretive abilities.[77] We can test McConachie's and Plantinga's hypotheses by analyzing the behavior in contemporary sporting arenas, where the lights are deliberately left on and where, as a consequence, the active physical (visual and aural) relationship between spectators and their subsequent involvement in social interpretive practices is perhaps the dominant characteristic of the pleasure of sports-going and an essential component of engagement.

Despite the historical evidence to the contrary, contemporary understandings about arts reception (significantly tied up with rules about arts etiquette and the legacy of sacralization) continue to support the notion that we cannot fully understand a work of art unless we are quiet and still. As musicologist William Webber puts it, we are conditioned by a "post-Romantic point of view," which distrusts any fusion between arts consumption and "mundane social activities which are felt to violate the integrity of the musical experience."[78] From a cognitive perspective, just how accurate is this assumption? Is it really true that sports spectators are not being attentive when they talk or move around or do the wave? And, more to the point, why do we care about being quiet at a symphony hall when we don't care about being quiet at a jazz club? Are we arguing that symphonic music is more sophisticated (and thus requires more attention) than jazz? In chapter 4, I survey recent work in attentional theory, where new understandings of brain function are allowing scientists, teachers, physicians, therapists, and perhaps arts workers to approach the notion of "attention" differently from in the past.

SELF-CULTIVATION

It is easy to understand why arts workers would promote sacralization and all its behavioral accommodations. But why would late nineteenth-century and early twentieth-century American audiences nurtured on active behavior and bred to assert control over their cultural experiences go along with the sacralization campaign? One theory points to the rise of a professional class in large US cities, which brought with it calls for "self-cultivation," an aspect of progressive era social reform "conceived as the dominance of reason and intellect over emotions."[79] The self-cultivation movement eventually came to encompass many aspects of American middle-class life, including personal hygiene, dress reform, aesthetic expression, and even sex education (euphemistically referred to as "self-knowledge"). Not surprisingly, self-control over personal emotions also extended to audience behavior: "One had to learn to respond with studious thought rather than spontaneous feeling to music, art, and ideas."[80]

The call for an internalized processing of an audience member's reactions went handily with the need for a new kind of elite interpreter ready to offer guidance for those seeking higher cultural status. The proliferation of daily newspapers and popular journals during the late nineteenth and early twentieth centuries fed this perceived need by producing numerous critics and self-appointed curators of "art appreciation" whose role was to evaluate the social and aesthetic value of arts products for the average reader (as opposed to earlier generations of critical gatekeepers, who thought and wrote for a small, educated elite). Scattered journalistic arts criticism first began appearing in US publications toward the end of the colonial era. A largely ad hoc process for the better part of the next two centuries, newspaper "reviews" were mostly unsigned "puff" pieces—the term for predetermined reviews written by press agents and theatrical managers in exchange for buying advertising space. Or they were moralized harangues focused on artistic content and audience behavior. In 1796, for example, a group of scholars calling themselves the "Company of Critics" published critiques that were little more than scathing indictments of ostensibly indecent behavior taking place inside the New York playhouses.[81] Even well into the nineteenth century, the relationship between journalistic arts criticism and serious aesthetic analysis was a loose one; most newspaper critics and arts columnists had scant training in the disciplines they covered and were primarily charged with reporting on the social milieu surrounding the arts event.[82] Writing in a familiar, often chatty style, these writers established authority by providing breaking news about the performing arts, including dates and times of upcoming concerts and productions, and offering insider gossip, such as how many trunks of luggage Sarah Bernhardt brought across in 1900 for her American tour (four) and her shoe size (she wore a two, apparently).

Chief among those journalist-critics' self-conceived duties was the dissemination of rules of behavior, reframed as "arts etiquette," and the dissemination of the rules of taste, reframed as "aesthetics." Toward the former point, columnists provided cues by scolding some members of the audiences for their lack of decorum in the playhouse while applauding others (usually the economic elite) who demonstrated their capacity to literally embody sophisticated understanding by sitting still and keeping quiet. Toward the latter point, columnists often lambasted the "public" for its insufficient appreciation of great art at the box office. Readers capable of responding to this emerging critical mandate were privy to entering a new club, one that recognized the relationship between acquiring aesthetic taste and climbing the social ladder. Ultimately, then, the key to controlling (that is, quieting) the emerging professional class of the early twentieth century proved to be relatively easy: tap into anxieties about social mobility. As Richard Butsch notes, the acquisition of proper etiquette became preferred "among the middle and upper classes to audiences exercising sovereignty, which became a mark of lower class."[83]

In some ways, these first few generations of journalistic arts columnists and artist gatekeepers functioned as the advance guard of the arts appreciation movement, an aspect of education reform that came of age during the Progressive Era. Inspired by educational theorists such as John Dewey, practitioners of arts appreciation believed that bringing culture to children would by default bring culture to parents and thus to the average working-class home. This trickle-up effect was implemented using techniques such as picture study, a secondary school pedagogy in which teachers handed out tiny reproductions of Western masterpieces for examination and discussion and allowed students to take them home. The picture cards also contained quotes from literature, equating visual aesthetics and canonical poetry, plays, novels, and scripture with a higher (but achievable) level of human behavior and interaction. The preface to a widely distributed Picture Study text from 1927 noted, for example, that the "subject matter of a picture is more than its execution, style or technique. The good picture from an educational standpoint of view is either like a sermon teaching a great moral truth or like a poem, idealizing some important aspect of life. It must palpitate with human interest."[84] In the early twentieth century, a second modality for teaching arts appreciation introduced the concept of participation in studio activities (painting, sculpting, playing an instrument) on the theory that applied study was a more authentic way to create a lifelong individual relationship with the arts.[85] I have in my personal library a book from 1904 titled *Textbooks of Art Education: Book Two (Second Year)* that combines both modalities. It contains classic Picture Study reproductions coupled with poetry (Longfellow, Christina Rossetti, Robert Louis Stevenson) *and* drawing instruction ("Draw a circle. Fold and cut it into two equal parts. Each is a semicircle"), color chart wheels and home decorating advice: All of it geared toward second graders.[86]

Music appreciation first originated in Europe in the early nineteenth century as an adult education initiative intended to "instruct ignorant lovers of music."[87] In the United States, W. S. B. Mathews, editor of the journal *Music*, published *How to Understand Music* in 1888, followed a year later by Henry Krehbiel's widely distributed *How to Listen to Music: Hints and Suggestions to Untaught Lovers of the Art*. These early music appreciation texts were designed for adult listeners, according to the early twentieth century musicologist Percy A. Scholes, because "Love for a thing may come (and very often does) as the *result* (italics original) of understanding it. What we do not understand is generally repellent."[88] In his study of the origins of music appreciation as a secondary pedagogy, Scholes argues that the term itself wasn't formally used in print until music education instruction was introduced into the public school curriculum after 1906, aided by the widespread availability of the phonograph as a teaching tool.[89] As arts education took its institutional shape over the first half of the twentieth century and became associated primarily with children, the notion of adult-centered arts appreciation mutated from a learning construct (understanding what elements distinguish a good painting, being capable of quoting a passage from Shakespeare, having the confidence to articulate a theory about why an arts-going experience was emotionally moving) to a strategy by which the professional class could climb the next rung on the social ladder. Salaried white collar workers might not be in the economic position to buy a season subscription, for example, but they could gain cultural capital by occasionally attending the symphony with the boss and demonstrating that they knew enough not to clap between movements. Gradually, the notion that the arts-going experience might also include discussion and debate about the meaning and value of the arts event faded away. For the average professional-class American of the mid-twentieth century, it was enough to be appropriately dressed and politely present.

This emerging definition of a sophisticated adult audience as a passive, silent mass remained in place even as the commercial high arts industry was replaced by the not-for-profit, tax-based arts economy after the Second World War. This shift—the result of a wave of foundation money dedicated to increasing supply and broadening the geography of "culture" to include a network of American cities beyond New York—could have had a leveling effect on the power dynamic between arts makers and audiences.[90] But, as I have written elsewhere, despite the rhetoric of democracy implied by terms like *public* theater and *civic* orchestra, the high/low binary that first emerged in the late nineteenth century was not erased, just reassigned. From the perspective of audience sovereignty, public funding did not desacralize the arts.[91] Instead, arts professionals at the helm of publicly funded institutions—artists, arts administrators, and board members—became the new gatekeepers. Today the nineteenth-century "raising the masses" ethos remains intact, seemingly peacefully coexisting with newer ideologies, such as multiculturalism and postmodernism, that deliberately erase distinctions between high, middle, and low in the effort to democratize what constitutes appropriate content or structure for making art. I cannot be the only observer to note the irony in this fact. Why has there been no correlative effort to redefine what constitutes appropriate audience behavior or to reexamine audience rights while consuming that multicultural, postmodern art? In the final analysis, the not-for-profit engine didn't empower audiences; rather, it increased the "need" for gatekeepers. One way or another, contemporary arts workers are still in the twentieth-century business of delivering meaning, ascribing value, and quieting audiences. I offer two possible explanations for this phenomenon in Chapter 6.

Chapter 3

Geographies of Social Interpretation

Magic…is about so much more than just playing the game. For example, add up the hours you spent on Magic in the last week—and I'm talking everything you did that was Magic related. How many of those hours were actually spent playing the game? You see, with Magic there is a lot more than the game itself. There is deckbuilding, metagame comprehension, community engagement, article reading, just talking about Magic. I believe the majority of players spend more time on Magic not playing than playing.

—*Mark Rosewater*, Head Designer, *Magic: The Gathering.*[1]

"Playing" Magic, a popular trading card game with both physical and online platforms, is a vivid example of the way social interpretation operates in twenty-first-century American culture. Many aspects of our culture fit this definition of engagement in which the players spend more time on the topic "not playing than playing." Think, for example, about the average sports fan and the hours spent preparing to watch a game (reading stats, analysis, and opinion in newspapers and online, listening to sports-related talk radio and television, talking to coworkers and friends) relative to the hours spent actually watching it. As Magic players and sports fans know, deep pleasure resides in those opportunities to prepare, process, and analyze in order to be ready to interpret in a social setting. In contemporary American life, consumers of popular culture are constantly invited to articulate meaning and are regularly provided with surrounding experiential opportunities that facilitate that process. And for good reason. There is a clear relationship between a given participatory community's interest in attending a sporting event, watching a television show, or playing an online game and the opportunity to construct its meaning; the resulting engagement is a product of the felt value of participating in *an experience*. As noted in Chapter 1, an experience is defined by the satisfaction we feel when we bring a level of consciousness to a process, thus allowing it to, as John Dewey said, "run its course to fulfillment." Though Dewey may not have envisioned playing Magic as the kind of aesthetic experience he set out to illuminate in *Art as Experience*, I argue here that the parallels are real and the analogy is valid for twenty-first-century American culture.

To that end, Chapter 3 is devoted to a synchronic analysis of a few selected contemporary practices (what I call geographies) in popular culture that demonstrate an authorized audience engaged in an experience that leads to social interpretation. These alternative geographies are not usually considered in the arts industry discourse on "participation" because they involve competition (sports, reality television), because they mix the role of spectator with the role of active participant (gaming), or because the audience is not constituted as a live assembly but rather is connected via alternative routes and mechanisms (the Internet or broadcast bands). As noted in the introduction, however, part of the book's methodology is to cross traditionally understood boundaries by making regular and serious comparisons between arts interpretation and hermeneutic processes from other cultural arenas. By analyzing culturally embedded interpretive practices outside of the serious arts realm, we are better situated to understand the mechanics of social interpretation and to apply those mechanics to an Arts Talk ethos. This is because the fundamental components of meaning making have universal cognitive characteristics and as such exist across subject matter and conditions of assembly. We don't learn to walk exclusively in order to be able march in formation. We learn to walk because it serves a wide range of human activities, including marching, and also running, jumping, climbing, etc. Similarly, we learn to interpret because making meaning is part of the human condition, and once we have those basic tools we are free to apply them to a wide range of topics.

Twenty-first-century popular culture is fertile territory for understanding the nature of interpretive agency because where there's an engaged consumer there is also evidence of how meaning is constructed and institutionally supported. And it is an important location for the taste-talk-pleasure calculus leading to engagement. In the cultural experiences discussed in this chapter, I find evidence of engagement through those operations; engagement defined by a deep connection to the event's value and place in shaping community life. Furthermore, this engagement is often intellectually critical, which is to say that there is clear evidence of audience participation in conceptualizing, analyzing, synthesizing, and evaluating information gathered from observation, communication, and reflection. This does not mean that there are no important differences between consumption patterns around the arts versus sports, gaming, etc. I readily acknowledge that sports spectatorship—with its emphasis on competition and tribal affiliations—serves a set of individual and collective impulses arguably distinct from those serviced by our contemporary definition of art. (Though I also take the opportunity to underline the point made in Chapter 2 that many forms of Western art, including theater, began in a competitive, tribal environment.) Competition does breed a particular type and level of engagement, as is evidenced by the success of contest-based reality shows and their ilk. But engagement comes in many packages. In sports, the inherent drama is tied up with who will win, but in the arts an equally compelling dramatic tension is born from the unraveling of plot, the virtuosity of performers, the flush of feeling that accompanies both beautiful and painful images, and the power of physical copresence (audience to audience, audience to artist, audience to arts object). Regardless of the differences between sports-going and arts-going, we need to look for the connections between them rather than refuse to acknowledge that most people enjoy both. For arts workers, there is a lot to be learned by looking carefully at how these cultural operations work and mining them for ideas and strategies. At its core what we are examining is human experience and the desire to talk about it, in order to talk it through, in order to know it.

    In the first part of chapter 1 I look at the structure of contemporary cultural participation and analyze how opinion formation, venues (live and digital), and paratextual materials inform both cultural consumption and audience engagement. Later in the chapter I turn to description and analysis of the ways in which social interpretation operates within selected areas of contemporary cultural activity. How does interpretation function, for example, as a recognized aspect of the sports industry? Who enables these functions, how, and why? Similarly, how are interpretive practices supported in television, gaming, and the emerging social reading industry? My goal is to locate characteristics that demonstrate an authorized audience involved in an experience that leads to deeper engagement through social interpretation. In particular, I underline the ways in which the operations of taste and talk are incorporated into both long-standing and emerging protocols for social interpretation, including discussion, debate, ranking/voting, information sharing, opinion uploading, remixing, and other recent forms of aesthetic commentary. What makes these consumer-centered protocols effective, and why? How are they operationalized through various forms of talk? And, critically, how do they lead to pleasure (and thus engagement)?

PARTICIPATION NATION

The term participation connotes both sharing an experience with other people and having an ownership interest in that experience. Of the two connotations, ownership seems particularly key today. As noted in the Introduction, our current culture's fascination with participation is spurred on by a new wave of do-it-yourself social energy and the wide array of digitally powered engines that have helped to engender a sense of ownership in cultural practices ranging from science to politics to journalism to creative expression. In this context, literal participation is the key component of engagement and the way in which participatory cultures are formed and governed. As media scholar Henry Jenkins defines the phenomenon, a "participatory culture is a culture with relatively low barriers to artistic expression and civic engagement, strong support for creating and sharing one's creations, and some type of informal mentorship whereby what is known by the most experienced is passed along to novices. A participatory culture is also one in which members believe their contributions matter, and feel some degree of social connection with one another (at the least they care what other people think about what they have created)."[2] Jenkins offers various forms of participatory culture, including affiliations (online communities such as Facebook), expressions (producing new creative forms such as digital sampling, zines, etc.), collaborative problem-solving (working in both formal and informal teams to develop new knowledge), and circulations (shaping the flow of media by blogging, for example).[3]

The primary focus of much of the scholarship around the participatory culture phenomenon is on young people. Increasingly, however, adults (including senior citizens) are active in these communities of practice, a large percentage of who have embraced the interactivity of Web 2.0 culture in ways that parallel their children and grandchildren. In the citizen science movement, for example, volunteer astrologers engaged in collaborative problem solving not only patrol the heavens performing research tasks in conversation with other citizen astrologers, they also network with professionals who increasingly rely on data gathered in this public manner.[4] Similarly, citizen journalists, in addition to shaping the flow of professional media outlets through blog posts and tweets, provide significant content; it is no longer startling, for instance, to see traditional media outlets such as the *New York Times* running tags on the website asking readers to submit photographs and video of breaking stories. This definition of public engagement through participation has of course been facilitated by wide access to and the ease of use of social media platforms. Facebook, Twitter, and tumblr invite plugged-in Americans to weigh in on breaking news or to participate in back-channel discussions while the topic under examination is unfolding in front of them. Posting a wall comment on an organization's Facebook page allows entry into worlds previously impermeable to the average American, as does tweeting or uploading a Vine or joining a feedback string at the end of an article in your local newspaper or pointing fellow readers to a particularly interesting article on reddit or pinning your latest find on Pinterest.

Other structures use the exponentiality of the Internet to leverage mass collaboration on specific projects, many of them with a civic orientation. Think, for example, of the Occupy Movement's use of the Internet as a tool for fund-raising and as a site for organizing the rhetoric of social change. Then think about the way in which that very rhetoric ("we are the 99%'ers") was disseminated and reformulated through participation in online social interpretation of the movement. Or look at the community response to Mitt Romney's "binders full of women" comment during the presidential debate on October 16, 2012. Within a few days, Amazon.com became a repository for open political opining when a page devoted to selling plastic binders (the Avery Durable View Binder) was appropriated for social commentary in the form of hundreds of customer "reviews" of the product satirizing Romney's statement.[5] The Amazon page engendered waves of water cooler discussion and layers of social interpretation as the electorate talked through the dynamics of the election season.

Adult participatory cultures can be broken down into user cohorts identified by their level and type of activity. Media theorists have developed multiple (often competing) taxonomies, from the oft-cited "groundswell ladder" for typing the trajectory of participation in social technology ("inactives, spectators, collectors, critics and creators")[6] to Nicholas Abercrombie and Brian Longhurst's framing of the television fan in *Audiences: A Sociological Theory of Performance and Imagination.* Abercrombie and Longhurst begin their study by observing that the place of television fans within popular, mass media disseminated culture is defined in terms of dominance and power. They go on to introduce the concept of the fan as "petty producer," an audience member *"skilled* or *competent* in different modes of production and consumption; *active* in their interactions with texts and in their production of new texts; and *communal* in that they construct different communities based on their links to the programmes they like."[7]

The concept of the petty producer is obviously closely related to the participatory ethos of contemporary culture and to recent definitions of identity within the construct of fandom. But what, exactly, is a fan? In sports, definitions range from "an affiliation in which a great deal of emotional significance and value are derived from group membership"[8] to a person who "thinks, talks about and is oriented towards sports even when [the fan] is not actually observing, or reading, or listening to an account of a specific sports event."[9] The association with obsession is an important marker (the term itself is, of course, derived from *fanatic*), as is a quality of devotion to a particular game, or team, or player. In popular culture, the term describes someone who is "obsessed with a particular star, celebrity, film, TV programme, band..."[10] As the examples of highly authorized historical audiences in Chapter 2 illustrate, fans (or aficionados, as they used to be called in the arts world) have always played a significant role in the economies of leisure industries, including the arts. But as television critic Adam Sternbergh points out, the Internet has profoundly boosted their impact, serving as a "kind of electrocharged amniotic fluid for the gestation of...what I'll call the superviewer. These people are engaged, passionate and vocal, an online jumble of professional critics and opinionated amateurs who gather together to watch and discuss and dissect their favorite shows. Early fan forums like Television Without Pity gave these viewers a voice; now sites like Twitter have given them a megaphone."[11]

Are there superviewers for today's serious arts forms? There is some evidence that skilled audience members (petty producers) have gained an increased presence in the arts sector in recent years—empowered by social media platforms and a variety of backchannel modalities that by their nature facilitate discursive practices in an unusually democratic (or, at least unusually unregulated) manner. Nevertheless, it is also clear that the not-for-profit arts industry has not been able to produce fan communities that match the energy of those associated with competing forms of leisure time entertainment. Why is this the case, especially given the relatively recent history of fanatical conduct of arts audiences outlined in chapter 2? I explore some possible explanations in chapter 6.

OPINION FORMATION AND SOCIAL INTERPRETATION

As this brief overview demonstrates, the contemporary concept of "participation" in popular culture is predominantly oriented around the invitation to make meaning through opinion sharing. "People want meaningful opportunities to participate and contribute, to add their piece of information, view or opinion," argues Charles Leadbeater in *We Think*, his treatise on the power of digital culture. "They want viable ways to share, to think and work laterally with their peers."[12] But what does it mean to share or think laterally? Leadbeater's use of the term "opinion" invites us to probe more deeply into the word's definition and its potential role in social interpretation. Given the opinion-centric quality of twenty-first-century life for most Americans, the question here is whether opining is a proper (as in formal) part of the hermeneutic function and thus a legitimate aspect of the taste-talk-pleasure calculus. In what manner does opinion formation inform the meaning-making operation and lead to the sense of fulfillment that defines pleasure?

The most commonly cited dictionary definition of the word opinion (from the Latin *opinari*, "to mean") refers to a view or judgment qualified by a lack of evidence; that is, an opinion is not a fact. Further, an opinion is differentiated from a theory in that the former is a feeling while the latter can be supported by evidence. If something is "a matter of opinion," then it has a subjective quality limited by the belief system of an individual or group. In Western culture, opining is seen as a kind of birthright of democracy. Americans say that we have a "right to our opinion," and by that we mean that we are free to choose and to express our beliefs in certain matters, regardless of who is seen to control the facts.

Other usages of the term, however, go beyond the purely subjective. The formal *opinion* issued by a court of law is a summary of facts and applicable law used as supporting evidence for a legal decision. These opinions form the basis of the common-law system and are used as evidence in future arguments coming before the bench. In a similar manner, religious doctrine is often handed down via a system of interlinking opinions. The Talmud, for instance, is a collection of the opinions of thousands of rabbis on a range of subjects from law and ethics to history, customs, and cultural lore. As the basis for rabbinic law, these opinions hold great weight and are not understood as individual feelings but rather as links in the learned discourse that defines Judaism. In everyday life, an *informed* opinion signals that the opiner has crossed the feeling/fact divide and is capable of providing evidence to support his or her assertions.

The concept of *public* opinion—that slippery term for the aggregate of individual beliefs or attitudes held by a defined group—extends the complication over subjectivity further. What precisely is public opinion and who is in the position to define it? The nature and function of public opinion in Western culture has been the subject of ongoing theorization since Montaigne first coined the concept in the sixteenth century and Jeremy Bentham developed the first unified theory under his notion of utilitarianism (the greatest happiness for the greatest number). Much of the ensuing theory has been associated with political life and the way in which democracy is operationalized via public debate designed to "establish the meaning and interpretation of issues" in the midst of "opposing frames that are intended by opinion leaders to influence public preferences."[13] In contemporary America, public opinion is also clearly shaped by mass media and the power of commercial consumerism. Historians trace the emergence of consumer culture in the United States to a shift at the turn into the twentieth century as people moved from a preference for leisure time to a preference for the additional income that comes with working longer hours.[14] This shift in preference was, of course, spurred on by the invention of advertising and marketing strategies targeted at the rising middle class and the cultural conflation of social status with the ability to consume. Accordingly, public opinion is highly subject to the manipulation of the free market and the taste makers and other trend setters it engenders.

But how are *private* debates, those internal conversations we hold in order to work out our opinions for ourselves, structured? Are we the sole arbiters of our own opinions, or are the interests and attitudes that shape them also controlled by outside frames, including those constructed by consumerism and mass communication? To update Samuel Johnson's oft-cited observation ("The majority have no other reason for their opinions other than that they are in fashion"), are our personal opinions highly subject to mass media-directed fashion?

Yes and no. As mentioned in Chapter 1, opinion formation in the form of taste and taste making is clearly related to the effect of authority on the process of social judgment. We process information in order to formulate our tastes or opinions, and in so doing, we assign different degrees of authority to different sources. "Source expertness" (the degree to which the source has been credentialed as an authority on the topic) and "source trustworthiness" (the degree to which the source intends to speak the truth) both affect the way in which individuals form opinions on everything from commercial products to arts events.[15] But recent studies of how social judgment operates complicate the matter by citing the effect that individual predispositions (which of course are themselves culturally constructed) have on opinion formation, thus questioning the absolute power of outside frames to leverage opinion. These studies find that an individual frame in thought (an individual's cognitive understanding of a given situation), for instance, is capable of overcoming the suasion of a media frame if he or she possesses a strong prior belief or interest.[16] The psychology of interest further complicates the discussion, because, as cognitive psychologist Paul J. Silvia points out, interest is now understood in two ways: (1) as *interest,* an aspect of emotional experience; that is, a "feeling" of interest defined as a momentary motivation) and (2) as *interests,* a part of "personality, individual differences, and people's idiosyncratic hobbies, goals, and avocations."[17] In terms of opinion formation, then, both an individual's interest and interests play a foundational role. Our opinions could be said to represent our interest/s in life, from the political or religious beliefs we inherit from our parents to the way in which a personal interest in singing influences our support for more arts education in the public schools. For most people, a self-inventory of our opinions is also an analysis of who we are as a person (I am a liberal, I am an artist, I am a feminist) and what we have experienced in life. But as David Bohm stresses, it is "important to see that the different opinions that you have are the result of past thought: all your experiences, what other people have said, and what not...Opinions thus tend to be experienced as 'truths' even though they may only be your own assumptions and your own back ground. You got them from your teacher, your family, or by reading, or in yet some other way. Then for one reason or another you are identified with them, and you defend them."[18] In the best sense, we offer our opinions because we feel we have information to share with others that might help them, or might help society. In the worst sense, we conflate opinion with ego such that when someone disagrees with us we feel negated. The latter hurts, so much so that we are prone to what psychologists refer to as the "false-consensus effect," a cognitive bias suggesting that people "see their own behavioral choices and judgments as relatively common and appropriate to existing circumstances while viewing alternative responses as uncommon, deviant, or inappropriate."[19] We tend, in other words, to overestimate how much other people agree with us just as we tend to classify our own opinions as the "normal" ones. (Shades of Kant's *sensus communus*.)

Opinions, then, are clearly emotional. But what, exactly, are emotions? Most people would say that emotions are feelings deriving from circumstances, mood, relationships with other people, etc. But as discussed in Chapter 2, contemporary neuroscience challenges this folk wisdom, instead defining basic emotions as biological response patterns rooted in species survival and activated by electrical and chemical stimulation at a precognitive level.[20] Emotions aren't free-floating feelings but rather embodied neural affective processes; that is, they exist empirically as part of our mind/brain. Understood in this manner, the relationship between opinion formation, emotion, and self-esteem is seen as a complicated social, psychological, and physiological web. Understanding how one thread of the opinion web informs and supports another is an important task for anyone interested in facilitating social interpretation.

PARATEXTS AND SOCIAL INTERPRETATION

Knowledge acquisition is an essential part of the Arts Talk model's taste-talk-pleasure calculus because it supports the journey toward fulfillment that an *arts experience* provides. Knowledge acquisition is also essential to the enjoyment of a variety of other social activities. In most popular culture contexts, productive and enjoyable participation relies heavily on preparation in the form of what media scholar Jonathan Gray calls "paratexts" (a term he borrows from literary theorist Gerard Genette, who coined it to discuss the cultural materials that surround a literary text).[21] Gray's examples focus primarily on film and television industry materials—ads, previews, trailers, interviews with creative personnel, entertainment news, reviews, and merchandising that "tell us about the media world around us, prepare us for that world, and guide us between its structures."[22] A film, for example, cannot be adequately analyzed without taking into account its paratextual proliferations because, Gray argues, they fill it with "meaning, take up much of our viewing and thinking time, and give us the resources with which we will both interpret and discuss that world."[23] These materials include "entryway paratexts" (those that try to control the way a viewer enters a media experience) and "in medias res paratexts" (those that come to the viewer during or after the media experience).[24] For Gray, there is no such thing as film for film's sake; movie spectatorship is a complicated sociocultural reading/viewing process made up of all the materials that contribute to the "meaning" of a motion picture.

Industry-produced paratexts are not just apparati of the marketing structure of commercial enterprise (e.g., the advertisements designed to sell the event in question), they are part of the meaning-making structure—they give consumers the resources to talk about the subject at hand and the tools to interpret its meaning. Seen this way, paratexts are de facto *learning supports*, a term I borrow from learning science, where they are defined as resources, strategies, and practices that provide physical, social, emotional, and intellectual supports "addressing barriers to and promoting engagement in learning and teaching."[25] Paratexts *cum* learning supports align with this definition, operating as resources, strategies, and practices that enable cultural participants to address barriers to engagement.

The idea that active and productive participation in a cultural event could include the consumption of materials related to but not a formal part of the event itself is not new to the arts, of course. Engaged arts audiences, particularly those involved in social interpretation of the work, have historically relied on paratextual materials to aid their meaning-making process and their capacity to participate in socially prescribed interpretive acts. These materials include artist statements in both oral and written forms (e.g., the *proagon* at the City Dionysia, playwright's prologues read by actors at the beginning of a performance, visual artist's and composer's statements disseminated through pamphlets), lectures given by critics and other experts before and after arts events, program essays, arts appreciation journals and books, newspaper articles (previews, reviews, artist interviews, industry news columns), newsletters issued by producing organizations, and audience league materials (critical bulletins, informational newsletters). Artists and arts institutions of the past not only used paratextual materials to enrich audiences but also, at times, to literally build them from the ground up. Between 1767 and 1769, for example, playwright Gotthold Lessing published a series of short critical essays on productions being staged at the Hamburg National Theater in serial pamphlet form (now referred to as the *Hamburg Dramaturgy*). And musicologist Johann Nikolaus Forkel gave free public lectures on music history before his concerts in Gottingen in the 1770s and 1780s. Both Lessing and Forkel designed their paratextual offerings for self-serving reasons; charged with running a public arts organization in an era without an organized public audience, they responded to the crisis of the interregnum by attempting to assist the aesthetic and intellectual growth of the citizenry as a way of growing an audience base. For both of these innovators, the need to address barriers to engagement caused by the audience's lack of prior knowledge informed the course of their plan of action in terms of enterprise and aesthetics.

In twenty-first-century America, the rapid social change brought on by the digital turn and the subsequent screening of the culture have introduced a new kind of "in medias res" paratextual practice. "Second screening" (or "two screening") refers to the practice of having a second screen in front of you as you watch the primary screen in order to support your understanding and engagement with the primary text and, in some instances, to interact with it. The cognitive implications for second screening are fascinating to ponder: split focus, hyper attention to certain details (because the viewer can look up supporting information while watching the unfolding action on the primary screen), and a kind of engagement fueled by personal choice (because the passivity inherent in the viewer's experience of the primary screen is disrupted by the opportunity to critically employ the second screen or to digitally connect with other users of the primary screen). The applications for live performance/gallery spectatorship are intriguing. While live performance is not a screen, cognitively there is no difference between the behavior described above and the opera buff who follows the performance (primary "screen") with the score in hand (secondary "screen"). As I asked in the book's introduction, could access to the Internet and social media platforms actually inform and advance social interpretation not just on line but also in physically co-present environments? Can arts workers expand the definition of arts-based paratexts to include iterations of second screening as part of the audience experience? Chapter 6 includes examples of experimentation with this concept.

VENUES IN THE LIVE | DIGITAL ERA

Cultural participation does not occur in a physical vacuum. Arenas, stadiums, music clubs, comedy clubs, gaming parlors, television studios, even some movie theaters, are, like the active auditoriums of the past, places where live audience reaction is prized as a critical component of the experience and where participation is enhanced by social convention that encourages an active response. The important role that social interpretation plays in this kind of a live environment is critical to the quality of engagement that people feel. Liveness sets off a kind of chain reaction that informs the shaping of public opinion and public taste and releases individuals to begin their own journey toward meaning making.

But in the twenty-first century, the quality of liveness is not strained. Digital liveness is a factor of contemporary cultural phenomenology and, in a way, the apotheosis of the modern quest for immediate contact with physically distant people that began in the nineteenth century with wired technologies like the telegraph. Today's live streams and other forms of real-time interfaces and networks have replaced physical copresence with social copresence, a form of human connection that does not require literal proximity. For many arts workers, this replacement is understood more as a displacement—taking audiences away from the three-dimensional immediacy of live performance and stripping people of fleshly access to other people in a way that flattens the experience for everyone involved. But is that really true? Is the wireless brain capable of being present in a digital capacity in ways that replicate physical copresence? In other words, if the affective experience *feels* live, does that make it live? Some media theorists believe that it does, arguing that liveness in the twenty-first century is the fact of *always being connected* (via mobile phone, for example). In this definition (and context), physical copresence is not required, nor is temporal immediacy. Instead, as media theorist Nick Couldry describes it, we have "on-line liveness," defined by social copresence, and "group liveness," defined by constant contact with acquaintances via mobile devices.[26]

Given the Internet's unparalleled ability to link up previously separate contexts, it is useful (indeed necessary) to look at the delivery mechanisms that inform contemporary popular culture: namely, social media computing platforms and related application softwares (apps). In the live | digital era, separating the medium from the message is truly impossible. Information channeling (gathering, sorting, dissemination) has always been the route to power, but social media platforms have adjusted the nature of that power structure. In particular, these postanalog platforms have increased individual access to paratextual data and as such profoundly altered the role and capacity of paratexts to facilitate the meaning-making operation. Social media using RSS feeds, for example, provide access to a constantly evolving array of paratexts by virtue of file sharing (videos, texts, graphics, photographs, sound files) and the ease of site linking and sorting features. Similarly, application software sorts through those files and provide streamlined access to specific paratexts supporting the performance of specific tasks.

While the digital turn has radically transformed the delivery system, the real revolution here (as many cultural theorists have noted) is the introduction of unparalleled opportunities for consumer-led interactivity. New media vehicles offer their audience the chance not only to talk back but also to actively shape individual experience. Henry Jenkins calls this process *convergence culture* and points to the way in which content (including paratexual learning supports) flowing across multiple media platforms is used and transformed by the "migratory behavior of media audiences" in their quest for certain types of entertainment experiences.[27] Jenkin's central thesis has to do with the reconfiguration of these media platforms to support two key characteristics of contemporary consumers: the belief that their contributions matter and the sense of social connection that their participatory behavior engenders. Today every industry-produced paratext has the potential to be appropriated and recirculated by the consumer in increasingly influential ways. And consumer-produced paratexts (blogs posts, tweets, mash-ups, etc.) are facilitated by handheld technology, access to processing and production software and, of course, free 2.0 distribution channels.

Among the key ideas here is the way in which convergence sites renegotiate power structures between producers and consumers. As Charles Leadbeater analogizes it in *We Think*, over the past 20 years the sorting and dissemination power of the commercial Internet has radically transformed us from what he calls a boulder to a pebble culture. In the mid-1980s (prior to the advent of the commercial Internet), information access looked like a beach, with crowds organized around a few boulders (big media empires controlling all access to information and information processing). Just five years later, only a few very big boulders were still showing, drowned out, he writes, "by a rising tide of pebbles. As you stand surveying the beach every minute hundreds of thousands of people come to drop their pebbles...in no particular order, as people feel like it. Pebbles are the new business."[28] Leadbeater's pebbles—reddit redirects, blog posts, tweets, instagrams—are channeled through social media platforms that operate as both identity sites ("here are the facts about me!") *and* as sites of assembly where users convene to share paratextual learning supports and to engage in social interpretation without the aid of hired gatekeepers.

In terms of social interpretation, digital venues now play an even larger role than brick-and-mortar venues. This is largely due to two factors: (1) the face-to-facelessness of the digital channel, offering a 2.0 version of anonymity and with it a new kind of liquid courage when it comes to stating an opinion; and (2) the stop-time effect of the digital channel, offering the ability to participate in and out of real time and thus allowing the user to step out long enough to formulate and reformulate affective reactions, including emotional responses ("that made me feel good"), opinions ("I hated it"), and tastes ("it's just not my kind of thing"). In the age of mass media and ubiquitous screens, cultural consumption as spectating happens in a wide array of sites, from arenas to living rooms to bars to interactive computer platforms placed inside those arenas and living rooms and bars. Because of this new paradigm, the definition of physical venue in this book includes discrete use of brick and mortar or digital sites of assembly *and* their simultaneous use.

TASTE, TALK, AND PLEASURE: SPORTS

Spectator sports thrive in contemporary America at least in part because they consistently invite social interpretation in a variety of forms. Before launching my analysis and support for this statement, I want to step squarely into the first person for a moment to state what may not be obvious to the reader thus far: I am not a sports fan. I don't attend or watch sports events and I don't consume sporting paratexts. As a child I did compete briefly as a speed and synchronized swimmer, but I left both sports at the age of 14 when forced to choose between attending rehearsals for a school play and making afternoon team practices. I am a fitness practitioner but spend most of my work-out time alone on machines. I am in my mid-fifties and I rarely read anything from a newspaper sports page or anything sports related online. I have never studied sports culture (prior to writing this book). I rarely choose to watch sports events on television. And I have only very sporadically (and reluctantly, except for the beer and the chance to sing "Take Me Out to the Ballgame") attended amateur or professional sporting events.

And yet I know a lot more about spectator sports than most other Americans know about, say, the serious arts. I know about sports by virtue of my participation in mediatized culture and in social life writ more broadly. I, like many Americans, cannot attend a family event without in some way overhearing or being absorbed into a discussion about sports teams, industry news, and personal news about athletes. I can't live in my own house without overhearing a sporting event on television or the radio. I can't listen to "Morning Edition" on NPR while working out in the morning without also hearing at least one news item about sports. I can't peruse the front page of the *New York Times* without some reference to a recent sporting event or the sports industry. I can't flip channels in a hotel room without passing through three or four ESPN channels. I can't go into bars and restaurants without seeing screens showing an array of broadcast sports and industry-produced paratexts. I can't go into a department store without confronting shelves of industry-related clothing and other fan items. And I can't get through a week of social activity without hearing sports talk. In other words, though I am not a direct sports consumer, I am still exposed to the *sports experience* and to the ways in which that experience facilitates social interpretation. The ubiquity of sports-related paratextual materials profoundly shapes contemporary culture, enables the talk that comes out of that culture (helping sports audiences to prepare, to process, and to analyze), and, ultimately, provides the kind of pleasure that so many people associate with sports.

I grew up in the city of Pittsburgh and spent two decades working and living there as an adult. I never cared, on a personal level, about the Steelers' season. But I did care on a community level, because every fall the city's talk (and, let's face it, the city's mood) was informed by what happened the previous Sunday afternoon (Monday night, Thursday night...). In other words, by virtue of my living circumstances, I was socialized into sports awareness (if not sports fandom). Pittsburghers do not hesitate to study, analyze, discuss, and debate a football game. They do not hesitate to formulate an opinion based on taste, data, and emotional response. They do not hesitate to share that opinion in a variety of social settings. In short, they don't hesitate to make meaning when it comes to the Steelers.

Why? Because they have been given the cultural "permission" to express their opinions openly and the tools they need to back them up. For most Americans, "watching the game" is not limited to the time spent actually watching the game, but rather has come to define the time spent consuming the paratextual material surrounding the sporting event and participating in the resulting sports talk. But where does this permission—what I call cultural space—for sports talk come from? I would argue that it is sourced in the three key ingredients of sports spectatorship and its pleasures: play, citizenship (including leadership), and competition. Play is characterized as a free activity outside of ordinary life and without material interest; it relates to the participatory nature of sport and the clear biological roots of social games that involve bodily performance.[29] As children we all participate, on some level, in physically oriented games whether or not we develop any level of expertise or whether or not we join teams. Citizenship relates to the long-standing cultural belief in the link between education and sports, wherein the relationship between sports participation and human development has consistently been posited as critical to creating productive citizens. Pierre Bourdieu traces educational sporting activity to late nineteenth-century English boarding schools, where participatory sports were created by the elite "as a training in courage and manliness, 'forming the character' and inculcating the 'will to win' which is the mark of the true leader, but a will to win within the rules. This is 'fair play', conceived as an aristo-cratic disposition utterly opposed to the plebeian pursuit of victory at all costs."[30] While Bourdieu's class analysis might not be fully relevant to the contemporary American context, a similar brand of character formation rhetoric is very much in operation today. Millions of dol-lars of tax money and philanthropic funds go into sports programs in public schools and not-for-profit community centers because of a deeply felt cultural belief that playing sports promotes good citizen-ship and leadership qualities in children.

Competition (the *will to win*) is the most commonly understood pleasure associated with sports spectatorship; indeed, many theo-rists argue that the definition of sport (as opposed to leisure and play) must involve competitive physical activity. For sports theorist Alan G. Ingham, agonal games that produce winners and losers are closely tied with engaged spectatorship because they create "pleasur-able, controllable, and creative tension."[31] Competition introduces external urgency and the drama of anticipating outcome—we don't know what will happen and that tension is fundamentally pleasurable. Sports anthropologist Kendall Blanchard observes that competition is sourced in conflict and aggression. This is amply demonstrated by the frequent use of war metaphors to describe professional team sports as well as by anthropological analyses showing that societies with higher frequencies of warfare are more likely to engage in combat-ive sports.[32] There is clearly a kind of cultural necessity tied up with structuring aggression, as Dwight D. Eisenhower must have known when he famously stated that the "true mission of American sports is to prepare young men for war."[33] Even pure spectatorship (without an element of participation) has what economists call an exchange or surplus value: As spectators, we buy our pleasure through consum-ing other people's participation and by aligning our identity with the professionals who will, we hope, win for us. In either instance of direct participation or of spectating, the elements of competition and conflict (tension, urgency, anticipation) produce pleasure.

These fundamental pleasures of play, citizenship, and competition are facilitated by the embodied nature of sports consumption and the physical copresence of spectators to one another and to the athletes they are there to watch. Inside sports venues spectators not only see each other as easily as they can see the sports event, but they can also express themselves physically by moving individually (standing, gesticulating, moving between the seats and other public areas) and communally (doing the wave, stomping in unison). And, of course, they can talk. Our physical response to a sports event includes talking about the event in real time. In sports culture, talk is not a by-product of spectating, it is an aspect of it. Spectators are expected to talk to one another during a sports event—this is understood as fundamental to the social nature of the sports experience and to its larger phenomenology. Spectators arrive in the arena talking to their companions (comparing statistics, discussing the latest sports news, making predictions, debating opinions), they talk in direct response to the unfolding action on the field during the game (to the referees, the players, other spectators), and they talk during breaks in the action (assessing, analyzing, arguing). Spectators also arrive in the living room of a friend or a neighborhood sports bar talking to their companions, and just as in the arena, they talk in direct response to the unfolding action, this time on the screen. Even before the broadcast and wireless eras, sports consumption sometimes occurred in facsimile, as this amusing description of a turn-of-the-century baseball game illustrates: "While the Pittsburg Club is away the games played by them will be reproduced on the Stage of The Avenue Theater. Identically the same in every detail as they are played on the field. The diamond is there, perfect and complete, and dummy figures play the game precisely like the players themselves, their movements being controlled according to the detailed description of the game sent direct from the grounds where the club is playing, by wire to the stage of the Avenue Theatre."[34] The Pittsburgh Pirate fans crowding into the Avenue Theater in 1900 undoubtedly talked their way through the virtual baseball game just as they would have in the ball park.

Regardless of whether the spectating is happening in the arena or the living room, sports audiences use their established tastes and opinions to launch sports talk—they carry allegiances, preferences and supporting critical analysis into the spectating environment and, through talking, they measure them against competing allegiances and preferences. Sometimes this talk leads to a change in point of view (and occasionally to fisticuffs); mostly, however, the tastes that walk into the arena or the living room are the tastes that walk out. (As many have observed, sports taste is significantly defined by the spectator's social class habitus—those aspects of culture that are anchored in the body or daily practices. As such, the spectator is not likely to give them up easily.) The issue here is not really about taste as an end in itself, however; rather it is the fact that sports fans, empowered by their ownership over their sense of taste, can enter into healthy debate. They aren't afraid to defend their allegiances and preferences—as sports fans, they know themselves.

Sports spectators rely heavily on paratexts to launch sports talk. Indeed, sports paratexts have long played a crucial role in engendering and facilitating all manners of sports-related social interpretation, from water-cooler talk to blogging. In the early years of organized baseball (during and immediately after the Civil War), for example, newspapers, in an effort to attract readers, began including a statistical summary of the previous day's game in the form of box scores. Conceived as a discrete item separate from the sports writer's analysis and other sports section offerings (such as player interviews), box scores offered readers a summary of both individual and team performance. In the era of ubiquitous penny papers, easy access to box scores launched the habit of data analysis that is so central to the social interpretation of sports. Other paratextual materials such as *Beadle's Dime Base-Ball Player* (1860–1881), the earliest set of guides on public sale, offered similar learning support for nineteenth-century fans of the game.[35] The Beadle's booklets were issued annually and contained the current rules of the sport and the previous year's statistics. Unlike the first iteration of arts-related paratexts, which were produced by artists and arts presenters to increase audience attendance, however, many of the early sports learning supports were produced to sell the audience something other than the sports event itself. This relationship between retail commerce and sports culture goes back to the 1890s, when "a new urban culture of entertainment, which included the sports press, magazines and journals, was formed. Sport sold newspapers and newspapers sold sport. Newspaper owners often invested in athletes, teams, stadia and advertising. The professionalization of core sports occurred because of this."[36] Over time, as sports sociologist Grant Jarvie notes, the relationship between sport and the media expanded beyond its economic basis to became "social and cultural, and while it might not be of equal parts it is one of interdependency."[37]

Today every major spectator sport has corresponding paratextual materials produced by organizing leagues, professional teams, big media corporations, advertisers (that is, businesses) and, last but most certainly not least, sports fans themselves. Analog-era paratexts continue to influence the sports experience: Newspapers still print large sports sections and network television still broadcasts sports analysis in a variety of formats (from talking head shows to sports news). But digital-era paratexts have introduced important additional layers of information gathering and sharing. The Pittsburgh Steelers' Gameday PLUS app offers to "make your Android device a unique part of your game-day experience" with smart phone access to breaking news of the team, video-on-demand clips of press conferences and player interviews, pregame previews and postgame blogs plus "real-time statistics for every drive."[38] The NBA.com Pulse, a trending analytical column featured on the organization's home page, constantly sorts the top ten basketball news stories (with updates every 15 minutes). Major League Baseball offers the At Bat app, the At the Ballpark app, and text messaging accounts for stats and news updates. And so on.

Industry-produced paratexts continue to be extremely useful in the digital age because they allow spectators to enter into the culture with the kind of confidence brought on by a sense of authority over the facts. The competency of that authority is contestable, obviously, and there's plenty of resistance to fan authority in certain channels of sports discourse. Nevertheless, the commercial foundation of sports in American life is a powerful ally of audience sovereignty because commercialism, by nature, must respond to consumer demands. The direct and indirect economic stimulus of sports-related industry ranges from ticket sales to advertising rates to product sales. The nondirect economics of sports also matter a great deal to American culture: influence, prestige, and other forms of social capital are firmly tied to the sports experience. As a result, the sports consumer experience is and has always been closely tied to the very definition of spectator sports in the United States; in a fundamental way, sports is its fans. This is in fascinating contrast to the serious arts industry, where the process of sacralization in the late nineteenth and early twentieth centuries encouraged a pulling away from the consumer experience, including any direct acknowledgment of audience opinion beyond that expressed through "appropriate" forms of in-venue approbation (which is to say, polite applause).

Fan-produced sports-industry paratexts come in a variety of forms (blogs, Facebook pages, discussion boards) and facilitate a range of activity, from collecting, collating, and organizing sports-related information to interpreting the blitz of media surrounding a particular topic. An example of the latter is the amusingly titled "Puckin' Idiots," which bills itself as "North America's Favorite Hockey Related Humor Site" and boasts that it is filled with "interesting stuff that happens behind closed doors in the NHL."[39] This revolution in both the production and exchange of paratextual learning supports is accelerating the sovereignty of Abercrombie and Longhurst's "petty producers," those consumers whose active involvement in interpreting texts is facilitated by emerging democratic discursive practices that include being able to produce meaning. The value proposition of fan-produced paratexts to social interpretation is obvious: Every Facebook page or Twitter stream is filled with layers of description and reaction and links to other sites of description and reaction, creating an exponential interpretive chain.[40] This activity (and related behavior) is fuel for sports talk because, to paraphrase Jonathan Gray, it tells us about the sports world around us, prepares us for that world, and guides us between its structures. Most importantly, it gives us the resources to interpret and discuss that world. Sports talk clearly matters in our society, particularly when it comes to male relationships, where it supports the development of masculine self-identity, reinforces social bonding, and sometimes helps (at least ideally) fans to cross class, race, and professional identity boundaries.

Women's status in this paradigm is more problematic. The same study that identifies the ways in which male-to-male relationships are culturally reenforced through sports talk also points out the fact that women "experience feelings of marginalization and possibly denigration in their consumption of organized sports."[41] Women in the business world feel the impact of this socially prescribed marginalization in myriad ways, from missing out on locker room negotiations to being unable to bond with coworkers because of a lack of interest in sports-related events. To address the latter, business consultant Diane Darling offers a networking product called Water Cooler Football, a one-off workshop designed to teach the basics of football in order to better participate in work-related events that include sports talk and thus "expand and leverage their network of professional contacts."[42] Or consider Jean M. McCormick's book, *Talk Sports Like a Pro*, which promises "99 secrets to becoming a sports goddess."[43] The need for these products is supported by the findings from a recent study of Harvard Business School graduates revealing that men initiated 85 percent of the sports talk in their environment.[44] There are clear parallels here with patterns of arts consumption and arts talk during the eighteenth and nineteenth centuries, when active auditoriums were profoundly populated by men. As recent scholarship into the relationship between leisure and gender reveals, this is likely because women have historically had little choice about how to spend their time and little leisure time to spend. Despite this history of marginalization, there is some evidence that women are beginning to enter into the sports talk sphere. Recent Neilson data show increasing numbers of female viewers for professional sports (particularly for championship games) and blogs such as "WomenTalkSports" and "Diane's Sports Talk" promote dialogue and debate about sports between and among female sports fans.[45]

TASTE, TALK, AND PLEASURE: NEW MEDIA

The term "new media" is widely used to refer to digital media practices that contain an on-demand element and the capacity for interactivity, creative participation, and community generation. This stands in contrast to the one-way dissemination that characterizes analogue-era vehicles for mass media, including broadcast and cable television, radio, feature films, and print journals. According to media theorist Vin Crosbie, old media operates via "one-to-many" vehicles designed to offer exactly the same content to all recipients and to maintain absolute control over that content.[46] New media vehicles, on the contrary, are characterized as "many-to-many." Crosbie identifies two revolutionary characteristics of new media technology: (1) "individualized messages can simultaneously be delivered or displayed to an infinite number of people"; and (2) "each of the people involved—whether publisher, broadcasters, or consumer—shares equal and reciprocal control over that content."[47] It is the second characteristic that most significantly impacts the meaning-making process. Without the restrictions of one-to-many vehicles, consumers can consume content from a far greater range of sources, they can manipulate and network that content, and they can (re)produce that content to aid them in their own interpretive journey.

This is not to suggest that the flow of information and promise of power sharing generated by 2.0 interactivity is in practice as democratic as Crosbie envisions. As cultural critics around the globe argue on a daily basis, big media corporations regularly coopt interactivity as "a revamped strategy for surveillance and control."[48] With that caution in mind, we should not deny the importance of the cultural reciprocity that has occurred as the result of web-based interactivity, even if mediated. I think, for example, of the changes in the culture of journalism in the past five years. As a long-time daily reader of the *New York Times*, I've watched the role of consumer feedback move from a few carefully selected letters to the editor to a range of protocols that eschew traditional gatekeeping in favor of real-time reader interactivity: posting responses to articles and columns at will, voting on issues and cultural events (your favorite presidential debate moment, for example) and contributing to online polling. The impact of digital interactivity and the expectations of a newly engaged audience on journalism have been eye opening; faced with financial ruin, the industry is constantly adjusting its gatekeeping ethos when it comes to "reporting" the news. Reader taste/opinion is far more visible than it was before the digital shift, and reader taste/opinion is clearly playing a role in the ways in which the news is both disseminated and consumed.

Web-based interactivity produces, whether consciously or not, interpretive behavior rooted in the taste-talk-pleasure calculus. In this section of the chapter, I look at how this functions within three very different corners of the old and new media universes: television, social reading, and gaming. Here we have distinctly different audiences all linked by a similar desire to make meaning in a community context (as opposed to a private context). We also have a clear illustration of the ways in which new media vehicles have redefined "talk." In these examples, talk is a form of written communication, yet it displays the discursive function and quality of oral talk. People use digital vehicles to share their immediate thoughts in the same way that casual talk operates among people who are physically copresent. The ease of digital connection produces prodigious amounts of talk—some of it annoyingly facile and some of it quite probing. On the facile end of the trajectory is the Facebook "Like Box" function, offering users a "way to give positive feedback or to connect with things you care about on Facebook."[49] "Liking" is an audience gesture for the digital age—a gesture that eschews substantive feedback for quick, almost guerrilla-style intervention. On the other end of the spectrum are the layers of thoughtful and innovative remarks that appear in every corner of the digital universe, from bulletin board discussions of world events to intelligent commentary on popular culture (explored later).

Regardless of its quality of orality, though, digital talk is phenomenologically different from in-person talk. Physical distance, coupled with the disembodied nature of internet use, removes a layer of inhibition to the meaning-making operation. Psychologist Sherry Turkle cautions that this is not necessarily as productive as it might seem. She notes that our "always-on/always-on-you" devices enforce three powerful fantasies about communication in the digital era, "that we will always be heard; that we can put our attention wherever we want it to be; and that we never have to be alone."[50] Turkle goes on to warn that this new way of being alone together, in which we customize our relationships by having the capacity to be with one another while simultaneously being elsewhere (through our digital devices), is dumbing down the quality of conversation in our lives. In face-to-face conversation, she argues, we tend to one another, paying attention to tone and nuance and all of the emotional undercurrents that accompany human connection. And, importantly, face-to-face conversation "unfolds slowly. It teaches us patience. When we communicate on our digital devices, we learn different habits. As we ramp up the volume and velocity of online connections, we start to expect faster answers. To get these, we ask one another simpler questions; we dumb down our communications, even on the most important matters."[51] Turkle's important observations should serve as cautions for arts workers thinking about the role of digital devices in constructing meaning around the arts; still, we cannot avoid the reality of digital communication in the lives of our audiences nor the potential for using digital copresence as a means of shaping productive talk around the arts in support of an Arts Talk culture. Connectivity is reality.

Like other forms of old media, broadcast and cable television have co-opted new media advantages by incorporating digital platforms as complements to their core broadcasts (becoming what some are calling a matrix or "many-media related" medium that operates in conjunction with other forms of media).[52] As a result, most television shows are now classified as "social television," replete with associated websites and opportunities for consumer-initiated interactivity. Television producers routinely employ web division staff whose responsibilities include shaping the show's web content and facilitating audience interaction with that content. The paratexts that make up the content of contemporary television show websites include blogs, audience forums/bulletin boards, episode guides, polls, video clips, photo galleries, celebrity news, show-related games, and links to a variety of social media platforms that help the viewer to connect with other viewers. Viewer engagement is enhanced by the opportunities to learn more about the show through these online paratexts. As AMC was ramping up for the return of its popular *Mad Men* show in the spring of 2013, for example, the network began a campaign entitled "6 Ways to Get Ready for Mad Men Season 6 Premiere." AMC viewers were pointed to six paratexts available through the network's website: video trailers for the new season, sneak peek photos, a timeline photo gallery, *Mad Men*-themed games ("Which of Don's Women Are You?" and "SCDP Job Interview"), a sweepstakes, and a newsletter. These aspects of the *Mad Men* campaign are examples of what Jonathan Gray calls "incorporated paratexts," because they "add to the storyworld" of the artistic product itself.[53] Importantly for our purposes, the "6 Ways to Get Ready" pitch ends with the following reminder: "You can also join the ongoing conversation with fellow fans in the *Mad Men* Talk Forum."⁵⁴

The show's talk forum is one of many industry-facilitated viewer-to-viewer sites built around social interpretation that allow for a back-and-forth style discourse. The Showtime cable network's *Homeland* site offers its own message board forum exclusively dedicated to audience talk that is not mediated (besides the fact that it appears on the Showtime website). During the second on-air season of *Homeland* (fall 2012), the forum was very busy, proof perhaps of the show's popularity but clearly also evidence of its audience's eagerness to engage with other viewers in conversation as a means of working out interpretations and developing community meaning structures to support their isolated viewing experience. The pleasure produced by working through the mysteries of the show's plotting, character development, and politics is clearly on display in both the range of opinions and, frankly, the quality of some of the forum talk, which in some instances rivals that of professional television criticism.⁵⁵

Industry-produced paratexts and structures for social interpretation seem to be seeding audience-controlled social interpretation as well. Look, for instance, at the amount of talk generated about the HBO series *The Sopranos* in the six years since it stopped airing in 2007. Googling the phrase "Is Tony Soprano dead?" brings up a wide range of fan-built and fan-managed discussion sites, including one called "The Chase Lounge," which bills itself as a "discussion forum dedicated to one of filmed drama's greatest masterpieces, HBO's *The Sopranos*, and its creator, David Chase. As a once-avid participant and lurker at numerous other *Sopranos* forums, I think you'll find the contributions and analyses here to be among the most passionate, insightful, and mutually respectful of any *Sopranos* discussions on the Net."⁵⁶ All of these discussion sites, whether industry-managed or fan-built, facilitate authentic social interpretation in the form of online talk: viewers opining, listening to one another, and working through the data to come to new levels of understanding. And it is "talk" that we can assume moves fluidly between digital and live presences, between people and their screens and people with other people. A recent Showtime ad highlights the true pleasure of contemporary television social interpretation: After showing soundless clips from their original programming (*Homefront, Nurse Jackie, Weeds*, etc.), the images fade out to reveal the following printed message: "You know what to talk about."

Pleasure through meaning making and evaluation is also present in other types of television programming, including the myriad reality shows that clutter the television landscape. In the arts realm, *The Voice* and *Dancing with the Stars* use the pleasure of competition as a structure that invites participation in decision making and acknowledges the audience's taste as an important component of that process. These shows provide paratextual learning supports in the form of the celebrity panels; the judges offer expert analysis from an industry/professional context. They also offer a route for audience judgment and evaluation to take place through online or call-in voting. Here, voting operates as a way to evaluate and thus to participate in the meaning-making operation. (Both of these shows, as with the other reality television series, also have a web division producing interactive paratextual learning supports and talk forums.)

Perhaps the most interesting recent development in the realm of social interpretation in the television industry is what appears to be a new kind of paratext in the form of discrete television shows designed to facilitate audience discussion of other discrete television shows. Cases in point, AMC's *Talking Bad* and *Talking Dead*, live "aftershow platforms" for discussion of the latest episodes of *Breaking Bad* and *The Walking Dead*. The format features a host "spending time with fans, actors, producers and TV enthusiasts," and taking questions and comments from viewers."[57] The core of the shows is audience talk in the form of real-time comments and questions streamed in via phone, Facebook, Twitter, and the shows' websites. Audience members weigh in by commenting on the plot developments, character relationships, and performances. They also talk to each other, without professional mediation, by using the "Blog & Talk" forum on the AMC website.

In a different corner of the digital realm stands social reading, defined as a networked reading experience designed to complement the solitary nature of pleasure reading, or, as the Open Bookmarks project site puts it, "everything that surrounds the experience of reading electronic books." Like live book clubs, social reading venues offer readers the opportunity to test their taste against the tastes of other readers and to evaluate and interpret the text in a community forum. And like live book clubs, social reading venues rely on reader talk (albeit in written form) to fuel connectivity and to create composite meaning. But, unlike live book clubs, social reading venues have the ability to incorporate an exponential range of paratextual material to aid in the learning and interpretive process. Importantly, they also open up the definition of community in ways that dismantle traditional gatekeeping structures (or at least have the potential to do so). Social Book, for example, is an online social reading platform created by the Institute for the Future of the Book, which allows readers to "add their own commentary to texts, share these ideas with others, follow others' comments, and create communities of interactive reader/writers."[58] The goal is to give a new kind of privilege to the dynamic layering of interpretation that defines any book's cultural meaning and to more transparently acknowledge its multiplicity of potential meanings.

The first entry in the project is called *Open Utopia*, a browsable version of Thomas More's *Utopia*, where readers can add their own commentary (as electronic marginalia), read comments left by others, discuss the book with the Open Utopia community, and create smaller groups for specific users (a classroom, for example). *Open Utopia*'s author/conceiver, Stephen Duncombe, notes: "We live in a world where people can talk back to their books."[59] Of course, we have always lived in that world, but access to the conversation has been largely determined by class, education, race, and other restrictions imposed by economic social structures. Not surprisingly, the concept of a networked reading experience has been co-opted by the online publishing industry: Kobo Reading Life is an app that offers similar capacities (sharing commentary, posting questions, talking on an online forum) to commercial users of Kobo Books.[60] Yet another iteration of the concept of social reading comes in the form of a product called Wattpad, an online reading and writing community offering the chance to "connect, collaborate and share interactive stories or stumble across the newest trends in fiction."[61] The idea behind Wattpad is to promote a relationship between writers and readers that includes critical commentary while the book (story, poem, essay) is being written. Wattpad members can upload drafts of their work and ask for comments from other users of the service, including other writers and also, importantly, lay readers. Perhaps the most famous member is Booker-prize winner Margaret Atwood, who supports the site's interactivity in an essay for *The Guardian* from 2012. "We hear a lot these days...that young people aren't reading, but are playing video games instead," she writes. "However, you don't get that impression from Wattpad, possibly because the site emulates features of video games: participation. Like Dickens during his serial publication of *Pickwick*, Wattpad writers get feedback from readers, and may shape their stories accordingly."[62]

The final geography of social interpretation under analysis here is gaming, a vast universe of player communities that includes both online and co-physical structures for participation. Gaming came of age in the 1970s as a form of adolescent entertainment but is now

emerging as a new form of sport, replete with a governing association (Major League Gaming) and live competitions that fill sports
arenas with spectators willing to pay to watch professional gamers
compete with each other. Despite this fascinating paradigm shift
from entertainment to sport (or perhaps in tandem with it), for the
average amateur player the *gaming experience* is, as the quote from
Mark Rosewater that begins this chapter makes clear, "bigger than
the box." Gamers know that their status as members of a given community offers them myriad opportunities for engagement that go well
beyond the game itself. Critical to this understanding is the belief that
the meaning-making function is squarely in their domain and that its
operation is made pleasurable through social interaction. According
to comparative media theorist Jesper Juul, multiplayer game designers
use three frames for evaluating a game's action: game as experience,
game as a social event, and game as goal orientation.[63] Interestingly,
only the final frame references competition, suggesting that game
designers understand the social nature of gaming and the importance
of a wider experience beyond the will to win. In *A Casual Revolution:
Reinventing Video Games and Their Players,* Juul describes the growing prominence in recent years of what he calls social games, a form
of casual gaming that is designed to create "interesting interaction
between the players."[64] Social games (e.g., Bejeweled or Wii games)
appeal to a significantly larger demographic than so-called hard-core
strategic games (e.g., World of Warcraft), which have traditionally
been male dominated. Recent statistics show, for example, that "girl
gamers" make up 40 percent of the population of social game users
(34% are over the age of 18), with 43 percent playing online.[65]
    Talk is obviously critical to establishing the sense of belonging that
informs these communities and to enabling the pleasure associated
with playing the games. Some of the game platforms that are strictly
digital feature live voice connections (using headsets) that allow players to talk to each other while playing. Other games are played both
online and in live settings. Magic players, for example, can talk through
physical copresence while playing in tournaments held in storefront
game vendor sites or they can talk in online discussion forums. Role-
playing games by their nature facilitate talk as players work together
with or against other players to organize and strategize. But they also
engender concentric layers of what might be called auxiliary social
talk; that is, talk that does not directly relate to playing the game but
nevertheless supports the culture of the game and becomes an aspect
of an individual player's social performance. (Bridge players have long
enjoyed the way in which strategic talk is mingled with auxiliary

social talk while playing. And many Bridge players would argue that the game's pleasure is measured in the way in which these two forms of talk interact with and deepen each other.) Another level of social performance occurs when knowledge and information gained from playing digital games is used to "inform conversations or social interactions based around other subject matter."[66] This is the kind of talk that happens all of the time in the sports and popular entertainment realms, where a type of applied intertexuality is a natural part of the learning process and a productive way to build status in a participatory community.

Rosewater's assertion that Magic players spend more time on the game "not playing than playing" alerts us to a basic fact about participatory culture in contemporary America: Pleasure is rooted in engaged activity surrounding the core activity. Engagement is not a momentary phenomenon but rather a process, one that relies on opportunities to build authority (through the use of paratextual learning supports) and to use that authority in a productive manner (through the opportunity to engage in social interpretation). The pleasure of "playing" an online game is the same as the pleasure of "watching" sports or reading a book with others: It begins with those opportunities to prepare, to process, and to analyze, and it reaches its climax in the act of social interpretation.

In Part II, I turn to an exploration of the building blocks of social interpretation. What cultural structures support and facilitate social interpretation? And how can arts workers and arts audiences apply these structures to the contemporary arts industry?

Part II

Facilitating Arts Talk

Only Connect

What do we want from our audiences? Beyond ticket sales and subscription commitments, what is it that we are seeking from the intimate exchange at the core of the artist/arts event/audience triad? For many arts workers, the answer is simple: We want to connect. We want our audiences to respond both emotionally and intellectually to our work. We want our audiences to happily partake in the nuance and complexity of our artistic endeavor. We want them, finally, to revel in this meaningful exchange between one human and another. I am reminded here of a passage from E. M. Forster's *Howard's End* in which the novelist equates the fundamental power of love to our ability to connect with the human activity that surrounds us. "Only connect!," Forster writes. "Only connect, the prose and the passion, and both will be exalted, and human love will be seen at its height. Live in fragments no longer. Only connect."[1] In his fine essay on the values of a liberal arts education, William Cronon muses on Forster's charge, noting that a liberal education is about "gaining the power and the wisdom, the generosity and the freedom to connect."[2] "Liberal" in this context properly means of or pertaining to freedom. It also connotes dignity, honor, generosity, and bounty. According to educational administrator Christopher B. Nelson, liberal learning is distinguishable from utilitarian learning because it "helps us understand what a good life might look like, in order that we might live it well."[3] To live well (that is, ethically and with full engagement), a liberally educated person must have the capacity to engage in Socratic self-examination, asking "Who am I?" in relation to the surrounding world.

The implications for arts audiences are obvious: Knowing one-self is a necessary first component of any engagement process, and understanding what a good life looks like—one filled with authentic human expression—is fundamental to the arts instinct in all societies. Audiences too are liberal learners, engaged in a process of making sense of the world through their connection with the arts event unfolding in front of them and with the community that surrounds it, artists and fellow audience members alike. People who experience the arts in an engaged hermeneutic manner find opportunities for critical and imaginative thinking, learn how to exercise and defend their own aesthetic judgments, and revel in their capacity to feel, to think, to communicate, to wonder and ponder, to share, to listen, and, perhaps, to collaborate toward the common good. With regard to arts audiences, however, perhaps the highest value associated with a liberally educated mind is the capacity to reflect into the heart of things. Reflection is the sine qua non of interpretation; the starting point for positioning, defining, and creating meaning. People who can reflect on their arts experiences and talk about them with others can also talk about the world.

All true learning begins with a need—an "intention to learn" so vital that the learner can "concentrate *attention* on the important aspects of what is to be learned and differentiate them from noise in the environment."[4] Productive talking begins, similarly, with a need—in this case to arrive at a shared appreciation of the multiple perspectives being voiced in an authentic conversation. As philosophers tell us, whatever is interpretable is, in principle, open to an infinite array of interpretations.[5] Engineering productive talk about the serious arts means uncovering its nature and identifying the environment(s) in which it is most likely to be produced. It also means accepting that facilitating authentic conversation about the meaning and value of the arts is more important in the production of a healthy arts ecology than teaching people to mimic the opinions of interpretive gate-keepers. This turning away from the values imposed by sacralization implies a rethinking of authority in the domain of arts workers and a rethinking of the definition of what it means to be entertained for audiences. How do we arts workers loosen our grip on meaning making and encourage our audiences to move beyond passive spectating and toward more intellectually engaged forms of audience engagement? How do we encourage our audiences to sustain complexities in our dialogues about the arts—to be comfortable with colliding truths and mindful about how complexity leads to both individual and collective insight? The answer, I propose, is to find structures for acknowledging the validity of their taste, encouraging their talk, and igniting their pleasure.

In Part II of *Arts Talk*, I explore the relationship between practicing the values of liberal learning constructs and an audience's power to (re)connect with the arts. The Arts Talk model is a call to build audience-centered learning communities as spaces (physical and digital) offering programming that (1) creates a conscious relationship with the audience that is transparent in its goals; (2) offers productive facilitators and/or facilitation structures that ask, listen, and request rather than tell, lecture, or direct; and (3), begins and ends with the audience's interests in mind. Chapter 4 offers an analysis of adult learning from both a biological and a cultural perspective, identifies a set of values associated with effective learning environments, and explores those values as structures for implementing a culture of Arts Talk. Chapter 5 is an analysis of the role and function of productive talk—what it is, how it operates, and what it takes to get it going. The book's final chapter explores the idea of audience learning communities and looks closely at the role of taste, talk, and pleasure in establishing a culture of Arts Talk within organizations and communities. My goal in Part II is to provide the resources for arts workers and audiences to connect through a rich and complex conversation about the arts in their lives. All three chapters offer values and approaches that can, when used effectively, trigger actions allowing arts workers and audience members to reflect into the heart of the arts. Live in fragments no longer.

CHAPTER 4

BUILDING AUDIENCE LEARNING
COMMUNITIES

He does not teach his pupils his knowledge, but orders them to ven-
ture into the forest of things and signs, to say what they have seen
and what they think of what they have seen, to verify it and have
it verified.

—Jacques Rancière[1]

No sentient being stops learning, regardless of age. Learning equals
adaptation, and adaptation is survival. Likewise, no collection of sentient beings ignores the role that learning plays in the foundation of
a civil society. Without the capacity to learn a community cannot
sustain itself, nor can it adapt to changing cultural circumstances.

Arts audiences are de facto learning communities, gathered
together to take in and process new information about the world of
art that surrounds them. As arts lovers, they too must adapt in order
to sustain and survive; in other words, they too must be learners.
Audiences are successful learners when they take charge of their own
interpretive process and are happiest when that process of meaning
making is social. But the history of sacralization of the serious arts has
left us with a social structure for arts-going that readily discourages
the formation of learning communities among individual audience
members. This is a serious problem for the arts industry, for, without the capacity to learn together, a given audience community cannot sustain itself (since learning equals adaptation and adaptation is
survival). In contemporary America, the dwindling audiences for the
most sacralized forms of art make this fact painfully clear.

THE BIOLOGY OF LEARNING AND KNOWING

Among the myriad revelations emanating from neuroscience and the field of learning science over the past quarter century is the fact that learning changes the physical structure of the brain and "with it, the functional organization of the brain."[2] Critical to this biological understanding of how learning/knowing operates in the physical brain is another often startling fact: New knowledge must be constructed from existing knowledge. As James Zull notes, learners do not begin with a blank slate; indeed, "There is a neuronal network in our brain for everything we know...prior knowledge is a thing."[3] The physical brain is "the whole story" and the neuronal networks that operate the brain are the engines that allow for cognition. Importantly, evidence supports the idea that activity in the nervous system causes nerve cells to create new synapses.[4] Synaptic connections are added to the brain in two basic ways—via overproduction in infancy and childhood ("Synapse overproduction and loss is a fundamental mechanism that the brain uses to incorporate information from experience. It tends to occur during the early periods of development.")[5] and through the addition of new synapses, which occurs throughout the human life span.[6] According to biologist Gerald Edelman's theory of "neural Darwinism," we lose synapses through a selection process when we don't use them.[7]

This evidence-based understanding challenges earlier theories of learning and knowing, including the behaviorist view of knowledge as being outside the learner. As a result, the contemporary science of learning redefines "knowing" from "being able to remember and repeat information to being able to find and use it."[8] Embedded in the latter definition is the notion of transfer, or how knowledge, skills, and attitudes learned in one setting can be used in another context. All new learning involves the transfer of previous learning, made biologically possible through synaptic attachment. But the efficacy of transfer is profoundly affected by our given circumstances as learners, including our attitude toward learning and the way in which we are treated as learners. Transfer is a delicate process, easily diminished by an environment that refuses to acknowledge the legitimacy of existing neuronal networks. Learners have to feel that they are free to use the neuronal networks they already have because "we cannot create new ones out of thin air or by putting them on a blackboard. And we cannot excise old ones."[9] This biological reality flies in the face of long-established traditions of teaching (and misunderstandings about how learning happens), which tend to operate on the belief that experts deliver meaning to a tabula rasa brain. Another long-established tradition of teaching is the notion that control over the learning process belongs with the expert teacher. But again, neuroscience is dispelling that notion and revealing that among the most important qualities for knowledge acquisition is a sense of the learner's sovereignty over the learning process. A helpful taxonomy for understanding this phenomenon is outlined in Jurgen Habermas' notion of the three domains of knowledge: technical (acquiring information about cause and effect relationships), practical (understanding social norms, values, political concepts, and also making ourselves understood), and emancipatory (gaining independence through critical self-reflection).[10] The acquisition of emancipatory knowledge suggests that the learner achieves an important kind of freedom from the pressure and control of outside forces.

What this means for the arts is that any audience enrichment program designed to enhance audience pleasure and engagement—from talkbacks to backstage tours to visitor-friendly pull content at museums—must begin and end with the audience in mind and with audience-centered learning as a goal. More specifically, it means that the program must start with what the audience already knows and it must end with the audience identifying, labeling, and evaluating the outcomes of what has been learned. Another way to frame this is in terms of insider/outsider status. Learning communities operate best when all participants are able to identify as insiders whose presence is deeply felt to be necessary to the process. When the talkback, for instance, becomes a space for discovery, reflection, and meaning making, it moves from a mere transaction of information to an opportunity for transformative learning. Transaction of information is fine, but it is not, as discussed earlier, to be confused with learning. Many contemporary audience members aren't all that interested in information for its own sake; instead, they seek the pleasure of applying that information to the processing of an art work's ideas, concepts, problems, themes, and issues. As I explore later, knowledge transfer and learner control play a critical role in the process of adult learning and in the construction of audience learning communities.

Another condition of adult learning among audiences is attentiveness. Generally speaking, attention is defined as the "focusing of sensory, motor, and/or mental resources on aspects of the environment to acquire knowledge."[11] Attention allocation is "deciding what to focus those resources on, whether the decision making is conscious or subconscious, based on current task needs and the benefits and costs relative to what is known."[12] There are many theories about how this decision-making process (called "selection" or "filtering") occurs. Selective attention, it is thought, allows us to choose from among the constant barrage of stimuli that surround us all the time—visual, aural, and kinesthetic. Recent research has focused on two processes for attention selection, described variously as "bottom-up/bottom-down" processing and "System 1/System 2" processing. In either description, the first process is largely nonvolitional and happens to us whether we want it to or not, while the latter is goal driven and under our control (or under what is known as the "executive function."). As cognitive psychologist David Kahneman describes it in *Thinking, Fast and Slow*, System 1 (also referred to as "automatic system") runs fast and is based on intuition, metaphor, impression, and other automatic functions. System 2 ("effortful system"), on the other hand, runs slow, making deliberate and effortful choices and analyses. We have to choose to operate System 2, and we have to put in effort if that operation is going to be successful. Kahneman's thesis is based on the idea that, despite the cultural value placed on System 2, it is actually System 1 that defines our psychological profiles and, importantly, the choices and judgments we make. According to Kahneman, we are far less in control of our decision making (and thus of ourselves) than we like to believe. The essence of his theory is that because System 2 tires very easily, it is quickly superseded by System 1. "A general 'law of least effort' applies to cognitive as well as physical exertion," notes Kahneman. "The law asserts that if there are several ways of achieving the same goal, people will eventually gravitate to the least demanding course of action."[13] This leads him to question the general accuracy of intuitive thought, which for Kahneman is filled with systematic errors traceable to the "design of the machinery of cognition rather than to the corruption of thought by emotion."[14]

What does this have to do with adult learning among audiences? For one thing, it points to the dual operation of the mind/brain and its ability to move between cognitive categories. For another, it highlights the way in which decision making (and thus opinion formation) really happens for human beings. We do not come to our opinions "objectively," we come to them through a combination of intuitive (System 1) and rational (System 2) processes, with the emphasis on the intuitive. Silence in an auditorium may enable System 2 cognition, but System 1 cognition will inevitably play a role in an audience member's judgment of the arts event in front of him regardless of the conditions of the spectating environment. Silence or stillness alone cannot overcome the dance between System 1 and System 2. Further, Kahneman suggests that stillness and concentration are not necessarily synonymous; allowing that limited physical arousal "may spill over into mental alertness."[15] In other words, sometimes we concentrate better when we are physically active.

The complexity of defining an attentional state is also treated in the field of learning science and the practice of active (or cooperative) learning. In an active learning environment, information processing is emphasized over information delivery, or, to state it more directly, learning happens when students work at understanding the information rather than simply receiving and storing the information. (This distinction between explaining and understanding traces back to the discussion of the emergence of hermeneutics as a field of inquiry in Chapter 1.) Modalities for active learning vary widely among school-aged children, from discussion groups to "think-pair-share" modules where a small group of students discuss an idea and then present their findings to the class. But they have in common one important quality: peer-to-peer talk. What learning research reveals is that information is often processed into learning more effectively in circumstances where ideas are run through the verbal mill.

The emphasis on peer-to-peer processing of information through talk as integral to the learning process has very interesting implications when thinking about the role of silence and quiet attention in social interpretation. The talk-filled auditoriums of the past were rife with peer-to-peer learning, as audience members worked through the experience in real time and in active interchange with fellow audience members. Jeffrey Ravel asserts that some eighteenth-century observers "implied that the chaos of the pit only heightened the intellectual and emotional intensity of the theatergoing experience."[16] This is certainly in line with what we know about cognitive multitasking, which makes parallel processing of concurrent stimuli possible, including a spectator's ability to switch focus from stage to auditorium or from the playing field to the bleachers without losing the thread of the event and without disengaging. "Even without a proscenium arch, our audience member could easily separate the world of the stage event from other events happening at the same time," notes Bruce McConachie. "Conscious attention can process several realities within a few milliseconds."[17] There are no absolutes here, scientific or otherwise, about the nature of attention and its impact on audiences' social interpretation. And that is just the point. The long-standing arts industry truth promoting attentive listening as a correlative to engagement is no more "true" than any other theory. We need to get over it so that audiences can choose individual paths to engagement and find their way back to the arts.

ADULTS AND LEARNING

The ideal of lifelong learning in American culture has its roots in the lyceum movement of the 1820s and 1830s, begun by social reformers espousing popular enlightenment through community discourse in an era before the introduction of our tax-based secondary public education system. Because many adults lacked basic academic skills, early nineteenth-century American cities and towns hosted Chautauqua-style institutions that sponsored programs offering a range of educational opportunities: reading, writing, and public speaking classes, lectures, library circles (using some of the first circulating public libraries), and, as described in Chapter 2, aesthetic education in the form of art and music appreciation.[18] Today the value of lifelong learning is still linked to a particular Americanized style of self-cultivation through personal betterment. It is also increasingly identified with the globalization of labor—touted by corporations and government officials as a critical component to our future economic success.

As neuroscience explains, learning is an embodied process. But biology is nevertheless conditioned by sociocultural factors as varied as an individual's economic circumstances, access to information/data resources, demographics, and value positions within those demographics (who is supposed to learn, when, why, and, importantly, what). Adult learning is particularly coded by societal norms and value positions related to both authority and democratic ideals. On the one hand, adulthood signals that we are complete and thus done learning; on the other hand, a free society is one in which liberty and the quality of a free mind are equated with the opportunity (indeed the civil right) to acquire new knowledge over the course of a lifetime.

Andragogy (as opposed to pedagogy) is the art and science of helping adults to learn. There are, not surprisingly, multiple and competing theories regarding how adults learn,[19] but several recurring themes provide an interesting point of departure for an analysis of the collective learning needs of adult audiences. The first has to do with the maturation process and the way in which we move from dependent to self-directed learning as we age. The second has to do with a change in our perspective on time as we mature, moving from the expectation that facts are stored for future application (I will need to know these things when I graduate and get a job) to the expectation that they be acquired for immediate application. The third has to do with motivation, which moves from external (I have to get good grades so I can get into a good college) to internal as we age; in other words, adults are ready and eager to learn when new information/ skills can be seen to directly impact their social roles. And, finally, in order to learn effectively, adults need transparency—they need to know up front *why* they need to learn something. Educational theorist Jane Vella points out that adults learn most effectively in an atmosphere of mutual respect and safety, where learning is understood as a dialogue—a two-way process of communication—between teacher and learner, and where learning is driven by the learner.[20]

In American culture, adult education occurs through three primary sites or opportunities: formal education, nonformal education, and informal learning. Formal education is institutionally structured, hierarchical in design and operation, and formally evaluated (grades, certificates, etc.). Generally speaking, formal education on academic, job skills, or otherwise economically significant topics ends with entering a profession and does not resume unless circumstances (e.g., losing a job) warrant it or unless professional development is required.[21] Nonformal education, on the other hand, is part of the lifelong learning tradition and is seen as appropriate in a variety of contexts and thus offered through a variety of structures. Usually voluntary and short term, nonformal education nonetheless revolves around an instructor of some sort and a set of learning objectives, however "soft." These can include programs that complement formal education, such as an adult literacy class, or programs that work as alternatives to traditional modalities, such as the great variety of community-based initiatives set up by churches, community centers, libraries, etc., and organized around social change of one form or another.[22]

The third structure for adult learning, labeled informal, is defined as the "spontaneous, unstructured learning that goes on daily in the home and neighborhood, behind the school and on the playing field, in the workplace, marketplace, library and museum, and through the various mass media."[23] Informal learning practices can be broken down into three forms: self-directed (intentional and conscious), incidental (learning is a by-product of doing something else), and socialization or tacit (neither intentional and/or conscious).[24] As Chapter 3 illustrates, sports fans participate in informal learning every time they check box scores online (self-directed), turn on the television and catch a reference about a recent sporting event on the news (incidental), or engage in an off-the-cuff debate about a particular play or coaching decision at the water cooler (tacit). Because they are embedded in everyday activities, however, most adults don't recognize or label these practices as "learning."[25]

The relationship between self and society always informs the learning process: adult learners are affected, as children, by a range of historical and cultural determinants as well as by issues of access. According to the National Center for Education Statistics, formal adult education is used primarily by white members of the professional class; that is to say, Caucasian Americans with full-time salaried positions, a high level of prior educational attainment, and an above-average household income.[26] This statistic is hardly surprising given the pressures on working-class American adults, notably the amount of disposable time in average hourly workers' days and the amount of disposable income in their budgets. Sociological factors also act as barriers to participation in various forms of adult education, including the lack of a support system for the idea of lifelong learning and, particularly among undereducated women and minorities in general, a "lack of voice" in the process overall.[27]

Traditional practices in adult learning often assume that learning is "value-neutral and apolitical"[28] and that adult learning happens in the same way for all individuals. But research confirms that adults retain the multiple learning styles that we identify and honor in school children, and, critically, that those learning styles are culturally informed. Studies of African American adult learners illustrate this phenomenon by pointing out the gaps between Eurocentric teaching modalities and Africanist practices. In Africanist culture, for example, knowledge is validated when it is "made public," whereas traditional Eurocentric adult learning protocols stress individual learning.[29] Acknowledging these distinctions is fundamental to a productive learning process; when adult learners are forced to conform to learning styles antithetical to their personal and/or cultural situation, they are effectively silenced.

Furthermore, the efficacy of formal and nonformal adult learning is often challenged by the fact that many of the teaching structures in use consistently "violate principles for optimizing learning" because they are not learner and knowledge centered.[30] Much adult learning continues to be organized around what education reformer Paulo Freire called banking education, wherein students are taught that their role is to be an empty container ready to receive the teacher's knowledge.[31] In classrooms, the least effective teachers assume that if their lectures reflect the highest standards of their respective fields (high-end inquiry, cutting-edge research, etc.) then their job is done. They have delivered the currency, and if students don't "get it," well, that's on them. Similarly, if audiences don't "get it," arts workers often wash their hands of the problem, because in offering artistic excellence, we've delivered the currency and thus we've done our job. I argue here that we have not.

LEARNING COMMUNITIES

Many arts industry gatekeepers say that their audiences don't want to think or to talk for themselves, they just want to be told what to think. In my experience, this is not really true. Invited properly, audiences will push beyond the discomfort of "thinking" to get to the interpretive sphere. As illustrated earlier, however, adult learning is a delicate business requiring the right environment. This is especially true in the arts sphere, where learning (long constructed as "arts appreciation") has traditionally been focused primarily on school-aged children. Adult audience members do not think of themselves as learners per se, unless they are what I call an Affinity type; that is, arts goers who self-identify as aficionados or fans and bring a kind of expertise to their spectating experience. The Affinity Type has long been a fixture of the serious arts and still exists today, though in ever-decreasing numbers. A more prevalent contemporary audience type is what I label the Tourist, an arts goer who can bring specialized knowledge or interest but is more often motivated by a sense of occasion. A trip to New York City, for example, often includes taking in a Broadway show and visiting art museums regardless of the person's spectating habits at home. And a blockbuster traveling art exhibit or road show will invariably bring new faces to the local museum and performing arts center. Tourist type audiences are notoriously easy to please because, having purchased something "good" by virtue of a high ticket price and/or a special occasion, they tend to "like" whatever they see in the same spirit that allows even an awful wedding band to get over on its crowd of family and friends—the stakes are just too high *not* to have a good time. (The nightly routine of standing ovations for Broadway blockbusters is surely a testament to this, as many cultural commentators have observed.) In both cases of the Affinity and Tourist types, however, the level of front-loaded enthusiasm does not necessarily produce capacities for productive talk, and enthusiasm does not inherently lead to social interpretation. Nor does the occasional trip to the theater or the museum to take in a marquis arts event lead to steady arts going. For that to occur, we need environments that foster learning in and through opportunities for social interpretation. We need audience learning communities.

The term "learning community" surfaced in the 1980s as a way to define a shift in attitude acknowledging learning as a cultural practice as opposed to an individual process. Based on the "communities of practice" work of social learning theorists Jean Lave and Etienne Wenger, a learning community operates via a sense of shared experience and a culture of praxis, a term defined in educational theory as "doing with built-in reflection."[32] In this model, learners take new knowledge, skills, or attitudes and practice them by sharing their experience with others in the community and by actively reflecting on their process. In doing so, learners are thought to be participating in the negotiation of meaning. A learning community by definition crosses boundaries, is highly adaptable, has resiliency, thrives on knowledge sharing, and knows how to capture learning so that it can be used in subsequent learning. The emphasis is not solely on the exchange of meaning, but rather on the process of making meaning collectively. In the next section of the chapter, I look at three qualities of effective learning communities—transfer, data acquisition, and sovereignty—and discuss some strategies for building them into an arts environment.

TRANSFER

Transfer, as already noted, is the process by which knowledge, skills, and attitudes learned in one setting can be used in another context. Audiences enter the arts space with many preconceptions about what they are about to see—preconceptions that are literally part of their brains. Cognitively speaking, if their initial understanding is not engaged, they will fail to connect with and thus to grasp the new information in any meaningful way. Arts workers interested in creating an audience learning community have to learn to draw out and engage with the audience's preconceptions and preexisting understandings of the arts event or object. As learning researchers note, sometimes a learner's current knowledge supports new learning and sometimes it hampers learning, but nevertheless "effective instruction begins with what learners bring to the setting; this includes cultural practices and beliefs as well as knowledge of academic content."[33] In order for the transfer of knowledge to occur and to spark engagement with new experience, then, we cannot in good faith ignore what an audience member brings with her into the arts venue. In *The Emancipated Spectator*, philosopher Jacques Rancière argues that the act of spectating, contrary to conventional logic, is not inherently passive but rather "our normal situation. We also learn and teach, act and know, as spectators who all the time link what we see to what we have seen and said, done and dreamed."[34]

DATA ACQUISITION

Effective data acquisition is closely tied to analytical skills (the ability to recognize patterns, generate arguments, explain phenomena, draw analogies) and thus to the learning construct. While process is paramount, there is plenty of evidence that we do indeed need to know the facts as part of effective and meaningful learning.[35] The same holds true for audience learners, of course; new data acquisition is an essential part of the Arts Talk model's taste-talk-pleasure calculus, because it supports the journey toward fulfillment that an arts experience provides. But in mainstream contemporary America, the kind of paratextual learning supports described in Chapter 3 that so profoundly enrich sports, gaming, social reading, and television cultures are not nearly so available to the average arts goer. Of course, it is true that digital platforms are offering a greater and greater array of paratextual materials in and around the serious arts—for audience members who are motivated to spend the time and energy to find them in obscure corners of the Internet. Without a commercial context for the serious arts or a state-supported system for promoting an arts-based cultural life among Americans, there simply isn't enough headwind to fuel the production of these materials in the mainstream media. Even a program such as National Public Radio's "Fresh Air," which advertises itself as a "weekday magazine of contemporary arts and issues," rarely does stories on the serious arts, instead focusing on commercial forms such as film and television. In this climate, the not-for-profit arts industry operates largely without surrounding, culturally produced paratexts.

And it shows. Americans are not well informed about the context of the serious arts—historically, aesthetically, hermeneutically. All of the money and effort that go into arts education programs in and around the secondary system have not changed this fact or kept the downward slide in the amount of culturally produced arts paratexts from deepening with each passing decade. Nor has that same arts education effort seemed to alleviate cultural skepticism about the arts among Americans at large (a skepticism that surfaced when the Continental Congress outlawed "expensive diversions and entertainments" in 1774 because they were thought to detract from the war effort). It is certainly notable that two recent National Endowment for the Arts chairmen are openly critical of our societal lack of support for the arts. Bill Ivey (NEA head under Bill Clinton), for example, has targeted some of his ire directly at government officials, noting that "authentic, West Wing-style 'hard' public policy only mixes it up with the arts by accident, though trade promotion or media regulation or when Congress rises up in a snit over offensive television programming or unsettling government-funded art."[36] And Rocco Landesman (NEA head under Barack Obama) recently spoke of the American public's "fundamental, visceral distrust of the arts"[37] on the eve of his departure from the post. Both of these experienced arts insiders express a hard truth about the place of the arts in American culture. Given this cultural and economic reality, the arts industry needs to take more responsibility for creating informative paratextual materials and for finding new and vibrant ways to distribute them.

Sovereignty

I use the term sovereignty to strongly suggest the relationship between learner control and a successful learner-centered environment. In learning science, this is referred to as a metacognitive approach to instruction, or one that puts students in charge of defining their own learning goals and taking responsibility for monitoring their own progress in achieving them.[38] There are several key conditions to learner sovereignty, starting with the choice to join a learning process and, significantly with adult learners, the choice to continue to stay in the process. That is why most effective learning experiences begin with locating a connection between the content and the learner's personal experience. As James Zull notes, metaphors, parables, and stories are powerful when teaching a concept because we "cannot understand anything unless we create internal neuronal networks that reflect some set of physical relationships that accurately map the relationship in the concept. At a minimum, we must be sure that our students have connections of this sort. We must push them to tell us their metaphors or stories."[39] Zull's comments about the classroom environment resonate nicely with the goal of productive talk about the arts. The personal stories that audience members sometimes share in postperformance dialogues, often treated as off-topic distractions by discussion facilitators, are in fact a sign of positive engagement with the arts event and/or artist. The desire to tell these stories should be understood as a signal that the process of transfer is beginning to happen as the audience member attaches prior knowledge to their spectator experience. And these stories should be embraced, by audience members and arts workers alike, as a necessary component of productive talk about the arts. Effective facilitators know how to acknowledge those personal connections (metaphors, parables, stories) and to push the audience member to use them as tools for analyzing and interpreting the art work under discussion.

Another way in which adults decide to stay with a learning process is through transparency: They need to know up front what they are going to learn. Many recent studies illustrate the importance of clearly identifying what is to be learned at the start of any given learning session. This is because transparency of the learning plan offers learners the opportunity to appropriately organize their thinking and to prepare their expectations accordingly. In an important way, prior knowledge about what is to come greases the learning wheel and enhances not only the learner's capacity to grasp the new information but also their pleasure in receiving it. A recent study by researchers at the University of California, San Diego, for example, shows that, contrary to conventional thought, spoilers make reading a short story more enjoyable rather than less. In the study, three types of stories were presented in their original format (that is, without a spoiler), with a spoiler paragraph added as a preface to the story, or with that same paragraph incorporated into the story itself. The results are startling: "Subjects significantly preferred the spoiled versions of ironic-twist stories, where, for example, it was revealed before reading that a condemned man's daring escape is all a fantasy before the noose snaps tight around his neck. The same held true for mysteries. Knowing ahead of time that Poirot will discover that the apparent target of attempted murder is, in fact, the perpetrator not only didn't hurt enjoyment of the story but actually improved it. Subjects liked the literary, evocative stories least overall, but still preferred the spoiled versions over the unspoiled ones."[40] One explanation for this unexpected finding, according to the researchers, is that "once you know how it turns out, it's cognitively easier—you're more comfortable processing the information—and can focus on a deeper understanding of the story."[41] This research helps to explain a finding in Alan S. Brown and Rebecca Ratzkin's "Understanding the Intrinsic Impact of Live Theatre: Patterns of Audience Feedback across 18 Theatres and 58 Productions" in which audience surveys reveal a strong correlation between "anticipation and respondents' levels of familiarity with the story, cast, and playwright."[42]

That kind of anticipatory pleasure certainly seems to have been a factor for the Greeks attending the City Dionysia annual festival in ancient Athens, whose experience was "spoiled" when the plot as well as the intended themes of the competing tragedies were outlined by the playwright during the *proagon*. It was also true for audiences at Jacob's Pillow Dance Festival in the summer of 1997 at a Merce

Cunningham Dance Company concert. In order to lessen the number of walk-outs during the concert (by then a well-established pattern during Cunningham appearances at the Pillow), the company's executive director, Bill Cook, took the opportunity to talk informally about the perceived difficulty of John Cage's musical score with audience members as they assembled to enter the auditorium. The impact was immediate in the form of fewer walk-outs for that particular performance. Cook's experiment coincided with the launch of Jacob's Pillow's "Audience Enrichment Program," a project originally developed by then executive director Sali Ann Kriegsman. One of the project components, "Pillow Talks," is a preshow lecture-discussion designed to "prepare an audience to meet the art and artist half-way; to bring more of the dance experience to them, and to bring more of them to dance."[43] At one Pillow Talk event in 1997, Resident Dance Historian David Gere discussed the way choreographer Mark Morris uses music in his work and gave specific visual examples from one of the pieces on the program to illustrate his points. At that evening's concert, the "audience spontaneously burst into applause right after those passages. There was a delight in that familiarity."[44]

As the ancient Greek and the contemporary American examples illustrate, transparency (delight in familiarity), however it is realized, impacts learning and thus the pleasure of experiencing a work of art. This seems to be of particular importance to the so-called Millennial generation (ages 18 to 35), where "behind the scenes, sneak peeks, and insider experience help these cultural consumers discover a brand's value and gain an intimate connection through content."[45] But it is also true about older audiences trained in a less self-determined protocol of arts going. Sixty-something symphony goers may not ask for a backstage tour as a condition of buying a ticket, or pull out their phones to download a composer's biography during a concert, but data currently being collected from a wide range of experimental programming are telling us that they too find the opportunity to look under the hood meaningful.

Finally, adults commit to learning when they know, based on a program's structure, that they can choose the point at which they are fully in control of their own learning. Or, as Paulo Freire puts it, "Only the student can name the moment of the death of the professor."[46] Freire is pointing to institutional power structures and the way that hierarchical social roles (teacher/expert over student/novice) must be inverted in order to positively impact the learning process. This is a particularly compelling concern in audience learning communities, especially with what I call the ambivalent audience member—the one who arrives in a state of willful skepticism out of which he must be pulled. A significant percentage of spectators from the professional class enter the serious arts arena with the expectation that they might find some interest in the work, or they might not. As in shopping at a supermarket, they are willing to test something out once but highly unlikely to buy it again if it isn't immediately satisfying.

So why do they bother to go in the first place? Another way to think about audiences (and to understand the ambivalent type) is in the context of social identity theory, or our understanding of who we are in terms of our social relationships with other people or groups of people. According to this theory, when meeting a new person or a new group of people we are inclined to locate these new acquaintances on a "social map."[47] Affinity audiences use social mapping to self-identify with people whose levels of sophistication match their own. These people often end up in a theater or concert hall because of a priori social relationships: A husband who loves symphonic music; a neighbor who is passionate about the opera; a business acquaintance who sits on the board of the local art museum. For them, the need to participate in arts-going is aligned with the human need to attach oneself to other individuals who are similar. But unlike earlier generations of American audiences who used arts-going as a method for climbing the social ladder, contemporary ambivalent audience members are unlikely to return for a second experience if they are not significantly engaged the first time (because there are better ways, now, to climb the social ladder). They may be willing to try out an arts event based on their social relationships, but they are not as inclined as their parents or grandparents were to submerge their own horizon of taste to the ruling tastes of their chosen cohort in subsequent visits to the concert hall or museum or playhouse. In other words, social alliances no longer trump personal interest when it comes to making decisions about how to spend Friday night.

Whether this is the result of a democratization of the culture or a trend toward risk aversion (especially of the intellectual kind), the fact is that a significant proportion of potential adult audience members are disinclined to repeatedly attend an event when its rules of operation do not fit within their existing knowledge framework. As neuroscience reveals, this disinclination toward intellectual risk-taking exists for sound reasons: The new information in front of them (the arts event) is just not in the brain. Therefore, when an ambivalent audience member enters a new learning arena (the unfamiliar arts event) and is not provided with data or tools for connecting what he already knows with what is new to his spectating self, he likely leaves the concert hall or playhouse or gallery with a failure to understand and thus a sense of personal failure ("I must not be smart enough to get it"). Personal failure unexamined often gets translated as disinterest or even distaste: The uncomfortable feeling that we didn't get it eventually surfaces in our psyches as an indicator of something we don't like. This kind of translation process (from confusion to distaste) has been quite destructive to the arts industry; with so many options for leisure, why would an ambivalent arts goer choose to return to a place where he has felt less than adequate?

One solution to this malaise is for arts workers to participate in creating culturally responsive environments that pay careful attention to the existence of previous knowledge by recognizing the attitudes and tastes that an audience member brings to the discussion and then offering that person opportunities to transfer their existing knowledge to the acquisition of new data as part of the meaning-making process. The Lincoln Center Institute's "Capacities for Imaginative Learning" program provides useful guidance on this point. Their training protocol counsels school teachers creating secondary arts curricula to advise students to "connect what you notice and the patterns you see to your prior knowledge and experiences." When combined with other hermeneutic practices such as "noticing deeply" (to identify and articulate the details in a work of art) and "exhibiting empathy" (to respect the diverse perspectives of others in our community), this protocol leads to a culture of social interpretation around the arts for school-aged children.[48] As Chapter 6 explores, these teachings can successfully be applied to adult audience members.

CHAPTER 5

FUNDAMENTALS OF PRODUCTIVE TALK

I talk in order to understand; I teach in order to learn.
—Robert Frost

In contemporary America there are many forms of talk: passive, agonistic, consensual, persuasive, and so on. And there are many venues for talking: home, work, school, leisure sites of assembly (bar, sporting arena, coffee house), online, phones, etc. Talk defines our culture and our daily lives (an average person talks from six to twelve hours per day).[1] Chapter 5 explores the social basis of talk by providing a review of the thinking about its nature and function. This includes an analysis of three forms of talk—dialogue, discussion, and debate—as they are understood through a variety of disciplinary perspectives, including, among others, learning science, behavioral psychology, conflict resolution, business communications, and religious practice. From these existing modalities, I glean techniques for listening, dialoguing, and debating as well as articulating ideas, feelings, and emotions—all elements of Arts Talk. The chapter continues with an analysis of the role that facilitation plays in producing productive dialogue and discussion. In my observation, the best audience-centered interpretive experiences are rooted in good facilitation. But here's the key—the facilitator is an instrument dedicated to creating a hospitable learning environment, not an ego looking to be fulfilled. The facilitator *does not make the meaning and give it to an audience.* The facilitator establishes the environment and the tools for artists and the audience to make the meaning together, and then gets out of the way. David Bohm states that it is useful to have a facilitator to get the group going and to watch over and support the developing dialogue. But, ultimately, "his function is to work himself out of a job."[2]

Defining Productive Talk

Evolutionarily speaking, human beings talk in order to get what they want. Even seemingly aimless social talk has a purpose: to engage with other people. "How are you?" is not a meaningless gesture even though we seldom stop to hear the answer—it is talk deployed as a way to acknowledge another's presence.

Talking is also a way of processing experience. As linguist Ronald Wardhaugh notes, "In a very real way language helps us to work out what we are feeling, what we are doing, how we are doing it, and how we must seem to be doing whatever we are doing...We not only observe others and their language and behavior; we also observe ourselves: our own acting, doing, behaving, and talking."[3] Talking in the form of conversation is a way of cooperating with other people in a public way; it is a reciprocal undertaking. In participating in a spontaneous social conversation, for instance, we engage in a culturally determined and understood set of rules (you talk and I listen, then I talk and you listen). A conversation is also a way to package and present ourselves to other people. It is, continues Wardhaugh, "not simply *about* something, nor is it merely a series of somethings, such as topics. A conversation *is* something. It is a performance, a kind of show in which the participants act out as well as speak whatever it is they are doing."[4] Wardhaugh's observations call attention to the fact that the term "conversation" refers to a structure of turn-taking between speaker and listener. The Latin roots of the word—*conversari* (to associate with) and *convertere* (to turn around)—are visceral reminders of this. Conversation brings us together and it can turn us around; that is, it can lead us to new information, new insights, and new opinions. Even in what we refer to as casual conversation, the human stakes are high. Conversations can, for example, become competitions of a sort—a parley of data, an exchange of wit producing a winner and a loser (the latter often suffering from what the French call *L'esprit d'escalier*—literally the wit of the staircase—or the frustration we feel when we think of a witty comeback only when we are on our way out of the building).

It is not surprising, then, that difficulties emerge when casual conversation moves into the linguistic territories of dialogue, discussion, and debate. As noted in Chapter 1, these three words, while often

used interchangeably in contemporary America, actually signify discrete forms of conversation. Dialogue, from the Greek *dialogos* (logos
meaning "the word" and dia meaning "through"), is organized
around the willingness to suspend personal opinions in order to listen and to learn from others. As David Bohm notes, the "picture or
image that this derivation suggests is of a stream of meaning flowing
among and through us and between us. This will make possible a flow
of meaning in the whole group, out of which may emerge some new
understanding. It's something new, which may not have been in the
starting point at all."[5] Discussion (from the Latin *discutere*, "to break
up") and debate (from the Old French *debatre*, "to beat down"), on
the other hand, imply a battle over territory as individual perspectives and opinions are presented and defended. The object here is to
engage in an analytical process (break up), and the underlying goal is
to convince or persuade others (beat down).

The Arts Talk model envisions an environment where all three
forms of talk are not only possible but also common. While dialogue
as a mechanism for achieving consensus and greater understanding is
a key goal for engendering engagement around the arts, thoughtfully
facilitated discussions and debates can also be fruitful. As we saw in
Chapters 2 and 3, tension surrounding the working out of meaning and value in other eras of arts going and in alternate contemporary geographies of cultural activity such as sports and television are
deeply pleasurable. For our purposes, then, productive talk, whether
in the form of dialogue, discussion, or debate, is talk that originates
in order to (1) communicate about a specific topic, (2) air publically
a range of opinions and perspectives on that topic, (3) listen and consider other points of view, and (4) work toward both collective and
individual meaning making. The productivity here is both literal,
involving the effective exchange of information and viewpoints, and
symbolic, in that people finish the experience with a new connection
to the information and ideas that came out of the exchange and a
new understanding between participants. In an environment where
productive talk is encouraged and supported, community spirit flour-
ishes, arising naturally out of the new understanding in the room.
This definition should hold regardless of whether that room is physical or digital.

So how do we move our complicated adult audiences into productive talk around the arts? There is much to be learned from educational theory, where the role of talk as a pedagogical tool and strategy
in the classroom is being explored through a variety of lenses (cognitive, behavioral, sociocultural). We can also learn by looking at various

constructs that rely on productive talk to achieve their ends—from therapeutic modalities to business negotiation to Quaker worship. In all of these cultures, the structure of productive talk looks remarkably similar and can be reduced to three main operations: open talk, powerful questioning, and effective listening.

Open talk signals a culture where talking is valued as a legitimate protocol for sharing information and ideas. In active learning classrooms, for instance, shared-inquiry discussion group protocol helps students to try out their thinking by inviting them to talk openly and without the fear that their ideas will be judged as unworthy. Here the notion of open talk is applied to the idea of testing out ideas, like a chemist tests a new formula. There is no judgment made on the correctness of the ideas—even if the chemical formula turns out to be faulty in some way, the data are still gathered and the process is furthered by the act of gathering data. Similarly, in an open talk environment, the ideas expressed build on each other and lead the group to new discoveries. A useful example of an open learning protocol is the University of Pittsburgh Learning Research and Development Center's "Accountable Talk" program for secondary school classrooms. In this protocol, open talk is structured with three prongs of accountability in mind: accountability to the learning community (encouraging students to build on the comments of others respectfully and inclusively), accountability to accurate knowledge, and accountability to rigorous thinking. When this model is followed, participants are more likely to share authentic reactions as opposed to canned responses and they are more likely to be open to other authentic reactions.[6]

Open talk can only occur, however, in a hospitable environment, that is, an environment that sincerely welcomes open exploration. As education reformers Parker J. Palmer and Arthur Zajonc articulate it in *The Heart of Higher Education: A Call to Renewal/Transforming the Academy through Collegial Conversations*, hospitable spaces promote learning "not merely because kindness is a good idea but because real education requires rigor. In a counterintuitive way, hospitality supports rigor by supporting community."[7] The authors call attention to the fact that an open talk environment, one in which we can admit our ignorance and encounter opposing viewpoints without losing the capacity to listen and learn, is "not going to happen in a class that lacks hospitality, a class where people feel too threatened to say anything that might get them crosswise with the professor or other students."[8] This is obviously true of adult arts audiences as well. As most arts workers have experienced firsthand, audience members

brought in from the cold without any preparation have a very difficult time talking about the arts, particularly when the work is new
to them. The difficulty is compounded when adult audience members are confronted by an environment that is inherently inhospitable
to authentic learning, such as a talkback dominated by an "expert"
facilitator or an arrogant (and sometimes defensive) artist. In this
kind of environment, very few adults will be willing to expose their
ignorance on the subject at hand or to risk being chastised for coming up with the "wrong" reaction or response. As adult professionals,
we are accustomed to being in control of the information around
us. Environments that challenge our control make us uncomfortable.
The psychiatrist and educational theorist Thomas Szasz understands
the phenomenon this way: "Every act of conscious learning requires
the willingness to suffer an injury to one's self-esteem. That is why
young children, before they are aware of their own self-importance,
learn so easily; and why older persons, especially if vain or important,
cannot learn at all."[9]

   Powerful questioning refers to the ability to frame questions that
can change the course of the conversation. These include open-ended
questions offered as a way to prime a dialogue and follow-up questions employed to deepen and expand discussion and to help clarify
ideas. In the Western tradition, the habit of using questions to engender learning is sourced in the Socratic Method, a dialectical process of
hypothesis elimination attributed to Socrates and formalized in Plato's
dialogues. Plato's Socrates is a negative questioner; that is, he elimi-
nates unfolding hypotheses by exposing their contradictions. This
style of Socratic questioning is still employed in law schools, where
(at least in the movies) oppositional questioning pushes the student to
defend her evidence. In the humanities, however, Socratic questioning is often employed not so much as a dialectical tool but rather as
means of producing the kind of "productive discomfort" that accompanies the complexity and difficulty of any attempt to understand
or know something. As educator Rob Reich describes it, the leader
of the dialogue "asks probing questions in an effort to expose the
values and beliefs which frame and support the thoughts and statements of the participants in the inquiry. The students ask questions
as well, both of the teacher and each other. The inquiry progresses
interactively, and the teacher is as much a participant as a guide of
the discussion. Furthermore, the inquiry is open-ended. There is no
pre-determined argument or terminus to which the teacher attempts
to lead the students. Those who practice the Socratic method do not
use PowerPoint slides. Without a lesson plan, the group follows the

dialogue where it goes."[10] In this modality, the leader (the professor) is a participant who must, by definition, also be a learner.

Powerful questioning plays a role in other modalities, including religious dialogue. In Quaker worship, for example, the Society of Friends follows a protocol for participating in a dialogue while avoiding the hierarchal aspects of much institutional discourse. Worship-sharing sessions (which are different from the regular worship sessions done mostly in silence) are based on a theme presented by one of the members. In this form of open talk, individual beliefs are "seasoned" by the feedback from fellow worshippers in the form of questions. The rules of a worship-sharing session include the call to "speak out of the silence, and leave a period of silence between speakers" and to avoid responding directly to what others have said "either to praise or to refute."[11] This open talk modality is interesting for our purposes for two reasons: one, because it does not rely on a designated leader but instead is driven by the participants; and two, because it is sourced in the Quaker belief that sharing an issue publically makes it smaller (that is, less threatening). It might be the case that the general silence that surrounds social interpretation of the serious arts in American culture makes our anxieties about speaking up larger than they need to be. It might also be true that public sharing of those anxieties would make them smaller.

Effective listening (sometimes referred to as attentive or active listening) is essential to productive talk, because without it there can be no synthesis of information or authentic use of the ideas being generated. An effective listener is listening for meaning as opposed to strictly recording what the other person is saying or, as often happens, simply biding time waiting for his or her turn to speak. An effective listener is an attentive listener who puts all of his cognitive focus on what the other person is saying. An effective listener is also a sincere listener willing to put aside her beliefs and values long enough to absorb what the other person is saying. As David Bohm understands it, true listening occurs "only if people are able *freely* [author's emphasis] to listen to each other, without prejudice, and without trying to influence each other. Each has to be interested primarily in truth and coherence, so that he is ready to drop his old ideas and intentions, and be ready to go on to something different, when this is called for."[12]

Effective listening is understood as a valuable tool within many industries, including the business sector. As business consultant Judy Brown points out, successful negotiation of the inevitable difficulties of workplace culture is predicated on listening for information rather than for confirmation. Effective listening allows people to engage hospitably with others, even in tense discussions or debates, and thus allows us to learn how to be provoked "and not close down."[13] Brown also points to the importance of honoring silence as part of the listening process in workplace situations, noting that silence often signals that people are reflecting on the topic at hand. It is generally the case that effective listeners are not afraid of silence. Instead, they embrace it as a tool for opening up space for thoughtful consideration (rather than knee-jerk predetermined responses). The ability to "settle into silence," as the Quakers put it, is necessary if one is to absorb what has just been shared. When used sincerely and with good intentions, silence is also a tool for leveling the dynamics within a discourse; periods of silence slow the pace and allow for a redistribution of power among the speakers.

Finally, effective listeners are able to feed back what they hear to the speaker as a way to confirm their understanding. In some modalities, this ability is referred to as "active listening." In the medical field, for example, the term is used in reference to a diagnostic technique called Active Listening Observation Scale (ALOS-global) and refers to a communication strategy for recognizing and exploring patients' cues in the examining room. Physicians are graded based on their facility with active listening. High scores are indicated when, for example, the physician shows an open body attitude with welcoming facial expressions, avoids distractions (such as reading the chart instead of making eye contact), "gives the patient time and space to present the problem," adjusts language to avoid use of unfamiliar medical jargon, uses silences "to give the patient a chance to think or to elaborate," employs exploring or open-ended questions "that do not invite any particular answer," and acknowledges "patient's feelings and emotions verbally by, for example, naming them, asking the patient to clarify the feeling(s) or emotion(s)."[14] Active listening by physicians in a clinical setting has been shown to be a better method of gaining information about a patient's status because "the very act of listening assumes that there is something to listen to, i.e. that the patient has the opportunity to talk and express himself."[15] Imagine the possibilities for strengthening our national dialogue around the arts if audiences too felt they were worthy of being listened to and had something of value to add to the conversation. Or if the authority to make meaning was authentically distributed among everyone in the room.

FACILITATING PRODUCTIVE TALK

The common qualities of productive talk described earlier are enabled by (indeed dependent on) good facilitation. Related to facile (easily

achieved) and facility (the quality of being easy to do), the word facilitation connotes the act of making easy or easier. A facilitator enables
another (usually a group of others) to function more effectively by
supporting all participants in their individual and collective quest to
move forward on a particular task or topic. Importantly, however,
the reference to ease should not be confused with a shallow process
or subject matter. In good facilitation protocols and practices, depth
and difficulty are addressed and worked through; indeed, facilitation
is often called for because of the particular difficulty in a given task
or process. And though the term facilitator is usually used to refer to
a person, in fact, facilitation can be enabled by structures as well as
by individual people. Quaker sharing worship sessions, for example,
can be conducted without a designated leader because the traditional
protocol (entering the room quietly, speaking only out of the silence,
listening deeply, using questions as a means of exploration, speaking
only once during any given session) is its own facilitation. Similarly,
sports talk is conducted through a variety of social structures that
automatically facilitate dialogue, such as water cooler exchanges in
which each participant offers his observations of the previous day's
game and then listens to the other participants before heading back
to his cubicle. Just like Quakers, sports fans know the rules of sports
discourse and tend to follow them as a function of class habitus
(again, those aspects of culture that are anchored in the body or daily
practices of individuals, groups, societies, and nations and that produce and reproduce the practices of a class). And, of course, much
online dialogue is celebrated for its conspicuous lack of an official
facilitator—the flow of the talk is often in fact predicated on a refusal
to be mediated in a hierarchal manner but is nevertheless facilitated
by the norms of the participating social group.

Whatever form it takes, good facilitation is the lynchpin of productive talk. And whoever or whatever is responsible, good facilitation is
grounded in framing and asking powerful questions that stimulate
response but don't tell people what they are supposed to be thinking
and feeling. In any productive talk environment, the most important
outcome is a collective appreciation of the meanings generated by the
participants—the sense that the "truth" is located not in this opinion
or that data point but rather in the quality of listening and observing.
Ironically, though, in the arts it is often the audience itself that stands
in the way of achieving this outcome. Because contemporary audiences have little or no experience with participating in productive talk
around the arts they often go into a talk session with the expectation
that the facilitator will tell them what to think and feel. This is only

natural in a culture that consistently reinforces hierarchal learning, especially in areas deemed "serious." The condition is exacerbated by the fact that most audience members come out of a system of higher education that cultivates, in the words of educational theorist Ken Bain, "the sense that only 'smart men can possibly comprehend this material and that if you can't understand what I'm saying, that must mean I'm a lot smarter than you are'."[16] Or, as we like to say in the arts world, if I have to explain it to you you'll never get it. In this kind of setting, creating the space for participants to see things differently from other participants and from authoritative voices outside of the group (such as artists or critics, for example), is particularly difficult. But in a healthy learning environment, oppositional perspectives are not seen as challenges to authority but rather as potential catalysts for productive talk. The ultimate goal is to authorize everyone in the room to feel, to think, and to understand.

For arts workers, helping audiences to move beyond this limited mindset is challenging but entirely accomplishable when sound practices for good facilitation are followed. In this section, I distil ten key values and strategies for facilitating productive talk. I caution, however, that simply reading down the list and using it as a quick do-this-don't-do-that reference guide will not make anyone a good facilitator. Like other skills, facilitation must be studied and deliberately practiced. The successful application of these values to specific contexts within the arts takes careful attention, imagination, and dedication.

1. Create a hospitable talk environment where everyone, including the facilitator, is interested in what other people have to say. The facilitator establishes hospitality by beginning with an invitation to contribute and then following through with behaviors that reinforce that invitation. These include taking the time to conduct introductory gestures such as asking people their names, what brought them to the event, etc. They also include establishing a conversational mode of interaction from the start (which generally means avoiding beginning with a speech), encouraging participants to talk to one another and not just to you, discouraging unnecessary deference to your authority and status, using gestures and body language that clearly convey your interest in what people are saying, and pausing to measure participant comprehension (rather than barreling along with a predetermined set of questions or points.)

Hospitality is more than a welcoming introduction, however. As Palmer and Zajonc intone, being hospitable is an iteration of being kind; as such it involves establishing a culture of respect for all participants and for the potentially different styles of talk they bring to the session. But, as we all know, that is easier said than done. Communications theorists William F. Eadie and Paul E. Nelson observe that conversation is by nature "fraught with difficulty. Even people in long-term relationships—where the individuals involved ought to know each other's attitudes, values, and uses for words—find that they are not always understood. Take away that knowledge in casual relationships and add differences in cultural experiences, attitudes, and values, and everything ranging from misunderstanding to outright hostility can occur."[17] When we add the challenges of living and interacting in a diverse culture full of diverse communication styles, having an authentic conversation becomes even more challenging. The resulting anxieties can lead to resisting and devaluing difference and the tendency to, as communications theorist Julia T. Wood asserts, "identify with and affirm the ways of our own social groups and to disparage those of other social groups." Wood goes on to point out that these practices occur when, for example, "European Americans refuse to consider the validity of African American communication styles," "Westerners judge Asians to be passive," and "men dismiss women's talk as trivial."[18]

Empirical and anecdotal research analyzing the differences in communication systems and conversational styles between genders, ethnic traditions, and various microcultures includes the study of gendered talk, or what psychologist Deborah Tannen identifies as "rapport talk" (female) versus "report talk" (male).[19] Tannen's easy-to-grasp (and oversimplified) labeling illustrates a hypothesized binary of the gendered perception of the purpose of talk: for men, talk is organized around communicating a specific piece of information (which can, then, build relationships or explore emotional status); for women, talk is organized around building relationships and exploring emotional status (which can, then, communicate a specific piece of information). These distinctions are obviously not essential and are likely not inflexibly biological either. A recent study from the University of Rochester, for example, asserts that the range of psychological differences (including conversational habits) that we perceive as binaric actually exist on a continuum between femininity and masculinity. In other words, some men prefer rapport talk while some women prefer report talk.[20] Still, perhaps Tannen's "men are from Mars, women are from Venus" application can shed light on the dynamics of some audience talkbacks where forms of "mansplaining" and reportage have been known to compete with personal anecdotes and seemingly off-topic emotional digressions to inhibit the free flow of ideas that mark a productive conversation.

There are also important differences between African American and European American conversational protocols that can cause confusion and introduce tension in conversations about the arts. In White culture, formal communication tends to adhere to a linear pattern in which the speaker delivers information to a quiet group of listeners followed by a highly structured question and answer period, after which the dialogue process is understood to be complete. As a result, White discourse incorporates a formal division between the designated speaker and the designated audience, a division that is often iterated in postshow discussion formats. People of Black African descent, on the other hand, participate in what is sometimes described as a circular discourse defined by rhetorical conventions such as call-response.[21] The circular nature of the call-response pattern evokes a communal experience in which "participation is considered by many to be a responsibility—not just an option—for listeners, who are supposed to do their part to make communication vigorous and effective."[22] As sociolinguist Geneva Smitherman notes in *Talkin and Testifyin: The Language of Black America*, call-response is a basic organizing principle in Black American culture wherein "there is no sharp line between performers or communications and the audience."[23] The call-response structure informs the rhythm, style, and tone of Black discourse, allowing for a construct where "virtually everyone is performing and everyone is listening."[24]

These cultural differences can become points of tension in the contemporary arts ecology, where Eurocentric definitions of "polite" behavior are understood by many gatekeepers and audience members as an absolute truth rather than as a culturally constructed condition. A more accurate assessment of audience behavior would acknowledge the fact that the Black idiom for being an audience member is simply different from that of the White idiom; and, apropos of W. E. B. Du Bois's famous theory of the "double consciousness" of African Americans, that some Black audience members might harbor a deep ambivalence about demonstrating "competence" in White audience etiquette. Chicago theater blogger Kelly Kleiman points to this distinction between the cultural protocols of White and Black audiences and suggests, wryly, that the unwelcoming rules in most contemporary theaters are off-putting to "black people . . . whose experience of performance is likely to include interactive church services and concerts of music where failure to clap hands or tap feet is the sign of someone's being dead."[25] A more clinical description of this gap comes from diversity consultant Bo Young Lee, who describes the traditional White arts audience as "low affect."[26]

This issue is surprisingly underexplored within the arts industry, perhaps the result of the habit of cultural proximity—the tendency to prefer cultural products from one's own culture or a similar culture. But I believe it must also be related to the ongoing cultural imperialism of large arts organizations, which continue to promulgate White middle-class tastes and values when it comes to signaling appropriate audience behavior in their venues, even at the risk of excluding prospective audience members holding different values. Despite the relative silence from the industry, however, there is a lively backchannel dialogue on the web among audience members interested in analyzing the "chasm between blacks and whites" at live performances in the serious arts realm.[27] Listening in on this backchannel audience-to-audience exchange might represent an opportunity for arts workers interested in gleaning some lessons about how audience members really feel. A culturally hospitable environment for Arts Talk must begin by acknowledging the legitimacy of alternate styles and manners of talk, and can only be achieved when the facilitation attempts to work productively with those alternate styles when they arise. Respect for difference in conversational manner as well as in styles of audience reception can lead to new understandings about the arts event or object under discussion. That respect must begin with the active acknowledgment of the privilege that structures and supports one form of audience discourse over another. As the wise person says: Privilege is invisible to those who possess it. The wise arts organization is willing to take off the blinders in order to examine the nature its own privilege in a rapidly changing culture.

2. **Begin transparently**. Effective facilitation starts with articulating the intended outcome(s) for the talk session. This introductory gesture, even if it comes in the form of a one-sentence statement, acknowledges that there are no mysteries in the works, thus removing any sense that a higher authority will slowly reveal (and thus deliver) the meaning or value of the subject under discussion. Instead, a transparent beginning establishes that the protocol for listening and talking is itself the intended outcome.

3. **Use body language that conveys your attention and focus**. It is easy to forget that our bodies (particularly our faces) convey as much if not more information than the words we say. Good facilitators are keenly aware that their facial and gestural responses need to reinforce the fact that they are focusing on each speaker. In Western culture, this is particularly true of eye contact. And, when the environment calls for it, good facilitators are physically active, moving through the space to show interest in individual responses and to make kinesthetic connections (I call it the Phil Donahue effect).

4. Listen authentically. This is by far the most difficult aspect of good facilitation. It is demanding to be in the position of needing to think one step ahead of the room (in order to run the meeting) while still being focused enough to stop and listen, authentically and attentively, to what is being said. Good facilitators err on the side of listening, trusting that they can rely on the structure of the talk session as a means of maintaining forward momentum. It is important to note here that authentic, active listening does not mean agreeing with the speaker. What it means is that the facilitator is willing to suspend her internal dialogue ("what am I going to say next?") in order to take in what the speaker is saying. When the facilitator models authentic listening, other participants follow suit. When the facilitator is not listening, the inverse is usually the outcome.

5. Operate on a "Yes, and..." basis. Here I am referencing the "Yes, and..." rule widely followed in contemporary improvisational performance practices. The idea behind this rule is to push performers (actors and comedians) to work with what is happening in the room rather than relying on a bag of tricks. When an improv performer says "Yes, and..." he is accepting what has just been offered and then adding to it in order to move the sketch forward. Similarly, when a facilitator says "Yes, and...," she is also accepting what has been offered and contributing to a collaborative process of defining the contours of the subject at hand. Many of the practices associated with artistic improvisation (in theater, dance, comedy, jazz) can serve as models for facilitators. In general, they remind us how important being in the moment (and bringing genuine mindfulness to that quality of "being") is to any community-building experience. They also reinforce the power of creativity. Bottom line, they concretize the fundamental necessity of authentic listening. A jazz musician who isn't listening is not a jazz musician. A facilitator who isn't listening facilitates nothing.

6. Welcome and celebrate indecision, struggle, and contradiction into the dialogue. Good facilitation is dependent on the ability to acknowledge that struggling with meaning is a central goal of the talk session. The facilitator's job is to open up the space for participants to struggle out loud with their experience, including their basic understanding. Attendant to that goal is to open up the space for those ideas to be challenged by other participants. This is not always a comfortable position to be in, and the impulse for many novice facilitators is to provide answers for participants who are struggling to articulate ("I think what you mean to say is") and to smooth over disagreements between participants. A useful approach to solving this dilemma comes from conflict resolution practices and the idea of "relational empathy," which emphasizes a productive rather than a reproductive approach to understanding another's point of view.[28] In this modality, all participants learn to acknowledge the validity (productive) of individual positions without having to agree to take them on personally (reproductive). The focus is placed on acknowledging the other person's position as a way to build trust and to work toward the construction of a shared meaning between the participants. This approach makes sense in the Arts Talk milieu, since it acknowledges that understanding is not "an all-or-nothing phenomenon"[29] and since it accommodates the inherent multivalence that is the very definition of good art.

Acknowledgment of the multiple readings in the room can also be a stepping stone for building new meanings collectively. In a productive talk environment, audience members are able to elaborate and build on each others' contributions in ways that can be deeply gratifying. The facilitator guides this building process, keeping the focus on the art work under discussion while allowing related topics to be introduced. Facilitators also help the participants work toward clarity by summarizing or paraphrasing others' comments to ensure that everyone understands each other.[30]

7. **Employ powerful questions**. As noted earlier, powerful questions can change the course of the conversation. These include open-ended questions offered as a way to prime a dialogue and follow-up questions employed to deepen and expand discussion and to help clarify ideas. Good facilitators are ready with questions that offer a point of discussion, pose problems for solving, explore the topic in ways that stimulate new thinking, and prime participants for brainstorming with freely formed (that is, new) ideas. Equally important are the kinds of questions that are employed in order to keep the talk productive—these are not so much substantive questions as guiding questions that help to maintain and enrich the talk environment. Guiding productive talk includes asking questions that keep the channels open ("Did everyone hear that?"), verify and clarify ("So are you saying...?"), link one speaker to another ("How does that comment strike you?"), and expand on a comment ("Why do you think that?").

8. **Be comfortable with silence**. I stated earlier that authentic listening is the hardest thing to learn and master. But really, the hardest thing for most facilitators to grasp is the beauty and power of silence as a tool for productive talk. As education theorist Robert Boice points out, while "talking nonstop appears a good way to maintain

control, it isn't in most instances."[31] The disequilibrium brought on by silence is a symptom of our chatter-oriented culture; a dip in conversation appears to signal a conversational group's failure to grease the social wheel. Facilitators often bring that sense of unease into their role, assuming that if the dialogue goes silent that means that the group has lost its coherence. To the contrary, learning science (and thousands of years of practice within various talking constructs) reveals that silence is a key part of the cognitive process, necessary in order to move ideas from the realm of thought to the realm of articulation through speech. Facilitators must allow for silence because it may well mean that the participants are in the process of thinking through to an articulate response. To that end, good facilitators find ways to make silent space (sometimes referred to as "wait time") comfortable for the participants. It bears repeating that the ability to settle into silence allows a group to absorb what has been said. If used sincerely and with good intentions, silence is also a tool for leveling the dynamics within a discourse; periods of silence slow the pace and allow for a redistribution of power among the speakers.

A case in point is an experience I had at the small New England liberal arts college where I teach. In the spring of 2013, I was asked to facilitate an audience postshow discussion because of concerns that the controversial style of the artist, Tamy Ben-Tor—whose character monologues involve commentary on risky issues relating to Jewishness and Israel (her home country)—might lead to misunderstandings among the audience. I began the postshow event with the invitation to reinvent the spacial dynamics of the performance space (we were seated proscenium style in an exhibition gallery) by putting our folding chairs in a circle. Once that was accomplished I welcomed the people who had elected to stay and invited them to listen and talk to each other or just to listen if they preferred. I stated that we were there to share our impressions rather than to receive information from Ben-Tor, who had deliberately chosen not to attend the postshow event. I also acknowledged that getting started on such a conversation might well be awkward. Then the large group (most of the 100 or so audience members had joined the circle) sat in silence for what felt like a long time. I reminded myself that silence was okay and stuck with my plan, using my body language and my facial expressions to indicate my comfort with the silence. After a time someone in the audience offered her emotional response to one of the images in the performance. Another period of silence followed, after which I offered one of my impressions. After another period of silence came and went (with considerably less anxiety attached to it), the rhythm of the conversation began to take its form. Soon this group of strangers understood that it was okay to sit in silence and okay to wait for their ideas to surface and emerge. That postshow session became an offering ("here's what I think I saw," "here's what it seems to mean to me") and an exchange ("can you please explain more about your observation?"). The participants expressed sincere appreciation for the opportunity to process Ben-Tor's layered and nuanced art work in a calm and democratic manner. There was no controversy about her work, just interest. Silence is a magic tool.

   9. Act as everyone's ally. In the 1980s, the psychologist Ivan Boszormeny-Nagy developed a methodology for conducting family therapy called multidirected partiality. In this approach, the therapist abandons the idea of impartiality and instead works to make sincere connections with the whole family in order to ensure that everyone's needs and concerns are being attended to. This notion of a multidirected focus (in contrast to a neutral or "unilateralpartiality" focus) requires an empathic acknowledgment of all members of the family. It also makes clear the expectations for participation and collaboration—all members must contribute their point of view in order for the process to be successful.[32] As Ken Bain observes in his analysis of higher education practices, the best college teachers speak as if they know and want to engage every student in the room.[33] The best facilitators have that capacity as well, especially when they begin with the understanding that adults have "enough life experience to be in dialogue with any teacher about any subject" and are best situated to learn new knowledge, attitudes, or skills best in relation to that life experience.[34]

   10. Check your ego at the door. All of the qualities and behaviors in numbers 1 through 9 are possible only when the facilitator leaves behind his or her own egoistic needs. Facilitation is always and only about the needs and goals of the participants and the participatory community.

THE ROLE OF THE PHYSICAL ENVIRONMENT IN PRODUCTIVE TALK

Some contemporary environments are built to signal that physically active interpretation is encouraged (a sporting arena). Some environments signal that the audience's experience is valued for its idiosyncrasies (a jazz club). And, of course, some signal a desire for collective stillness (traditional arts centers). Purpose-built, fixed arts spaces (concert halls, playhouses, galleries, and exhibition halls) began appearing in the United States during the colonial era and quickly became a marker for urban vitality and sophistication. By the mid-nineteenth century, all of the country's major cities boasted "cultural palaces" (a term deliberately deployed to reference the first arts spaces in Europe, which were, quite literally, the palaces of the nobility). Built by the economic elite for their own entertainment, most of these spaces sacralized the arts experience not only by enforcing a code of behavioral etiquette but also by predetermining the value of the work of art being presented inside their sacred walls. The selection of a symphony orchestra to perform in Carnegie Hall, for example, was a signal to audiences that they should expect something worthy of reverence. In other words, the social status of the space itself imbued the environment and thus its content (the arts events) with meaning.

After World War II, many American cities began another wave of conspicuous construction by building large, multipurpose arts centers designed by famous architects to be either grand or edgy (depending on the character of the city in question). Regardless of their architectural innovations on the outside, however, most of the postwar arts spaces in the United States are orthodox inside—the separation between artistic expression and audience presence is formalized and concretized by a proscenium or near-proscenium spatial organization. In the majority of our contemporary iterations of these cultural palaces we continue to adhere to a similar ethos: seating arrangement, lighting, sound, access to food, drink, and restrooms are all controlled in order to produce the best circumstances for the arts workers and the arts event. As such, we continue to institutionalize a kind of executive function where everything is "already under the control of somebody else."[35] Including, by default, if not by design, the audience's interpretive agency. For surely the meaning imbued by the sacred space has the power to influence, even impose upon, the potential agency of an individual's interpretive response. Highly controlled spectating environments where audiences are required to sit quietly in the dark or to remain physically detached as they move quietly through a gallery, restrict visual and aural access to the reactions of other spectators and thus disrupt what cognitive scientists refer to as *emotion contagion*, or the automatic way in which individuals partly or fully embody the emotional expressions of other people.[36] If embodying another person's emotions produces emotions in us (and, by extension, ideas and opinions), then there is a relationship between an inhibited spectating body and the lack of a fully realized hermeneutic process in today's arts goers.

This leads directly to one of the most significant barriers to productive social interpretation on the arts in contemporary America. Given the impact of the passive spectating environment just described, per-haps the most ineffectual space to talk about an arts event is exactly where it typically does occur—in the very seats or standing pos-tures where the audience has just spent a few hours as quiet, passive spectators inside the playhouse or concert hall or museum gallery. Emotionally *and* cognitively, you can't put people in a room that says "shut up and be still" and then turn on the lights and say "okay, now talk to us about your feelings (and hurry up because we only have 45 minutes)." Nor can you place audiences in a hierarchically reveren-tial relationship with artists or arts object and then expect those same people to easily and automatically reveal their personal feelings and intimate thoughts. This constitutes a jarring transition from passive to active status without changing (or challenging) the hierarchical power structure implied by the physical positioning of artists, arts event/object and audience inside the arts palace.

What, then, are the environmental implications for structuring productive talk and meaning making around the arts? To begin, the built environment must be hospitable for supporting the physical mechanics of talking, which include good acoustical quality for car-rying sound and the ability to control the ambient noise level. Just as important, though often overlooked, is attending to the psycho-logical mechanics of talking. In order to listen attentively to someone while they are speaking, for example, most people need to see the speaker's mouth as a reference point. Many people also need (psycho-logically speaking) to see the eyes of the speaker and, when speak-ing, need to sense that the listeners are looking at them in return. If the built environment restricts or prohibits the ability to look at a speaker's face, the quality of listening is significantly impacted. Think of a traditional secondary classroom. The room is intentionally set up so that all of the students are directly facing one vantage point (the teacher and the blackboard). The purpose of this physical construc-tion is clear—the students' attention should be solely on the room's lone authority figure and their reactions confined to noting down rather than engaging in a dialogic relationship with the information. Postshow talkback sessions that occur in the auditorium are iterations of this kind of educational modality. Audience members know with-out consciously thinking about it where the authority lies and where value and meaning are sourced. The result is a stilted session, one ori-ented toward the one-way delivery of information and one that does little to address the physical requirements for productive talk.

Equally important in creating an environment conducive to productive talk is attending to the way in which adults use their physicality while listening, absorbing, and processing information. Learning science has demonstrated that children need to use their bodies to process the acquisition of information; contemporary active classroom and active learning pedagogies acknowledge the importance of embodied learning. There is no reason to believe that some adult learners don't also rely on embodied processes to learn. As the Heinz Endowments' Arts Experience Initiative laboratory demonstrated, physical agency can be an effective dialogue generator. When Pittsburgh Ballet staff brought audiences into the studio to experiment with ballet technique at the barre (even trying on toe shoes), for example, people talked freely and asked many more questions of the facilitators than they typically did in talkback sessions occurring in the auditorium. The Heinz experiment also demonstrated how critical the mood or feeling of an environment is to productive talk. When Pittsburgh Symphony staff broke their talkback audience into small groups, moved them into a bar/lounge area adjacent to the concert hall, and invited them to lead their own discussions, for example, the nature of the talk changed from vague questioning to lively opinion exchange. And when the Pittsburgh New Music Ensemble audience group decided to meet on nonperformance nights in a series of local restaurants, their interactions with each other and with New Music Ensemble staff were animated by a newly charged ability to apply individual taste portfolios and fore-meanings to the ideas being generated in the conversation. Through productive talk, these subscribers came to see themselves as integral to the artistic and educational mission of the Ensemble. This kind of power redistribution allows arts producers and audience members to build trust and to develop a sense of shared purpose and community.

CHAPTER 6

ARTS TALK

A theatre that makes no contact with the public is a nonsense.

—Bertolt Brecht[1]

Arts Talk is a metaphor, an ethos and, ultimately, a call to arms. It is a metaphor for a way of moving through the world with art as an intimate companion. It is an *ethos* (a term derived from the ancient Greek word for character) promoting a set of ideals that characterize an arts-infused community. And it is a call to arms championing a move beyond the one-way delivery system that characterizes meaning making in most of the discourse around the serious arts in contemporary America. In this volume, Arts Talk connotes not just literal talk, but also a spirit of vibrancy and engagement among and between people who share an interest in the arts. Arts Talk connects us in the profoundest of human ways—as hearts and minds looking to make the world mean something through art.

Chapter 6 is an invitation for arts workers to invent their own Arts Talk protocol consistent with their own organizational identity. There will be different methods for different groups depending on genre, institutional style, cultural territory, community profile, and, of course, institutional mission. Regardless of those organizational preferences and distinctions, however, this book has focused on a shared goal: to provide the resources for arts workers *and* audiences to connect through a rich and complex conversation about the meaning and value of the arts in their lives. To that end, Chapter 6 proposes a twenty-first-century antidote to the legacy of the quietized arts audience: the audience learning community. A reconceptualizing of the arts appreciation model of the late nineteenth and twentieth centuries, the audience learning community is organized around the importance of access to knowledge acquisition and interpretive agency in contemporary participatory cultures. By looking under the hood to understand how taste, talk, and pleasure impact our experience with the arts, we are better able to explore the environmental, social, philosophical, and psychological conditions that *allow* us to talk, productively and pleasurably, about the meaning and value of the arts in our lives.

What makes this the mandate of arts workers? After all, we're not professional dialogue facilitators, we're artists and artistic directors and composers and directors and curators and administrators and marketing experts and education department staff members—all of us with big jobs that do not by definition and tradition include facilitating Arts Talk. True. And yet, here we are, facing a changing culture that is demanding a style of audience interface outside of the norms of twentieth-century-style industry protocols. Given this reality, what choice do we have? Without a commercial context for the serious arts or a state-supported system for promoting an arts-based cultural life among Americans, there is no other existing apparatus for facilitating an Arts Talk environment. We'll know the paradigm has shifted when Penguin publishing agrees to put out a book called *Talk Arts like a Pro* and business consultants offer workshops called "Water Cooler Arts." Until then, the arts industry needs to take more responsibility for creating opportunities for social interpretation of the art work we produce and present.

How? Encourage the citizen-audience to start talking about the arts. Give them rigorous, imaginative, and participatory enrichment programming to build up their knowledge. Follow that up with public opportunities to express their opinions about what they've seen, heard, and felt. And make sure that that public conversation is facilitated in a respectful, thoughtful, and democratic way (meaning, everyone gets to talk, everyone learns to listen). The more arts workers accept and encourage this idea, the healthier the arts industry will be.

Participation Nation Redux

Where does the arts industry currently stand within the participation revolution in American life? And how does this stance impact the role of social interpretation? As I stated in the book's introduction, there is surprisingly little evidence that the serious arts industry is adjusting to the expectations of our opinion-centric nation when it comes to facilitating public opportunities for meaning making about the arts. This does not mean, however, that the arts industry is not responding to the demand for "participation." As arts workers are abundantly aware, *arts participation* has been a buzz phrase for close to two decades. But what exactly do we mean by the term? Is it meant to simply describe someone who buys a ticket (as it does in the 2008 NEA survey)? Does it refer to literal hands-on arts events and programmatic activities "in which the participant is involved in artistic production by making, doing or creating something, or contributing ideas to a work of art, regardless of skill level"?[2] Or is it somewhere in between, functioning as an umbrella term for policy making that puts greater emphasis on the demand side of the industry?

At the policy level, definitions of what participation implies vary, though all seem to land on the issue of how to create more satisfied consumers among current and potential audience members. *Gifts of the Muse*, the influential RAND study from 2004, introduced a by-now familiar construct defining the instrumental (provides the means for producing something else of value) and intrinsic (valuable in and of itself) values associated with audience participation. *Gifts* and a later RAND report, *Cultivating Demand for the Arts: Arts Learning, Arts Engagement, and State Arts Policy* (2008), contributed important new vocabulary to the discussion about the socioeconomic value of the arts, including an exploration of the ways in which pleasure and satisfaction factor into the engagement process. The reports also made a strong case for the argument that the consistent privileging, in terms of resources, of the supply side (artists and art works) over the demand side (audiences) of the arts economy has contributed to the much bemoaned lack of engagement among American audiences. Other influential reports investigating the relationship between participation and engagement include arts management professor and blogger Andrew Taylor's "Cultural Organizations and Changing Leisure Trends, A National Convening, Online Discussion and White Paper" from the National Arts Strategies and the Getty Leadership Institute (2007) and the NEA's *Audience 2.0* (released in 2010 and based on data collected in its 2008 *Survey of Public Participation in the Arts*). The former asks a series of provocative questions about changing societal habits vis-à-vis an embedded industry infrastructure "often heavy on the 'hardware' of cultural experience—facilities, objects, technical production spaces—but thin on the human and financial resources required to make full and adaptive use of that hardware" and posits a related "growing disconnect between professional, established cultural organizations and the lives of their communities."[3] The latter, a study of the ways in which Americans participate in the arts via electronic and digital media, operates by broadly defining "arts participation" and then, under that rubric, teasing out media-enhanced arts consumption strategies (reading and viewing online, for example) that "reinforce other types of arts participation."[4]

In the past decade, a number of studies have responded to and built on the notion of instrumental and intrinsic value. Among the most insightful is arts consultants Alan Brown and Rebecca Ratzkin's "Understanding the Intrinsic Impact of Live Theatre: Patterns of Audience Feedback across 18 Theatres and 58 Productions." This survey-based study, published in 2012 as part of a larger book project called *Counting New Beans: Intrinsic Impact and the Value of Art* (edited by Clayton Lord), documents a relationship between "intrinsic impact" ("the core benefits that can accrue to individuals by virtue of experiencing an exhibition or live arts performance")[5] and the survey participants' expressed levels of engagement, over time, with select theater productions. In the report, the authors assert that "helping patrons achieve the 'moment of curatorial insight' (i.e., the 'aha' moment when understanding dawns) should be the focus of pre- and post-performance engagement efforts."[6]

University-based research centers are also contributing important data and analysis. The Curb Center for Art, Enterprise, and Public Policy at Vanderbilt University produced *Engaging Art: The Next Great Transformation in America's Cultural Life*, an edited volume of essays that approaches the concept of participation and engagement from a variety of disciplinary perspectives and offers data and theory to support new initiatives. And at the University of Chicago's Culture Lab—a think tank partnering academic researchers with a consortium of arts consultants—one of the stated goals is to create new pathways for sharing and using emerging research that will "disturb the status quo" and address the cultural sector's systemic problems (including the gap between institutional and audience priorities).[7]

Participation is also the key word for a wave of recent audience-oriented initiatives and products from foundations and research centers. As already noted, the Heinz Endowments' Arts Experience Initiative (2004 to 2008) was the first grants-based program devoted solely to supporting arts organizations interested in exploring how enrichment activities surrounding the arts event might deepen audience engagement.[8] In a similar vein, the Wallace Foundation launched its Excellence Awards in 2006 to support arts organizations in six target sites (San Francisco, Philadelphia, Chicago, Seattle, Boston, and

Minnesota) charged with pioneering "effective practices to engage more people in high-value arts activities."[9] More recent iterations of this funding practice include the Mellon-funded Audience Project, designed to help community-wide arts service organizations become "centers for cultural information and vibrant interactions among audience members, artists, and arts organizations;"[10] and Theatre Communications Group/Doris Duke Foundation's Audience (R) Evolution, designed to "study, promote and support successful audience engagement models across the country."[11] A slightly different but, to my way of thinking, very promising initiative, the Exploring Engagement Fund, was launched by the James Irvine Foundation in 2011. By aligning with the Foundation's "Who, How, Where" engagement pathways strategy, the Fund serves arts organizations willing to engage "low income and ethnically diverse populations" (who), to "utilize active participation" (how), and to "experiment with the use of non-traditional venues for arts experiences" (where).[12]

This rapid rise in grants supporting the exploration of audience enrichment programming (including many others not explicitly mentioned here) is an obvious by-product of the audience turn in cultural management occurring over the past decade or so. In some ways, it is reminiscent of the funding response to the arts education turn of the 1990s, wherein foundations began diverting general operating support to programming targeted at school-aged children. The result has been mixed, producing some fine examples of the state-of-the-art education programs and some examples of ill-informed, even cynical programming (with arts organizations taking the money without an authentic interest in arts education or an authentic intention to follow through with stated outcomes). A challenge for arts organizations responding to the current call for audience engagement initiatives is to begin and end with the audience's interests in mind by developing the kind of expertise necessary to support effective programming. In this respect, success equals expertise, and expertise equals people. Effective audience engagement programming is dependent (like all output—creative or otherwise) on human resources. Arts organizations that are truly interested in audience engagement will need to invest in audience enrichment specialists capable of creating, facilitating, and sustaining that programming.

Another challenge for funders offering grants-based support for audience engagement is to widen the aperture when it comes to methods for evaluating program efficacy. One radical aspect of The Heinz Endowments' Arts Experience Initiative, as I noted in the introduction, was the fact that participating organizations were not required to evaluate success using traditional metrics such as the number of audience members in attendance. Instead, they were encouraged to explore qualitative ethnographic methodologies, including anecdotal exchanges between team members and audience participants collected in a casual, interpersonal way. While this kind of measuring often flies in the face of industry values (especially in the era of "Big Data"), I posit that it is an important methodology that gives us a window into whether an enrichment experience has in fact influenced a person's level of engagement. I also posit here another perhaps radical assertion: When an audience member contributes to the social interpretation of a given work of art in a public setting (live or digital), she herself becomes the meaningful evaluative tool we are all so desperately seeking. If we cannot "measure" an audience member's engagement through the depth, creativity, and passion of her interpretation of our work, we are misunderstanding the very function of art in society. Want to know what your audience values? Listen to them make meaning. Social interpretation is a kind of impact assessment, one capable of contributing to the overall evaluation of the economic and social worth of the arts because it provides a way for audience members to do their own describing and thus to effectively communicate their individual, personal experiences of the arts.

From the perspective of contemporary arts institutions and individual artists, the concept of participation takes on many forms and means many things. Some arts organizations that regularly employ participatory strategies and protocols (e.g., Liz Lerman Dance Exchange, Cornerstone Theater, East Bay Center for the Performing Arts, and the Wing Luke Museum in Seattle) have long seen their *core* capacity as audience engagement. But since about 2004, an increasing number of organizations have been steadily introducing audience-centered engagement programming—from tweet seats to patron blogs to pull content to competitions to placemaking gestures—that offer spectators the opportunity to deepen their engagement with the arts event, the host organization, the artists, and even other audience members.[13] In Brooklyn, for instance, the Streb Lab for Action Mechanics, founded by choreographer and social innovator Elizabeth Streb, is promoted as a "gathering spot for exchange of creative ideas across cultures of kids, dancers, gymnasts, circus specialists and pedestrians. SLAM is a place to experiment, a place that examines the difference between public and private, a place that is all public, all the time."[14] In Chicago, Steppenwolf Theater offers First Look 101, a two-month experience that invites audience participants "on a backstage journey through all aspects of the new play development process—from the first rehearsal to the final performance,"[15] while the Chicago Symphony Orchestra produces a program called "Beyond the Score" featuring a multimedia "examination of the selected score—its context in history, how it fits into the composer's output of works, the details of a composer's life that influenced its creation—sharing the illuminating stories found 'inside' the music."[16] In Seattle, On the Boards, the first arts organization to organize a patron's blog, has experimented with other digital platforms (including a "t.v." station that rebroadcasts live performances) to "grow the contextual content around the performances in order to nurture our audiences' capacity to understand the work we present."[17] In New York, Jazz at Lincoln Center offers Swing University, an opportunity for subscribers to learn strategies for effective listening from accomplished jazz musicians.[18] In Grand Rapids, Michigan, ArtPrize is a community-driven competition for the "the world's largest art prize." Competing visual artists exhibit their work in downtown venues over a period of 18–20 days, and anyone who attends the event can vote (after registering in person or by using a smart phone). Winners of the public art component of the event are decided solely by public opinion, and the vote is billed "not as a way to discover the 'best' art," but rather as "the action to get everyone talking about art."[19] Competition-style events that encourage the use of crowd-sourcing protocols to curate arts events have been implemented in other genres as well, including (among many others): A.W.A.R.D.S. (Artists With Audiences Responding to Dance Show), a choreographic showcase initiated in 2005 by Neta Pulvermacher/The Neta Dance Company and originally produced by the Joyce Theater that invites the audience to choose the finalists and to comment on their performances; Click!, a photography exhibit mounted by the Brooklyn Museum in 2008 using an online forum for public evaluation of the open call submissions; and the New York Philharmonic's 2008 Central Park performance, where attendees voted by text message to choose part of the program.

In the commercial theater, the participation revolution has meant expanding the definition of marketing in ways perceived as audience inclusive. In 2009, for example, a year after the musical *Next to Normal* premiered, its producers began "performing" the play on twitter by tweeting a scene per day (accompanied by links to the show's songs). The musical was completed in 281 tweets over the course of five weeks, attracting over 361,000 followers and generating enough industry buzz to win an OMMA (Online Media Marketing and Advertising) award. More fascinating than the crossover dynamic between Broadway commercial theater and a professional marketing association is what happened next. "Librettist Brian Yorkey and composer Tom Kitt invited fans to collaborate on a new song via Twitter. Fans were asked to submit suggestions about who would sing the song, where in the story the song would take place, and ideas for lyrics. 4,000 suggestions were submitted and the song, 'Something I Can't See' was the result."[20] The song was not added to the show, but the audience was invited to submit questions to the creative team via Twitter, thus bringing the Twitter experiment full circle.

A more cynical example (to my historian's eyes) of the participation–marketing alliance was on display during the recent Broadway run of *Spring Awakening*, in which 26 on-stage seats were sold for each performance. As illustrated in Chapter 2, in past eras, audience members did sit on the stage, where they displayed themselves and sometimes reshaped the rhythm of a performance by interfering with the action or by forcing the performers to repeat an aria or a scene from a play. In the case of *Spring Awakening*, the participatory promise of such unusual proximity to the performers was constrained by a set of draconian rules for sitting in the midst of the action (dark clothing only, no programs or personal items allowed, clear instructions to pay close attention at all times). As a result, the historical reference (undoubtedly lost on the twenty-something audience anyway) was empty; the wealthy audience members who sat on stage from the time of Renaissance court performances through the eighteenth century would not likely have responded to any such attempts to restrict their "participation" in the stage action or their interpretive agency. Marketing-driven efforts like these push the sincere interest in reframing the industry's relationship with the audience in unfortunate directions, making participatory initiatives seem callow. I'm reminded here of a favorite recent *Onion* headline: "Struggling Museum Now Allowing Patrons to Touch Paintings."[21]

Certainly, the second decade of the twenty-first century brings more and more evidence of the blurring of the lines between performer and audience, whether as part of engagement programming with a creative agenda or as a redefining of the very structure of the arts event itself. Today the most visible examples of direct participation in an arts event involve what Alan Brown refers to as "crowd sourcing" ("audience becomes activated in choosing or contributing towards an artistic product") and "co-creation" ("audience members contribute something to an artistic experience curated by a professional artist").[22] While Brown's taxonomy is useful on many levels, what is most interesting to me is the way in which these changes in the power dynamic of arts-making and arts-presenting both invite and resist audience sovereignty when it comes to controlling the artistic product (and thus its perceived value). The recently revitalized realm of participatory (immersive, interactive, etc.) theater offers an interesting perspective on this.[23] Older versions of participatory theater such as *The Mystery of Edwin Drood* or *Tony and Tina's Wedding* used audience involvement as part of the performance—but in such a way that there was never any question about who was in control. Newer, hipper versions, such as *Sleep No More* (originally created by London's Punch Drunk theater company) and *The Donkey Show* (created by Diane Paulus and Randy Weiner), are necessarily more in tune with Millennial generation expectations about their relationship to an evening out; according to digital marketing consultant Patricia Martin, Millennials want to be at the forefront of information they can share (through real-time electronic exchange) because it "makes them influential."[24]

The American Repertory Theater's popular *The Donkey Show* is a case in point. Standing in the Studio 54-style line that begins at the Oberon Theatre's door and crawls down Arrow Street in Cambridge, the twenty-something crowds that line up each weekend are already texting, photographing, and posting on their experience. Once they enter the black box theater set up to look like a late 1970s disco (replete with bouncers and a full bar), the action of the play (a stripped down telling of *A Midsummer Night's Dream*) happens in and through the crowd and is managed by several floating characters who move people out of the way of the action, clear off tables that are soon to be used as acting spaces, and also get the crowd dancing and clapping and generally behaving like disco-era habitués. In this model, participation is tangible—the personality of the collective and of individuals is part of the meaning of the event. In a similar vein, the feet-on experience of *Sleep No More* (spectators spend two hours moving up, down, and across six floors of a warehouse space made to look like an old hotel) offers its audiences a sense of control in that each spectator chooses where and when to stop, look, and listen (and text). With that kind of corporeal autonomy, the narrative arc and thus the "show" is constructed by the individual spectator.

And, yet, truthfully, it's not. *Sleep No More* is billed as participatory theater, but in point of fact nothing the audience does alters the predetermined performance narrative (and there are plenty of black-masked attendants on hand to make sure it stays that way). Instead, what the *Sleep No More* experience enables is a kind of meta spectating, as audience members repeatedly negotiate each other's presence in ways that are unfamiliar in the quiet, still environment of most venues for the serious arts (though quite familiar in a sporting arena or at a rock concert). *Sleep No More* and kindred immersive performance events such as *The Donkey Show* invite audience members to actively shape each other's experience, even if that shaping is limited to shoving other spectators out of the way so that you can be the first to follow Lady Macbeth into the bath tub room. In this respect, they certainly generate a different order of enthusiasm among the spectator-participants. Though, interestingly, not of the verbal kind. In the case of *Sleep No More*, talking is strictly forbidden while the performance is happening (this prohibition is enforced by the requirement that all audience members wear three-quarter facial masks). And in the case of *The Donkey Show*, talking is basically impossible because the disco music is so loud.

Not so with contemporary African American performance forms such as Urban Theater (sometimes referred to as the Chitlin Circuit or Urban Circuit Play) and Hip Hop Theater, where communal talking is at the center of the aesthetic and thus the audience experience. Perhaps the most popular (and controversial) example of Urban Theater work is by Tyler Perry, who builds his plays around street stereotypes and spiritual tropes wholly dependent on call-response protocols derived from the Black church. Perry's audience is almost entirely African American and, by most accounts, made up predominantly of middle-aged women. Hip Hop Theater, on the other hand, caters to a younger, more culturally diverse audience and usually includes some aspect of Hip Hop music performance (certain dance forms, MCing, etc.) as part of its structure. Both Urban and Hip Hop theaters participate in the Black Arts aesthetic of orality, which, as discussed in Chapter 5, acknowledges call-response as an artistic structure and as an expression of cultural vitality and resiliency. As a consequence, both theater forms produce social interpretation as part of the performance itself, because, as literary critic Michael Awkward understands the phenomenon, not "only does the black audience listen to the text—it helps to create it."[25] Call-response is an ancient form of crowd sourcing that retains its cultural vibrancy among African American audiences and contributes to the pleasure and subsequent engagement of the spectator experience.

The question for all of these forms is whether crowd sourcing-style arts participation leads to social interpretation once the show is over and the audience collective returns to its status as individuals. Does deeper immersion into the physical environment of the performance push audience members toward analysis and evaluation of the arts event itself? Do spectators talk about the aesthetics of

The Donkey Show once they quit dancing? Do *Sleep No More* attendees work together in conversation to render meaning once they pull off their masks and sidle up to the on-site bar or during the subway ride home? Do Urban Theater audiences evaluate the value of the play's structure or the meaning of the character journeys after Sunday's worship service? I suspect not as much as they might. The celebratory atmosphere of the above examples is certainly a welcome relief from the constrained etiquette of the sacralization era, but on its own it does not seem likely that it will lead to social interpretation on the level called for in the Arts Talk model.

SACRALIZATION RECONFIGURED

All this evidence of the participatory nature of the serious arts industry makes it clear that the sea change is so well established that it might be argued we now live in a new climate. But while the initiatives cited earlier (among many others) are certainly markers of the arts industry's growing awareness of the importance of acknowledging audience needs, they do not address in a substantive manner the audience's cultural right to publically participate in the meaning-making process, nor do they actively pursue programming aimed at generating audience-centered talk about the meaning and value of the arts event or object.[26] Given the opinion-sharing nature of much of our participatory constructs in twenty-first-century America, this lack of hermeneutic opportunities in the arts stands out to me. In most engagement programming, the emphasis is on creating social connection and in some cases on providing paratextual learning supports, much of it in the form of talking head expertise delivered via traditional learning structures organized along the one-to-many model (and this is true regardless of whether that delivery is live or electronic). In many of these initiatives, there are plenty of opportunities for audience members to expand their knowledge and to gain a deeper perspective. Compared with the "it's great art because we say it's great" ethos of the sacralization era, this is a significant step forward. Still, most of these opportunities are not intellectually critical and thus do not invite conceptualizing and analyzing. And few provide structures for observation, communication, and reflection. In these examples and in hundreds of other audience engagement programs, there is little in the way of the free-form exchange of taste and talk that characterizes the audience behavior of the past or the audience-centered initiatives described in the sports, television, and new media sections in Chapter 3.

The exception to this generalization is the museum industry, which has on the whole been far ahead of the other serious arts disciplines when it comes to acknowledging the audience's cultural right to interpret the arts they consume and the industry's responsibility for facilitating that right. Museum engagement practices that involve some aspect of social interpretation have been theorized for decades and are implemented at a steady pace through education departments and curator initiatives. The explanation for the gap in attention to the hermeneutic aspects of audience experience between the visual arts and live performance forms is at least partially sourced in the structures for presenting the work. In a museum, the visitor selects his or her own time frame for the visit ("I'll go to the museum for three hours on Saturday afternoon") and can choose to devote as little or as much of that time to a range of activities beyond viewing the objects on display. In a live performance format, audience members do not choose the time frame for the visit, do not select when they'll engage in viewing the performance, and do not, as a rule, expect to remain in the building beyond the stated performance time. This of course increases the challenge for performing arts workers to locate the cultural space for social interpretation of their work. But that fact does not change the cultural imperative to do so.

By now, nearly every aspect of our culture has incorporated structural support for social interpretation *except* the serious arts. Why? As already noted, we do not have the kind of societal infrastructure that could readily facilitate opinion sharing on the serious arts and we don't have the kind of arts industry infrastructure necessary to make up for it. Perhaps another critical factor is that we arts workers are still very much engaged in the twentieth-century business of delivering meaning, ascribing value and quieting audiences. I have two theories on why this remains an industry truth: (1) the Authority Effect, a term I appropriate from a general concept in social psychology acknowledging the effect of authority on the way in which people formulate opinions[27]; and (2) the introduction of state-of-the-art marketing science professionals into the organizational structure of the not-for-profit arts industry.

A by-product of the sacralization project of the late nineteenth and early twentieth centuries, the Authority Effect uses the "standards" of "taste" to inhibit publically acknowledged discursive activities centered on meaning making. As discussed in Part I, anxiety over the relationship between taste and social status is long-standing and deep in the collective American psyche. So deep, in fact, that it is easily tapped by trained professionals who, according to cultural sociologist

Steven J. Tepper, "maintain and abide by a set of shared professional ethics and standards that are promulgated by national associations, licensing boards, and professional societies."[28] Tastemakers are not, by definition, democratic, even in this era of participatory democratization of culture. And most of what we call "audience participation" does not result in audience-centered meaning making or support the idea that the interpretive role belongs in the house among the spectators. With few exceptions, there is very little evidence that arts workers are involved in processes that encourage practices based on social interpretation. This is because the sacralized cultural model of arts attendance in the United States has been absorbed by both arts workers and audience members over more than a century of socially engineered practices. Somewhere along the way, this socialization became hardwired. As a result, our cultural logic entrusts only experts to make decisions about the meaning and value of an arts event or object.

Put differently, we aren't really talking about a true democratization of the American arts ecology because that would mean dismantling the Authority Effect that continues to dominate our cultural life and the way in which our cultural institutions operate. An amusing reference to the engrained nature of this kind of hierarchical meaning-making model comes from "The Pinky Show," a social-justice-in-education video site (with blog and YouTube links) using a variety of subversive performative techniques to share "information and ideas that have been misrepresented, suppressed, ignored, or otherwise excluded from mainstream discussion."[29] In a post from November, 2008, Pinky, an animated cat, offered the following analysis of contemporary museum culture's death grip on gatekeeping: "Museum people need lots of training so they can tell the difference between what's important and what's not important. They go to college to get trained how to think properly so that they can learn to recognize what has 'Value'. The valuable things will get into the museum where the public will be allowed to worship it. Sometimes museum fashion changes and something that was once worshipped will get kicked out, that happens. But that's okay because something else always replaces it so who cares."[30] As Pinky's ironic tone makes abundantly clear, the Authority Effect is ultimately no joke but an ongoing reality of American cultural practice.

The advent of marketing science within the not-for-profit arts sector plays an equally important role in this discussion. Commercial arts organizations are and have always been like any other business when it comes to selling tickets: Audiences are conceived of as consumers who operate both collectively (responding to persuasion aimed at group trends) and individually (responding to persuasion aimed at individual identity). The post-war Ford Foundation not-for-profit model was intended to disrupt the commercial imperialism of the aesthetic market place; with charitable status came artistic sovereignty for a new generation of artists and arts presenters. But, as Paul DiMaggio first pointed out more than 20 years ago, American arts organizations are "nonprofit" but not "nonmarket" institutions. They are required, in most cases, to earn at least 50 percent of their operating budgets and thus must compete in the arts marketplace. This has proven to be an awkward situation because "by definition the nonprofit arts organization sells a constantly changing, unknown, and unproven product."[31]

During the 1980s, rising overheads and diminishing ticket sales brought this institutionalized paradox to a head. The result was a widespread corporatization of the not-for-profit arts industry, a process highlighted by a new era of high-stakes (and high-cost) marketing science and the employment of teams of marketing professionals. "The twentieth century witnessed extraordinary growth in the nonprofit sector as tens of thousands of new nonprofit arts organizations formed in communities across America," notes Steven J. Tepper in *Not Here, Not Now, Not That! Protest Over Art and Media in America.* "These new organizations were increasingly run by professionals who boasted arts management, law, and business degrees and who were tied to other professionals across the nation through any of dozens of newly formed professional arts service associations... Such professionalism facilitated growing budgets, expanding facilities, and the perceived need for efficient and effective administration. As the cultural sector grew by leaps and bounds in the twentieth century, savvy administrators used their own authority and credentials to keep critics at bay, to secure the support of key community leaders and funders, and to build and entrench their organizations."[32] Over time, fundraising, communication/public relations, marketing/advertising, and corporate/foundation relations departments became more and more important to the definition of an arts organization because, in one way or another, they were thought to serve the bottom line goal of increasing the number of ticket buyers and donors.

Somewhere along the way, this "butts-in-seats" mandate was reframed as "audience development" and "cultural participation." When I attended my first public meeting on the issue of cultural participation in my then home city of Pittsburgh in the mid-1990s, I naively thought that I, as a cultural historian and playwright interested in the history of audience behavior and its relationship to the

contemporary arts scene, belonged with the audience development
cohort. I soon discovered that what I came to talk about was not what
the marketing professionals came to talk about. To them, "audience
behavior" was a demographic breakdown of who buys tickets, when,
and for what. To them, the audience was a marketing object to be
quantified and thus understood through statistical analysis. What I
came to understand is that the use of ostensibly empirical statistics-
based methodologies, long the province of the commercial entertainment industry, drove the way in which many large arts organizations
were organizing their "audience development" departments, programs, and strategies. In that environment, audiences were perceived
less as participants in the wider definition of an arts event (the triadic
hermeneutic relationship between the artist, the art object, and the
audience) and more as mass consumers, even if the scale of the "mass"
under analysis was numerically small (for example, the opera-going
community of interest in a medium-sized American city).

In his study of crowds, Richard Butsch points out that the word
mass first entered popular usage in the 1920s as a modifier for everything from audiences to communication and culture. "All of these
usages implied the same characteristics of mass: large numbers of
undifferentiated and interchangeable people; something of disdainful
low quality; and the isolated individual within the mass. Rather than
referring to class, as 'the masses' did, the 'mass' referred to an alleged
homogeneity among people."[33] This marketing-driven objectification
of the audience, when combined with the ongoing sacralization of the
artist *and* a hierarchical interpretive gatekeeping ethos rationalized by
the Authority Effect, makes for the ultimate one-two (three) punch:
not only is the audience member reduced to a wallet valued solely
for his ticket-buying capacity, but he is also expected to be a silent
receptor more interested in finding meaning from those in authority
than in constructing meaning from his own experience and with his
own interpretive toolkit. But this shouldn't be surprising, I suppose.
The cultural learning of the twentieth century taught arts workers to
despise the corporeal presence of the audience and all of the ways in
which spectators' bodies (including the mind/brain) might disrupt
the sacredness of the arts event and thus challenge the artist's and the
arts presenter's place in the hierarchy.

Twenty-first-century arts workers caught up in this marketing-
driven ethos routinely ask where is the audience? But once we have
sold them a ticket, do we ever ask what they think about the art
we offer them? Not really. Not authentically. Over the course of the
twentieth century, the idea of taking into account public opinion on

the arts morphed into the notion that listening to the audience would lead to changing ("dumbing down") the nature of an arts organization's programming—a distasteful compromise of "artistic integrity" known to some as "pandering to public taste" and to others as an abandonment of our responsibility to lead rather than follow. This notion is partially sourced in the sacralization ethos: Great art will automatically find its true audience without mediation of any kind and without the need for public discourse. Sentiments such as "Great Art speaks for itself" and "If I have to explain it to you you'll never get it" operate as a kind of short hand separating out the sophisticated few.

There is nothing new about elitism in the Western arts tradition, of course; segmentation and segregation among types of art and types of arts audiences have always been present. But in the past, the arts audience's access to social interpretation (and its greater sovereignty over the arts marketplace) tempered the Authority Effect and kept the gatekeepers in check. The contemporary bottom line mentality has disrupted this important equilibrium. As Bill Ivey notes in *arts, inc.*, "Today our expressive life is shaped within an arts system dominated by gatekeepers and market forces—by Target, Microsoft, Sony-BMG, the Metropolitan Opera, and lawsuits against students who download music or movies—a system with no mechanism to align action with the public interest."[34] Public interest is indeed the missing piece in this scenario. Where is the sense of common well-being in an industry obsessed with defending its worth to society while simultaneously refusing to articulate that worth in ways that the public can understand and embrace? The low barriers to personal expression (and thus to social interpretation) that Henry Jenkins identifies in participatory cultures such as television, for example, are difficult to locate in the serious arts industry. For many arts workers, providing the kind of audience-centered programming that could engender authentic dialogue around the arts is seen as an added financial, human resource, and environmental burden—one that would take arts organizations away from their missions and their core capacities. And they have a point. Andrew Taylor rightly warns, for example, that you can't solve a problem (in this case, a disengaged audience created by a hierarchical arts apparatus) with the same models that created the problem (the hierarchical arts apparatus).[35]

I believe the heart of the issue lies in the fact that many arts workers aren't really interested in partnering with the petty producers of the digital age when it comes to identifying the meaning and value of their arts products (some will even take offense at my use of the label

"product" instead of "work" or "piece"). Nor do they believe that
including the audience in the meaning-making operation will add
value to the arts as a whole. A closer inspection of the response from
the arts industry to one of the examples of crowd-sourcing curatorship referred to earlier in the chapter reveals, for example, how some
contemporary cultural gatekeepers resist efforts to bring the audience
directly into the evaluative process. When the A.W.A.R.D.S. program
was launched in Seattle in 2009, comments posted on the host organization's (On the Boards) website and in a variety of Seattle media
sites (local newspapers, online publications, and various professional
blogger sites) revealed considerable tensions over the notion of competition as a construct for concert dance. Some dancers voiced predict-
able opposition to the format: it's a beauty pageant, only the fluffiest
pieces will win, it could be rigged, a good/bad, yes/no judgment is
irrelevant when discussing serious art-making. But others saw participation as a complicated phenomenon with an interesting set of colliding truths, as in this blog post by Seattle choreographer Amy O'Neal:
"There is something equally humiliating and exhilarating about the
whole thing. But if dance was more like a sporting event where people
felt like they could invest more of themselves in a way that is familiar
and collective, maybe more people would go see dance."[36]

Expert commentators from a variety of local media venues (newspapers, online publications, and various professional blogger sites)
repeatedly stressed the "controversial" nature of the event within the
Seattle dance community. Running barely beneath the rhetorical surface in many of the professional blog and newspaper exchanges is the
question of whether a dance competition in the fine art realm disrupts the role of the expert in making meaning. These exchanges are
loaded with both explicit and coded references to the perceived high/
low binary, including a good deal of discussion questioning the validity of audience-centered interpretation/evaluation and the "problem"
of allowing popular taste to comingle with concert/aesthetic dance
sensibilities. Jeremy Barker, Arts Editor for *SunBreak*, for example,
cautions that the nature of the event "could wind up playing to a
sort of lowest common denominator in terms of allowing the audience to reward or, in a sense, punish choreographers."[37] Comments
like these express the anxiety critics feel over protecting their status as professional gatekeepers (and of course, their paychecks). It is
worth repeating Bourdieu's warning again: what is most intolerable
for those who are in control of cultural meaning is the "sacrilegious
reuniting of tastes which taste dictates shall be separated."[38] Why?
Because the audience's power to choose a winner through a system of

representational democracy unbalances our monopoly over "artistic legitimacy," revealing a fundamental truth about the ongoing elitist basis of our contemporary aesthetic constructs.

Contests are not the only source of anxiety over the expanding participatory ethos within the arts industry, however. In "The Death of Criticism or Everyone Is a Critic," Michael Kaiser, president of the John F. Kennedy Center for the Performing Arts and an influential policy maker within the arts industry, expresses alarm at the "growing influence of blogs, chat rooms and message boards" devoted to the arts because they give local professional critics a "slew of competitors." He appears astonished that some arts institutions "even allow their audience members to write their own critiques on the organizational website." This, he suggests, "is a scary trend."[39] Kaiser's fear of the Internet was quickly challenged by a variety of arts industry commentators, notably Andy Horwitz in *Culturebot*: "God forbid that the actual audience should have a place to voice their response to a work of art... The magic of live performance—even the most traditional forms—is that the audience is never really a passive watcher—they are engaged and their response informs the performance. The internet as a forum for authentic feedback and reaction is vital to the growth, development and continued relevancy of the discipline."[40]

Horwitz's comments are smart and forward looking, but Kaiser's are not as reactionary as they might seem (and in any case his comments certainly represent an attitude still very much intact within the industry). Perhaps Kaiser's alarmist rhetoric is rooted in his skepticism regarding the audience's ability to form meaningful opinions about the art work they consume; perhaps he fears that a kind of contagion will spread from one ill-informed consumer to another through the Internet. At the heart of the matter is the fact that arts workers like Kaiser see their sovereignty over meaning making and valuation as a professional right earned through expertise gained via training, experience, and talent. It isn't the audience's business to participate in social interpretation when it comes to the serious arts, because they simply aren't prepared to do so in a meaningful and productive manner. Understood this way, embracing the uninformed opinions of average audience members could not and would not push a given art form forward in the way that the informed opinions of trained critics ostensibly do.

Which leads us back to the discussion from Part I on the role of opinion formation in contemporary culture. Does the cultural habit of claiming our "right" to our opinions interfere with or even negate productive social interpretation because we rely on an emotional definition of "feeling" and of following our interests as opposed to reasoning through the effects of an arts experience? In other words, is saying "that's my opinion" another way to justify an intellectually lazy "like"/"don't like" attitude? These days, nearly every cultural operation, from public radio to professional basketball to the local town hall, has a mechanism built in for sharing "our" thoughts. But is this conversation? Are we turn-taking? And, more importantly, are we listening? Cultural critics such as Nicholas Carr and Andrew Keen argue, for example, that the kind of easy opining facilitated by digital venues reduces meaning making to its lowest common denominator.[41] The issue at hand for arts workers is whether we are beholden to audience taste or whether we are in conversation with them about meaning and value. If we are beholden to taste, then we are sunk, pure and simple. The lesson, then, is to be in conversation. Asking subscribers to use public talk to interpret the arts does not mean that business decisions will be made based on those interpretations. We listen to others as part of our daily lives: in the classroom, at work, at leisure. Listening does not mean blindly following. I think that the malaise of the arts in America is deeply connected to this confusion among arts workers. Aristotle claimed that all people delight in "learning and reasoning out what each thing is."[42] We can no longer move forward with an arts-going culture in which there is no opportunity for learning and no value placed on creating opportunities for audiences to reason out the aesthetics embedded in the arts event.

ARTS APPRECIATION FOR THE TWENTY-FIRST CENTURY: BUILDING AN AUDIENCE LEARNING COMMUNITY

As Chapters 4 and 5 illustrate, establishing a learning community and a protocol for productive talk for and among adults requires a particularized value set: emphasis on discussion rather than lectures or speeches, equal participation, inclusion of nonexpert-based dialogue and content, encouragement of multiple perspectives and diverse communication styles, and, importantly, comfort with unknown and unpredictable outcomes.[43] In this section, I distil five values for building audience learning communities and establishing productive talk leading to social interpretation that correspond with this ethos. It is important to state again that I am offering *values* rather than a list of best practices. As I have been stressing throughout the book, this is a deliberate choice, since I believe that the only way to create a culture of Arts Talk is through a fully conscious, determined effort on the part of the participating arts workers and arts organizations. Successful application to specific organizational contexts is not a question of choosing from a menu of options but rather of making the choice to enter into a fully conscious relationship with the audience and the community by applying the values discussed in the next section. Think of them as ideas for action (rather than activities for imitation).

Or think of them as survival tips. Changes in the experience of being an audience member have been constant throughout the history of Western performance, and the arts industry has always been subject to the laws of cultural evolution. Twentieth-century arts workers adapted to the expectations of the emerging sacralization ethos by quieting the audience. Twenty-first-century arts workers must now adapt to the expectations of a digitized participatory nation. Still, even in the midst of evolutionary change, core values can be retained. It is possible for the *arts experience* to fully participate in the live | digital era while also embracing its original, historical status as a collective action and a community initiative. And arts workers can revel in seeing themselves as coproducers, along with the community, of that experience.

1. Make the Environment Hospitable

In the commercial realm, how a customer responds to the physical environment of a place of business informs the particulars of the exchange that occurs inside of it. This is especially true in the "age of the hospitality economy," as one consulting firm describes the current business climate.[44] Potential clients need to feel that they belong in the space and that their purchase power is welcome not just because of the bottom line but also because by buying into a product they become part of the product culture. This is true of arts audiences as well; the arts temples of the late nineteenth and early twentieth centuries (all of those "opera" houses and "academies" of music) attracted working- and middle-class audiences because these spaces offered a rare opportunity to spend time in luxurious surroundings while consuming a welcoming range of arts events—high, low, and in between. After World War II, a new generation of sacred arts centers was built to position the arts as culturally important and was predicated on the assumption that local citizens would, as in the past, be attracted to splendid surroundings. But this time around the menu of arts events was considerably more restrictive, the lows were removed and the highs were further sacrilized. Then a curious thing began happening in the 1990s (or perhaps it just began showing up in the data): More and more people were opting out of the arts temple experience in favor of more comfortable (physically and emotionally) surroundings associated with other forms of public entertainment.

Sacred arts spaces are built to send a message about the elite status of the arts and, importantly, about appropriate behavior within the temple walls. As a result, they are not by nature hospitable environments and, by extension, they do not promote productive talk and social interpretation. That might have been okay in earlier eras, but in today's participatory culture the specter of increasingly empty seats haunts the industry. This means that arts organizations must actively work to turn their buildings into community spaces ripe for public exchange. There are many examples of this kind of work currently underway, of course. Recent building renovations at a group of venerable New York City institutions (Brooklyn Museum, Lincoln Center, The New York Public Theater) have been geared toward creating a campus effect that encourages visitors to view arts spaces as round-the-clock destinations. Food is often at the center, as are more comfortable lobbies and after-hour lounges that encourage people to sit down and to mingle long after the event has ended. The Library Lounge at the Public Theater, for example, features the original steel-frame bookcases (full of the vintage books) that were housed on the site when it was the Astor Library, free Wi-Fi, and a late-night closing time (2 a.m.).[45]

The other way to "renovate" is to deliberately desacralize the normative etiquette and participatory boundaries of an existing space in order to create a community feeling. To that end, the Baltimore Symphony's Rusty Musicians program invites nonprofessional adult instrumentalists and vocalists to play a concert alongside the orchestra and under the direction of Maestra Marin Alsop. Alsop created the program in 2010 in order to "attract new audiences through participatory opportunities for engagement as well as to enhance the BSO's position as an educational and social community resource."[46] Or the arts organization can elect to forego the arts palace altogether, as in the case of Classical Revolution, a Bay Area collective of musicians dedicated to performing "high-quality chamber music in non-traditional settings." According to founder Charith Premawardhana, "There's nothing inherently wrong with the concert hall setting, except that the institutions have a tendency to create an alienating effect between musicians and audiences (and management!). We're trying to put on concerts of great music with low overhead and high impact, reaching the audience on their own terms / level, and creating new connections that will continue to bear fruit over the years."[47]

Or the arts organization can challenge the normal boundaries of what constitutes their own identity. Flash mobs provide a useful example of a descralizing spirit wherein arts workers let go of their standard practices for building a performance or an exhibit in exchange for fueling a participatory ethos. A particularly beautiful example occurred in Sabadell, Spain, in May of 2012 when a hundred symphony and choral artists slowly assembled in the town center, instrument by instrument, voice by voice, to play and sing Beethoven's "Ode to Joy." The video of the event shows an audience made up of uninformed passers-by stopping to watch the unfolding action—a performance that slowly constructs itself, piece by piece, starting with a lone double bass player who is joined by a cellist who is followed by other string and brass and timpani players and, finally, the members of several choruses. Audience members and artists comingle in a circular performance dynamic in such a way that is is hard to tell who is a professional and who is just singing or conducting along for the pure joy of it.[48] In this instance, the work itself operates as a paratextual learning support, offering audiences the opportunity to watch a piece of art assemble itself and thus to get inside its engine.

Finally, the arts organization can embrace new technology as an aid to engagement rather than an annoying audience distraction. Second screening has been common in museums and performance halls since the widespread introduction of cell phones—that's a cultural reality that no amount of pre-show announcements is going to change. The question is whether that habit can be employed to enhance the primary "screen" (the live performance, the art object). There are and have been for some time a range of experiments with this concept, from the Concert Companion hand held device tested by a handful of major orchestras in 2004 and 2005 to tweet seat sections that glow in a variety of venues today. These examples of desacralization (and many others) acknowledge the need for hospitality, transparency, and individual agency in learning, pleasure, and, ultimately, in engagement. They also help to illustrate the way in which breaking down the separation between creative expression and meaning making engenders a sense of insider status in our audiences that inevitably seeds hermeneutic impulses. It is clear that, as formerly traditional boundaries are crossed in both live and mediated settings, alternate modalities for spectating are increasingly influencing mainstream audience experience and expectations.[49]

Hospitality as a concept for learning is considerably more than just desacralizing the physical space or creating participatory opportunities, however. For adults, a hospitable learning environment is one that is safe intellectually and emotionally. Trust is the key factor: trust in the competence of the leader, in the relevance of the learning goals, in the feasibility of learning the material under discussion, and in the structure of the learning protocol. But none of these is more important to adult learners than confidence that the environment is nonjudgmental. In an arts context, this means that a person's taste is acknowledged as a legitimate part of who they are and what they bring to the group. This notion of safety does not preclude expecting audience learners to be willing to experience new aesthetic ideas and structures, however. "Safety does not obviate the natural challenge of learning new concepts, skills, or attitudes," notes Jane Vella, nor does it take away the hard work that goes into accessing new data and acquiring new knowledge.[50] It means, instead, that audience learners must feel that their prior experience and their taste portfolio are welcome, as a starting point, for the new, often difficult learning that is about to occur. In an arts context, if we sponsor a postshow talkback program in which an expert of some kind (a scholar, a critic, an artist) lectures rather than listens and does not work to create opportunities for productive talk or authentic conversation, then we are sending the message that we aren't truly interested in the audiences' response. We do so at our own peril.

2. Acknowledge the Audience Participant's Themes

One aspect of adult learning that is routinely ignored in the arts industry is the necessity of addressing why the audience member has chosen to participate in a given enrichment activity. The assumption is that they are there because they are interested in the arts event/object and want to learn more about it. But as the literature surrounding the participation phenomenon reveals, the motivation for most adults to participate in surrounding events is far more complicated than simply wishing for a vague sense of enrichment. Participation is motivated by a wide range of social pressures and by an even wider set of individual needs. That is why learning theorists and educational reformers argue that adult learning should begin with what they call a "needs assessment," a soft introductory period designed to find out what each learner wants and needs from the program. This protocol complements what Paulo Freire called a "thematic analysis," which for him was a way to listen to the themes of a group before attempting to teach the group. As Vella points out, "When adult learners are bored or indifferent, it means their themes have been neglected...People are naturally excited to learn anything that helps them understand their own themes, their own lives."[51] In an arts context, starting with the themes of the learners means taking the time to hear why an audience member has joined the enrichment activity and what he or she hopes to gain from it. Techniques for eliciting this information include adaptations of story circling, a protocol most commonly found in community-based arts projects in which participants share a brief personal anecdote before beginning collective work on a community enhancement project. Storytelling as a form of personal greeting is as ancient as civilization and as current as the Moth Story Hour, Golden Gate Opus, and hundreds of ad hoc "Tell Us Your Story" programs favored by groups as diverse as undergraduate students and senior citizens.

The idea of beginning with the learner's theme is also applicable when accounting for different learning styles. Adults, like children, learn differently from one another and they process feelings and opinions in a wide variety of ways. For most, talking is crucial. For some, creative interaction leads more directly to social interpretation than talking does. For still others, socialization combined with discussion and/or information is the best way to contribute to an Arts Talk environment. Organizations committed to building an Arts Talk ethos need to begin by thinking of their audiences as a collection of individual subjects who think and feel—as opposed to groupings of "demographics" who consume. And organizations truly committed to creating an audience-centered culture will understand that effective engagement programming is made up of a series of small, interwoven, multilayered experiences serving a variety of learning styles and thus be willing to invest in a variety of approaches for building social interpretation into their cultures. If we start to think about adult audiences as individuals who crave an arts experience and not just an arts event, we are open to methodologies that account for individual taste and make room for the variety of reasons our audiences enter the arts environment.

3. Honor Emotion

Most learning theorists devote significant thinking to the way in which emotions impact the learning process, and for good reason. For despite close to 400 years of belief in the notion of a Cartesian duality, we are in fact *not* made up of a separate mind and body— our thinking process is fully embodied and inextricably linked to all aspects of the physical brain, including the limbic cortex (the emotion center). The limbic cortex is evolutionarily older than the neocortex (the cognition center), making it, according to James Zull, more fundamental than cognition. As such, he cautions, "If we want to help people learn we must expect to encounter emotion, and we must take it seriously."[52] In a learning situation, as in all our human experience, our sensory signals are first routed through the amygdala (the fear/danger center). "This so-called 'lower' route," continues Zull, "begins to make meaning of our experience before we have begun to understand it cognitively and consciously. Our amygdala is constantly monitoring our experience to see how things are."[53] When the material under examination is demanding or strange, the emotions tied up with the learning process, first filtered through the amygdala, will be felt as a form of danger.

So what does this have to do with audience learning communities? Plenty. As we know from our own personal experience, when fear and/or danger are triggered, we act differently. A learning environment, whether we understand it as one or not, can become rife with fear when we sense that we are out of our comfort zone, about to be challenged intellectually, or are facing a confrontation of some kind (for example, a debate based on a person's taste and/or the value of a particular style or type of art). In this context, the amygdala triggers the fight-or-flight response. Even when we choose not to take a literal "lower route," we often convert it into a kind of flight, as in, "I'm not going to say anything during this audience talkback session for fear of being wrong." The real problem with this situation is that a learning environment without any danger of the intellectual kind is, well, not much of a learning environment. Learning happens best when our strongest emotions are engaged and when we have to work to defend our point of view. That said, affective learning environments are built in such a way that participants can parse the difference between difficult material and a threatening situation. They are also built to help learners parse the difference between disagreement and personal confrontation.

This is a significant challenge for contemporary arts workers, most of whom are not accustomed to handling strong audience emotion beyond standing ovations and other normative approbative gestures. Our industry instinct toward conflict avoidance is rooted in the sacralization ethos, where disagreement over the meaning and value of a work of art is not really tolerated. Class issues also play a role in this phenomenon, loaded as they are with concerns over the perceived relationship between educational level and sophistication in terms of the construction of taste. When we add colliding cultural traditions, as in the differences between the linear Eurocentric audience behavior habits and the circular Africanist audience behavior habits outlined in chapter 5, we have a complicated mix of biological and cultural factors ready to undermine the healthy exchange of opinion. These all seem like very sound explanations for why there is no culture of arts talk in the United States. It is fascinating, then, to note that our culture of sports talk proves, on a daily basis, that we have the societal structures in place to argue, debate, disagree, and then shake hands over an emotionally charged topic.

4. Embrace the Inherent Subjectivity of the Arts

As this book has repeatedly stressed, locating meaning in an Arts Talk environment is not intended to be an objective or empirical process. When it comes to meaning making, there simply is no right or wrong answer. No one has a magic looking glass that can locate greatness existing beyond the cultural frame it exists within, and no one has the right to make the claim that they do, not even the artists themselves. Literary critics W. K. Wimsatt and Monroe Beardsley first pointed this out nearly 70 years ago in their essay titled "The Intentional Fallacy," declaring that "the design or intention of the author is neither available nor desirable as a standard for judging the success of a work of literary art."[54] In other words, in the hermeneutic process, it doesn't ultimately matter what the artist thought or thinks about his own work—an art work is not a monument revealing itself in a timeless monologue; meaning and value are not fixed at the point of origin or at any other point. Contemporary artists tend to embrace this ethos more purposefully than previous generations; many point out that they have no interest in conveying any particular set of lessons or meanings. Nevertheless, as Jacque Rancière notes, they "always assume that what will be perceived, felt, understood" is exactly the same as what they have put into their art work. "They always presuppose," he continues, "an identity between cause and effect."[55] Rancière understands this presupposition as a condition of privilege; the artist holds a fundamental belief that he or she is in the right.

When it comes to the serious arts in mainstream culture, the sacralization ethos has allowed the myth of artist omniscience and empirical standards for the evaluation of great art to survive. But as I have already stated, in this age of abundant postmodern relativism, the idea that a definition of "great art" can be tracked, identified, and fixed is ironic, to say the least. Nevertheless, it does survive; indeed, it is frequently the default platform in organizational mission statements ("advancing artistic excellence is at the core of our mission and goals") and business plans ("the way to keep people coming back is to do high-quality work"). But these old maxims won't help us now. The repeated truism that "quality" art is the best form of audience enrichment is simply untrue. Just because something is of high quality does not mean that people will instantly understand it or be willing to support it. As cultural theorist Diane Ragsdale points out, "Selling the superiority instead of the diversity of the arts; being exclusive and mysterious rather than inclusive and open; privileging the professionally performed and passively received experience over other forms of participation; and competing against one another to get people to consume one's particular variety of exclusive and mysterious art rather than collaboration to develop arts participation, *have not been particularly effective strategies*"[56] [my emphasis].

The fluidity of meaning in an arts context is a very complicated conversation, and I certainly don't mean to reduce the implications of this fact for arts workers interested in participating in social interpretation with their audiences. Interpreting meaning is a constant challenge for the serious arts because of the prevalence of what Umberto Eco calls "open" texts; that is, art that provides little in the way of response indications to its audience consumers. "Closed" texts, ones that consciously generate particular responses, are more common at the entertainment end of the arts spectrum. Nevertheless, I assert that a productive Arts Talk culture allows for a healthy, vibrant and enjoyable exploration of the relative difficulties associated with understanding open texts—those arts events/objects that refuse easy classification. Arts Talk aspires to be a setting for productive disagreement—for minds and hearts to meet over conflicting interpretations that don't cancel each other out but rather exponentialize them. In this environment, audiences are invited to explore the existence of multivalence not as a quandary ("just tell me what it means!") but rather as an opportunity. Understood in this way, disagreement over what makes an art work valuable (or not) is something we can not only tolerate, but also celebrate. The goal, then, is to encourage multiple readings in the course of a conversation and to embrace the sense of unease that accompanies nuance and multivalence.

So just how do we acknowledge the inherent complexity of the serious arts or of the many horizons of understanding that our audience members bring with them into a conversation about an arts event? I don't believe the answer lies in the common practice of writing a program note advising the audience to relax, sit back, and be "open to experiencing" the work rather than looking for meaning. In the first place, as I've established in earlier chapters, that sentiment defies human psychology and the realities of our cognitive condition, because the human mind is always looking for meaning—we are biologically incapable of "relaxing" in that respect. In the second place, statements like that are read by many audience members as patronizing—just more evidence of the elitist nature of arts workers. Instead of putting the onus on the audience, we need to take responsibility for creating a conversation around the arts event by employing the fundamentals of productive talk outlined in Chapter 5. These include establishing a hospitable environment where everyone feels valuable, asking open-ended questions offered as a way to prime a dialogue, asking follow-up questions employed to deepen and expand discussion, and, most importantly, listening for meaning (instead of for validation). Using these techniques, arts workers can turn confusion, conflict, and disengagement into authentic conversation centered on social interpretation. They can also help to build a culture that supports risk taking on the part of spectators. Building opportunities for the audience to participate in social interpretation around an arts event should not be confused with dumbing down the repertoire (as it often is). It bears repeating here that truly effective social interpretation experiences are more likely to support progressive, adventurous programming because they provide audiences with the tools for receiving unfamiliar art and the confidence to explore new terrains.

5. Work toward Building Community Partnerships (and Letting Go of Control)

Given America's cultural neglect of the serious arts, the responsibility for constructing audience learning communities and launching productive talk inevitably falls to arts workers and arts organizations. But it should not end with us. By definition, a learning community takes on a life of its own, moving from a kind of dependency on the structure (in this case, the arts organization) to a state of independence defined by the learning community's ability to function beyond institutional borders, expectations, boundaries, and guidelines. This kind of growth to independence is common in other geographies of social interpretation (think, for example, of the way in which discussion protocols facilitated by an institution like HBO quickly expand into audience-built structures like the "Is Tony Dead?" b-board thread). Transparently designed and praxis-based learning structures are ready made for launching independent learning communities because the learners have put into action all of the skills needed to create an autonomous community. Indeed, as learners they have, per Habermas' three domains of knowledge, been emancipated, and thus are ready and eager to take that autonomy to other parts of their lives. Our best hope for the future of the serious arts in American life is to encourage and enable this route to interpretive freedom. Today's engaged audience is the best breeding ground for tomorrow's emancipated audience.

Which leads us back, one final time, to a discussion about power. Learning communities operate best by treating the learner as a decision maker and holding the learner accountable for his own process. This, of course, necessitates a balance of power in the learning environment, or, in the case of traditional one-to-many learning models, a redistribution of power. Once that shift has occurred, arts organizations can engender Arts Talk by following the values (and strategies) of good facilitation outlined in Chapter 5. As noted there, in a productive talk environment, the facilitator is an instrument dedicated to creating a hospitable learning environment, not an ego looking to be fulfilled. The facilitator *does not make the meaning and give it to an audience.* Instead, the facilitator establishes the environment and the tools for artists and the audience to make the meaning together. In this respect, there does seem to be a power shift underway among individual artists, some of whom are working to facilitate more authentic interactivity with their audiences and are showing more interest in generating productive talk without using the presenting organization as a middle man. The choreographer David Dorfman, for example, includes a message in his show programs inviting audience members to "share their reactions" directly with him via e-mail.[57] This gesture signals that Dorfman is interested in his audience members' individual opinions, obviously. But it also signals that the choreographer wants a relationship with the audience that is distinct from the power structure represented by the presenter. In my view, Dorfman's gesture isn't intended to disrespect the presenter, but rather to acknowledge the audience's innate sovereignty over their arts going experience.

I want to stress again that facilitation protocols can be implemented through structures as well as through individuals. This can happen by providing what museum director and consultant Nina Simon defines as "hosted" participation; that is, programs in which an arts institution "turns over a portion of its facilities and/or resources to present programs developed and implemented by public groups or casual visitors."[58] Simon's context is the museum industry, but this kind of model is ripe for exploration in all types of arts organizations. And it is appropriately applied to productive talk and social interpretation as well. What would happen if we provided the bricks and mortar (and even the coffee and wine) but turned the meaning making over completely to the participants? What if each individual audience member was empowered to decide for herself what a given work of art means? Or if audience members themselves took over the facilitation of the meaning-making process inside our walls (or websites)? Would that change the definition of what makes that work of art valuable? And if it did, what would come of that? In an Arts Talk environment, sovereign perspectives are not seen as challenges to authority but rather as catalysts for engagement through productive talk. The ultimate goal is to authorize everyone in the room to feel, to think, and to understand.

Building community partnerships implies encouraging on-going audience learning outside of the arts venue and, in some instances, beyond the purview of arts workers. I am not the first to argue that the age of partnering with nonarts systems to create effective engagement opportunities is at hand,[59] although I may be the first to argue that those opportunities should also be focused on encouraging social interpretation. To make this feasible, arts workers and arts institutions have to want to let go of control because they believe that the future of the serious arts depends, significantly, on a sovereign audience. Then they have to be willing to commit the resources necessary to create community partnerships with existing structures (whether bricks and mortar or digital) that already have a place in mainstream American life. Arts organizations and arts presenters might look to partner with non-arts-based systems in their community that are either already fostering interpretive acts or are structurally ripe for taking on that function.[60] This includes libraries and community centers, colleges and universities, restaurants, bars, gaming stores, secondhand record stores, as well as the wide range of existing digital platforms that use two-way systems to share information. It also includes the ever increasing range of venues that are both physical and wired. Can the corner coffee shop, with its free wireless and ample seating, become, for instance, a place for Arts Talk?

That question is worth further reflection. Coffee houses have a long history as sites for social interpretation in both the East and the West. They first emerged in tenth-century Istanbul and began spreading westward, along with the drinking product itself, in the middle of the seventeenth century. By 1800, there were hundreds of coffee shops in London organized around reading the daily newspapers (which could be "rented" for a penny), conducting business deals, debating current politics and, as Chapter 2 demonstrates, passionately interpreting the value of the arts. In these venues, ideas were discussed within a structure but without a rigid hierarchy, allowing for working class and economic elite alike to espouse opinions. (Though not working class and elite women, since they were discouraged from entering most English coffee houses of the period.)[61]

Today's coffee houses have evolved into what urban sociologist Ray Oldenburg calls "third places," or the realm outside of the home and workplace where citizens participate in inclusive sociable practices. In his book *The Great Good Place*, he describes the third place as being hospitable in all senses—comfortable, accommodating, and playful—while also existing as a neutral space where social status is put aside and conversation is the main activity.[62] The latter point is salient. People seek out third places because they want to talk or to be around talk, as the by-now common coffee house scene amply demonstrates: individuals "talking" through their personal screens (from laptops to smart phones) sitting next to chattering groups huddled over their cups. The ubiquity of third places (bars, salons, restaurants, community centers, coffee shops, libraries) in urban, suburban, and exurban environments offers many possibilities for arts organizations to build partnerships centered on social interpretation of the arts. The question for arts workers is whether we can push the comfortable, accommodating, and playful nature of today's coffee shop culture into a more critical sphere where the values inherent to meaning making around the arts (conceptualizing, analyzing, synthesizing, and evaluating) are operationalized.

At the beginning of the chapter, I stated that Arts Talk is a metaphor, an ethos, and a call to arms. Arts Talk is also a way of doing business. The arts industry is awash in audience-centered engagement programs and initiatives that in one way or another are attempting to address the audience turn the industry has taken in the past decade or so. It would not require much to nudge these varied engagement programs into opportunities for social interpretation of the arts event or object. In many cases, it is a matter of only a slight adjustment to think of "engagement" and "participation" as a *hermeneutic opportunity* for the audience. And yet it is hard work to do this, because it necessitates a deep commitment to valuing the audience as a partner in the meaning-making process rather than as simply an appreciative consumer. It's true that we don't live in an arts talk nation in the way that we live in a sports talk, or television talk, or movie talk nation. But this is not an unchangeable situation beyond our control. Arts workers and arts audiences can and must influence the way the serious arts are positioned in contemporary culture.

I end by revisiting two concepts from Part I of this book. The first is John Dewey's definition of *an experience*: "when the material experienced runs its course to fulfillment." For contemporary audiences, *an arts experience* is not a drifting from one thing to another but a willful application of conscious analysis that concludes in a sense of satisfaction. Audiences want to engage in social interpretation because this is, for most of us, how we identify and subsequently narrate to ourselves and to others a "real experience."

The second concept is the original meaning of the term engagement, derived from the action of gears built into a mechanism. When the gears *engage*, the mechanism gets to work. Emotionally and intellectually, people engage with the arts when they feel a sense of involvement in the process. When they have the sense that they, too, are an element in what makes the gears of art work.

Conclusion: The Pleasures of Interpretation in the Live | Digital Era

Karl Marx had a pretty good idea. On a perfect day in a perfect world, he wrote, a happy citizen might "hunt in the morning, fish in the afternoon, rear cattle in the evening" and, finally and best of all, "criticize after dinner," perhaps with a bottle of wine on the table.[1]

Analog versus Digital?

When it comes to the makeup of contemporary arts audiences, we are in the midst of a culture war. I'm not referring to tensions between the high brows, low brows, and omnivores, or older and younger generations, or Black or White or Hispanic behavioral constructs, or people who eat wrapped candy versus everyone else. The culture war I'm talking about is between analog people and digital people. Analog people aren't Luddites—they mostly all have smart phones, iPads, and personal computers. And digital people aren't always rude twenty-somethings more engaged with their screens than with the physical world around them. The distinction between the two cultures lies in the way each thinks about how to use technology. Analog people enhance their daily tasks with technology. Digital people reinvent theirs with technology.

It might be argued that digital people think more creatively about how postanalog applications can enhance their daily lives and their capacities to analyze, debate, reflect, imagine, and wonder. Or it might be argued that they have given control over to those devices; that they suffer from what Nina Simon calls "technology rapture." But either way, the social change brought on by Web 2.0 capacities and the subsequent cultural migration to cyberspace is permanent. Arts workers (made up of both analog people and digital people) are not being offered a choice in whether to join the migration—that ship has sailed. What seems clear, though, is that we have the freedom (and an obligation) to think carefully about how to incorporate digital access into the arts construct in a positive and progressive fashion. Facebook pages and tweets are fine, but often they are employed as mere iterations of the one-to-many communication platforms that characterized most analog-era arts organization's "outreach" protocols. The vast majority of Facebook pages associated with arts organizations, for instance, aren't much different, structurally and operationally, from printed newsletters and brochures.

Which leads me to a question: What can arts workers and audiences gain from embracing the two-heads-are-better-than-one power of cyberspace collectivity? As media theorist Clay Shirky notes in *Here Comes Everybody*, the digital era has ushered in powerful new leverage for the crowd-sourcing protocol of most social achievement, a protocol that gave us the Sistine Chapel ("Michelangelo had assistants paint part of the Sistine Chapel ceiling")[2] and scores of other great works of art that are usually (and incorrectly) attributed to a single creator. Given our ongoing desire to live and work collectively, Web 2.0 technology makes organizing "without organizations" a finger swipe away. This suggests, then, that the digital possibilities for organizing social interpretation are also only a finger swipe away. I feel certain that new modalities for arts appreciation are being invented right now, on line, in ways I don't yet know about.

And that's a good thing. I believe that much will be gained from traveling the social media universe in search of information about the ways in which people are talking about their arts experiences. If we study online practices, we can learn more about how average audience members process their arts experiences after they leave the arts space. And that knowledge can help us to better understand how social interpretation of the serious arts functions in the twenty-first century. Can we improve the ways in which we support our audiences in their quest to use existing forms of digital talk (Twitter, Facebook, texting, smart phone photography) and sharing platforms (Digg, tumblr, flickr, instagram) to work through their personal responses? Can we invent new cloud-based solutions for disseminating greater context and richer understanding of the arts? I'm reminded here of the Amazon.com social retail business model, which is predicated on the fact that today's consumers are buying access more than they are buying content. Or, to put it in absolute terms, they are buying access to information *about* content. Information sorting has always been the route to power. If arts organizations become information sorters for their audiences, everyone gains. And if arts organizations can

combine that power to compile useful paratexts that support understanding and provoke thinking with structures that facilitate productive talk, the gain is exponentialized.

The best motivation for arts organizations to enter into an Arts
Talk protocol is, ultimately, a selfish one. The better our audiences
become at meaning making, the less we need to worry about the
"accessibility" of the content of our programming. The evidence cited
in earlier chapters about the learning process supports the notion that
audiences included in transparent and democratic learning operations
are more likely to respond well to progressive, adventurous programming, because they have better tools for making sense of that experience. When audiences are more fluid interpreters, they are more
interested in tackling difficult works of art. This should be very good
news for arts organizations and artists because it means we can leave
the arts event/object alone. In a productive, well-functioning Arts
Talk environment, it isn't necessary to change our repertoire or to
turn all of our work into participatory events. It also isn't necessary to
give over our galleries and playhouses to disruptive behavior.

Expanding on the latter point, perhaps this is a good moment to
admit something else about my personal predilections (besides the
fact that I don't like sports). The other side of my professional life
is as a playwright and stage director, and quite honestly, I go crazy
(inside my head) every time *anyone* makes *any* noise during *any* of
my productions. But I've learned over the years that that's the artist
me, not the spectator me. The spectator me (along with all the other
spectators in the house) can tolerate a reasonable level of ambient
activity; I can filter, focus, select, and organize surrounding stimuli
in the auditorium just as I can in other environments. That doesn't
mean that it isn't reasonable for audiences to expect a quiet auditorium during an arts event, if only because we are accustomed to this
reception environment and have learned, through experience, to need
silence to concentrate. I am not arguing that in order to be authentically participatory we have to undergo a wholesale reconstruction of
the arts-going experience, the performance environment, or the very
structure of the arts event. We just have to start talking, before, after,
and in between our arts-going experiences. Arts appreciation in the
twenty-first century is about understanding the mechanics of social
interpretation and being willing and able to apply those mechanics to
an Arts Talk ethos.

So what is keeping an arts-centered, audience-built conversation
from forming itself in twenty-first-century America? Why is it that the
serious arts industry (and the not-for-profit engine) has been unable

to produce fan communities that talk at every turn about their passion for the arts? This book has argued that it is a lack of confidence born of socioeconomic practices, societal habits, and entrenched arts industry attitudes. A vibrant Arts Talk culture would change this. Our goal must be to empower audiences to engage in constructive and pleasurable dialogue about the arts. We must celebrate those citizens who, by virtue of their vital and engaged presence, can turn arts spaces, Facebook pages, e-bulletin boards, living rooms and the local coffee shop into sites of public assembly ripe for intellectual and emotional connection over the arts.

TASTE, TALK, AND PLEASURE: THE ARTS

I end this exploration of the Arts Talk model where I began, asserting that our arts-going pleasure is deeply tied up with the opportunity to interpret the meaning and value of an arts object/event, and, further, that this pleasure is enhanced significantly when meaning making is made social. I have tried to demonstrate in the preceding chapters a phenomenology for the average arts goer in which **an arts experience** combines with the audience member's preexisting **taste** portfolio to produce productive **talk,** which arouses **pleasure** and thus engenders **engagement** with the arts. In this way, Arts Talk becomes a term for a new modality of arts appreciation for the twenty-first century characterized by a vibrant interest in social interpretation of, by and for the audience.

By acknowledging the role of **taste** in the meaning-making process, my intention has been to secure a safe place for individual arts goers to explore their knowledge and experience of the arts, to share that knowledge and experience with others, and, through productive talk, to extend that knowledge and experience into new aesthetic territories. As I have tried to illustrate, a given audience member's horizons of understanding significantly inform the way in which the ensuing interpretive process unfolds. And those horizons profoundly affect the nature, tone, and style of any dialogue that follows an arts event.

By acknowledging the critical importance of **talk** in twenty-first-century American life, my intention has been to direct our understanding of the role of dialogue, discussion, and debate as a means for seeding a deeper interest in the arts among existing and potential audiences. Talk is the corollary between the historical examples described in chapter 2 and contemporary behaviors described in chapter 3, and it is the through line connecting those behaviors to

Part II's exploration of how to produce arts experiences that have the capacity to unleash the **pleasure** of learning. As I have tried to show, my use of the term talk is intentional and purposeful. In contemporary America, talk is the term we use to convey the connection, through language, of ourselves to other selves. It denotes personal expression and opinion formation, and it connotes all manner of communication venues—from tweeting, facebook posting, and texting to bar chatter and water cooler conversation. Talk, because it is inviting and hospitable, is a lubricant for the operation of social interpretation. Arts workers have to harness this overwhelming human need to be socially connected through talk. We have to take that need and redirect it in ways that will enrich the arts and the audience alike.

By acknowledging the relationship between pleasure, learning, and meaning making, my intention has been to explore why social interpretation of the arts will lead to deeper engagement. As the previous chapters of this book have asserted (and as Karl Marx so helpfully elucidates in the opening quote of this conclusion), audiences are by nature and practice liberal learners engaged in a process of making sense of the world through their critical capacities to analyze, to debate, to discover, and to connect. We need to infuse our audiences with the ideal that art going can be a tool for thinking, living, and enjoying life. We need to help our audiences to see that when we talk about the arts, we talk about our lives and we discover new lives.

Let's build a culture of interpretive-oriented talk around the arts that rivals that of sports, television, gaming, and social reading. Let's find (let's rediscover) the heart of community in a conversation about what the arts mean in the live | digital era.

NOTES

Preamble: We the Audience

1. Hans-Georg Gadamer's concept of the horizons of understanding is defined as the "range of vision that includes everything that can be seen from a particular vantage point." In the hermeneutic process, a receptor's horizon is the point of departure for understanding and ultimately for meaning making. See Hans-Georg Gadamer, *Philosophical Hermeneutics* (Berkeley: University of California Press, 1976) and Gadamer, *Truth and Method* (London: Sheedand Ward, 1979).
2. See Lynne Conner, "Who Gets to Tell the Meaning?: Building Audience Enrichment," *Grantmakers in the Arts Reader 15*, no. 1 (2004): 13 and Lynne Conner, "In and Out of the Dark: A Theory of Audience Behavior From Sophocles to Spoken Word," *Engaging Art: The Next Great Transformation of America's Cultural Life*, eds., Steven J. Tepper and Bill Ivey, 116 (New York and London: Routledge, 2008).
3. The organizations included the Pittsburgh Symphony Orchestra, the Carnegie Institute Museum of Art, the Andy Warhol Museum, City Theatre, the Pittsburgh Ballet Theatre, Quantum Theatre, Pittsburgh New Music Ensemble, Pittsburgh Chamber Music Society, Silver Eye Center for Photography, Mattress Factory, Pittsburgh Dance Alloy, and the Society for Contemporary Craft. For more information on the Arts Experience Initiative, see Lynne Conner, *Project Brief: The Heinz Endowments' Arts Experience Initiative* (Pittsburgh: The Heinz Endowments, 2008), http://www.heinz.org/library.aspx
4. Film scholars complicate this assessment by using the term "spectator" in a theoretical way to refer to a "hypothetical entity, a 'position', 'role', or 'space' constructed by the text." See Carl R. Plantinga, *Moving Viewers: American Film and the Spectator's Experience* (Berkeley: University of California Press, 2009), 16–17.
5. Richard Butsch, *The Citizen Audience: Crowds, Publics, and Individuals* (New York and London: Routledge, 2008), 9.
6. For a look at a few selections from the range of disciplinary-based studies of historical and contemporary audiences, see Dennis Kennedy, *The Spectator and the Spectacle: Audiences in Modernity and Postmodernity*

(Cambridge: Cambridge University Press, 2009); Jonathan Gray, Cornel Sandvoss, and C. Lee Harrington, eds., *Fandom: Identities and Communities in a Mediated World* (New York: New York University Press, 2007); Nicholas Abercrombie and Brian Longhurst, *Audiences: A Sociological Theory of Performance and Imagination* (London: Sage Publications, 1998); Richard Butsch, *The Making of American Audiences: From Stage to Television, 1750–1990* (Cambridge: Cambridge University Press, 2000); and Steven J. Tepper and Bill Ivey, *Engaging Art: The Next Great Transformation of America's Cultural Life.*

7. Antonio Gramsci, Geoffrey N. Smith, and Quintin Hoare, trans., *Selections from the Prison Notebooks of Antonio Gramsci* (New York: International Publishers, 1971), 276.

8. "Live From Cyberspace: or, I was sitting at my computer this guy appeared he thought I was a bot," *PAJ: A Journal of Performance and Art 24*, no. 1 (2002): 17.

9. Nancy Cantor and Stephen D. Lavine, "Taking Public Scholarship Seriously" in *The Chronicle Review 52*, no. 40 (2006): B20.

10. Susan Bennett's widely read *Theater Audiences: A Theory of Production and Reception*, for example, provides a close reading of an array of theoretical platforms and thinking on reception theory from the 1960s through the 1990s by focusing on the audience as spectator-in-process. Her analysis of the way in which meaning making arises in the minutes, hours, days, and weeks after the event, however, is confined to about a page and one half of the monograph (London and New York: Routledge, 1997), 164–165.

PART I   DEFINING ARTS TALK

1. Paul Bloom, *How Pleasure Works: The New Science of Why We Like What We Like* (W. W. Norton & Company, 2010), 151.

2. Jean Grondin, *Sources of Hermeneutics* (Albany: State University of New York Press, 1995), 28–29.

3. Ibid., 26.

4. Gayle L. Ormiston and Alan D. Schrift, *The Hermeneutic Tradition: From Ast to Ricoeur* (Albany: State University of New York Press, 1990), 11.

5. Ibid.

6. Ibid., 14.

7. Roy J. Howard, *Three Faces of Hermeneutics: An Introduction to Current Theories of Understanding* (Berkeley: University of California Press, 1982), 2.

8. Ormiston and Schrift, *The Hermeneutic Tradition*, 16.

9. Hans-Georg Gadamer, *Truth and Method*, Second Revised Edition, trans. and rev. by Joel Weinsheimer and Donald G. Marshall (New York: Crossroads, 1991), 267.

10. Ibid., 268–269.
11. Hans Robert Jauss, *New Literary History* 2, no. 1 (Autumn 1970): 10. The article was translated by Elizabeth Benzinger.
12. Susan Bennett, *Theatre Audiences: A Theory of Production and Reception* (London and New York: Routledge, 1997), 49.
13. Terence Hawkes, "A Sea Shell," *That Shakesperian Rag: Essays on a Critical Process* (London: Methuen, 1986), 43.
14. Bradd Shore, *Culture in Mind: Cognition, Culture, and the Problem of Meaning* (Oxford: Oxford University Press, 1996), xv.
15. Ibid., 319.
16. Ibid., 315.
17. Suzanne Nalbantian, "Neuroaesthetics: Neuroscientific Theory and Illustration from the Arts," *Interdisciplinary Science Reviews*, 33, no. 4 (December 2008): 357.
18. Ellen Dissanayake, *Art and Intimacy: How the Arts Began* (Seattle: University of Washington Press, 2000), 73.
19. Bruce McConachie, *Engaging Audiences: A Cognitive Approach to Spectating in the Theatre* (New York: Palgrave Macmillan, 2008), 4.
20. Ibid.
21. Ibid., 20.

1 ROAD MAP TO PLEASURE

1. "The Hero's Journey: The World of Joseph Campbell," documentary film produced by Holoform Research Inc., Mythology Ltd., and William Free Productions, 1987.
2. *Oxford English Dictionary* (Oxford and London: Oxford University Press, 1955), 656.
3. Bradd Shore, *Culture in Mind* (Oxford: Oxford University Press, 1996), 319.
4. John Dewey, *Art as Experience* (New York: Minton, Balch & Company, 1934), 35.
5. Ibid., 37.
6. Ibid., 35.
7. See "Who Gets to Tell the Meaning?: Building Audience Enrichment," *Grantmakers in the Arts Reader 15*, no. 1 (2004): 12 and Lynne Conner, "In and Out of the Dark: A Theory of Audience Behavior From Sophocles to Spoken Word," in *Engaging Art: The Next Great Transformation of America's Cultural Life*, eds., Steven J. Tepper and Bill Ivey, 115 (New York and London: Routledge, 2008).
8. Dennis Dutton, *The Art Instinct: Beauty, Pleasure, and Human Evolution* (New York and London: Bloomsbury Press, 2009), 235.
9. George Lakoff and Mark Johnson, *Metaphors We Live By* (Chicago and London: University of Chicago Press, 1980), 3.
10. Ibid., 5.

11. Paul Bloom, *How Pleasure Works: The New Science of Why We Like What We Like* (New York and London: W.W. Norton & Company, 2010), 30–31.

12. Ibid., 34.

13. Ibid., 47.

14. http://www.csulb.edu/~jvancamp/361r15.html

15. Ibid.

16. Dutton, *The Art Instinct*, 36.

17. Immanuel Kant, *The Critique of Judgement*, trans. and intro. W. S. Pluhar (Indianapolis, IN: Hackett Publishing Company, 1987), 20.

18. Antoon Van den Braembusshe, "Sensus Communis: Clarifications of a Kantian Concept on the Way to an Intercultural Dialogue between Western and Indian Thought," *Galerie Inter/The Foundation of Intercultural Philosophy and Art*, http://www.galerie-iter.de.

19. See, in particular, Pierre Bourdieu, "The Habitus and the Space of Life-Styles" in *Distinction: A Social Critique of the Judgment of Taste* (Cambridge: Harvard University Press, 1984), 169–225.

20. Pierre Bourdieu, *Distinction: A Social Critique of the Judgment of Taste*, trans. Richard Nice (Cambridge, MA: Harvard University Press, 1984), 56–57.

21. See, for example, Paul Dimaggio and Toqir Mukhtar, "Arts Participation as Cultural Capital in the United States" and Bonnie H. Erickson, "The Crisis in Culture and Inequality" in Tepper, *Engaging Art*, 273–305; 343–362; For an analysis of the political ramifications of taste making in contemporary American cities, see Steven J. Tepper, *Not Here, Not Now, Not That!: Protest over Art and Culture in America* (Chicago and London: The University of Chicago Press, 2011).

22. See "Understanding Audience Segmentation: From Elite and Mass to Omnivore and Univore," *Poetics* 21, no. 4 (1992): 243–258. For overviews of the debate surrounding the cultural omnivore theory, see Alan Warde, David Wright, and Modesto Gayo-Cal, "Understanding Cultural Omnivorousness: Or, the Myth of the Cultural Omnivore," *Cultural Sociology*, 1, no. 2 (2007): 143 and Oriel Sullivan and Tally Katz-Gerro, "The Omnivore Thesis Revisited: Voracious Cultural Consumers," *European Sociological Review*, 23, no. 2 (2007): 123–137.

23. Richard Peterson and Gabriel Rossman, "Changing Arts Audiences: Capitalizing on Omnivorousness," Steven J. Tepper, *Engaging Art*, 313.

24. Somewhat recently the arts industry picked up Peterson's theory and began identifying omnivorousness as a positive force that is rapidly disappearing from the twenty-first-century arts economy. In a report released by the National Endowment for the Arts in the spring of 2011, for example, Mark J. Stern bemoans statistics that show

NOTES   179

cultural omnivores shrinking in numbers and becoming less active
as they age out of the arts system. See "Age and Arts Participation:
A Case against Demographic Destiny" (Washington, D.C.: National
Endowment for the Arts, 2011).

25. Robert W. Wallace, "Poet, Public and 'Theatocracy': Audience
    Performance in Classical Athens" in *Poet, Public and Performance
    in Ancient Greece*, eds. Lowell Edmunds and Robert W. Wallace
    (Baltimore   and   London: Johns   Hopkins   University   Press,
    1997), 98.

26. Ibid, 99.

27. Van Wyck Brooks, *America's Coming-of-Age* (New York: B. W.
    Huebsch, 1915), 18.

28. Russell Lynes, *The Tastemakers: The Shaping of American Popular
    Taste* (New York: Harper & Brothers, 1949), 310.

29. Ibid, 340.

30. Bill Ivey, *arts, inc.: How Greed and Neglect Have Destroyed Our
    Cultural Rights* (London: University of California Press, 2008), 24.

31. Merlin Donald, *A Mind So Rare: The Evolution of Human
    Consciousness* (New York: W.W. Norton, 2001), 253.

32. Ibid., 274.

33. Ibid., 277.

34. Gadamer, *Truth and Method* (London: Sheed and Ward, 1979),
    384.

35. Gadamer's somewhat romantic view of the power of conversation
    has been challenged by poststructuralist thinkers such as Jacques
    Derrida, who argues that meaning is made possible by absence and
    by confronting difference rather than by seeking consensus in cultur-
    ally predetermined and preordained strategies.

36. *The Oxford Universal Dictionary* (Oxford and London: Oxford
    University Press, 1955), 2126.

37. David Bohm, *On Dialogue*, ed. Lee Nichol (London and New York:
    Routledge, 1996), 30.

38. Quoted in Jeffrey S. Ravel, *The Contested Parterre: Public Theater
    and French Political Culture, 1680–1791* (Ithaca and London: Cornell
    University Press, 1999), 55.

39. Bloom, *How Pleasure Works*, 7.

40. Ibid., xi.

41. Kent   C.   Berridge   and   Morten   L.   Kringelback,   "Affective
    Neuroscience of Pleasure: Reward in Humans and Other Animals,"
    Psychopharmacology 199, no. 3 (2008): 458.

42. Ibid., 465.

43. Epicurus, "Letter to Menoeceus": wiki.epicurus.info/letter_to_
    Menoeceus

44. For two interesting yet opposite readings of Aristotle's meaning, see
    A. D. Nuttall, *Why Does Tragedy Give Pleasure?* (Oxford: Clarendon

Press, 1996) and Martha Nussbaum, *The Fragility of Goodness: Luck and Ethics in Greek Tragedy and Philosophy*, Part 2 (Cambridge: Cambridge University Press, 2001).

45. See Edmund Burke, *A Philosophical Inquiry Into the Origin of Our Ideas of the Sublime and Beautiful*, http://www.gutenberg.org/files/15043/15043-h/15043-h.htm

46. Kenneth A. Telford, *Aristotle's Poetics: Translation and Analysis* (Lanham, MD: University Press of America, 1961), 6–7.

47. James E. Zull, *The Art of Changing the Brain* (Sterling, VA: Stylus Publishing, 2002), 51.

48. Bloom, *How Pleasure Works*, 127.

49. Bertolt Brecht, "A Short Organum for the Theater" in *Brecht on Theatre: The Development of an Aesthetic*, ed. and trans. John Willett, 187 (New York: Hill and Wang).

50. John D. Bransford, Ann L. Brown, and Rodney R. Cocking, eds., *How People Learn: Brain, Mind, Experience, and School* (Washington, D.C.: National Academy Press, 2000), 118.

51. Tim Van Gelder, "Teaching Critical Thinking: Some Lessons from Cognitive Science," *College Teaching* 53, no. 1 (Winter 2005): 41.

52. See, among others: Kevin F. McCarthy, Elizabeth H. Ondaatje, Laura Zakaras, and Arthur Brooks, *Gifts of the Muse: Reframing the Debate about the Benefits of the Arts* (New York: RAND, 2004); Alan S. Brown and Jennifer L. Novak, *Assessing the Intrinsic Impacts of a Live Performance* (San Francisco, CA: Wolf Brown, 2007); and Laura Zakaras and Julia F. Lowell, *Cultivating Demand for the Arts: Arts Learning, Arts Engagement, and State Arts Policy* (Santa Monica, CA: Rand Corporation, 2008).

2   ERAS OF SOCIAL INTERPRETATION

1. Quoted in Leo Hughes, *The Drama's Patrons: A Study of the Eighteenth-Century London Audience* (Austin and London: University of Texas Press, 1971), 4.

2. My use of the term "exchange" is deliberate, evoking a sense of commerce that implies both the social dealings between people and also a kind of buying and selling occurring between artist/arts event and audience/arts consumption. Historically, most arts going has been a commercial endeavor, even when tied to civic life and civic obligations. Even the Ancient Greeks sold tickets to their annual civic festivals as a way to raise funds for future festivals and, importantly, as a way to mark participation as a form of support for community life and the role of art within it. The impact of commerce on the audience experience is, I believe, fundamental to the process of meaning making.

3. The earliest museums were founded by wealthy individuals interested in showcasing personal collections, or by groups of collectors

(trustees) who formed closed corporations allowing a few shareholders to set policy. As a result, access restrictions kept working-class visitors from attaining fully regularized admission until the nineteenth century, when the growing power of the public sphere began to put pressure on wealthy trustees to open their collections for public consumption.

4. Richard Butsch, *The Citizen Audience: Crowds, Publics, and Individuals* (New York and London: Routledge, 2008), 144.

5. Tony Bennett, *The Birth of the Museum: History, Theory, Politics* (London and New York: Routledge, 1995), 25–26.

6. *Theatrical Guardian*, March 5, 1791, as quoted in Leo Hughes, *The Drama's Patrons*, 5.

7. Terence, *The Mother-in-Law*, http://www.perseus.tufts.edu/hopper/text?doc=Perseus%3Atext%3A1999.02.0116%3Aact%3Dprologue%3Ascene%3D0

8. See Andrew Gurr, *Playgoing in Shakespeare's London*, Third Edition (Cambridge: Cambridge University Press, 2004).

9. Martha Feldman, *Opera and Sovereignty* (Chicago, IL: University of Chicago, 2007), 7.

10. Ibid., 13.

11. Susan Wollenberg and Simon McVeigh, *Concert Life in Eighteenth-Century Britain* (London: Ashgate Publishing, 2004), 80.

12. Arthur Pickard-Cambridge, *The Dramatic Festivals of Athens*, Second Edition. Rev. John Gould and D. M. Lewis (Oxford: Clarendon Press, 1988), 272.

13. Frederic William John Hemmings, *The Theatre Industry in Nineteenth-Century France* (Cambridge: Cambridge University Press, 1993), 129.

14. Quoted in Calvin Tompkins, *Merchants and Masterpieces: The Story of the Metropolitan Museum of Art* (New York: E. P. Dutton, 1970), 78.

15. See John A. Davis, "Opera and Absolutism in Restoration Italy, 1815–1860," *Journal of Interdisciplinary History* xxxvi, no. 4 (Spring 2006): 569–594.

16. James Johnson, *Listening in Paris: A Cultural History* (Berkeley: University of California Press, 1995), 16.

17. See Selma Jeanne Cohen, *Dance as a Theatre Art: Source Readings in Dance History from 1581 to the Present* (Princeton, NJ: Princeton Book Company, 1992), 21.

18. http://www.online-literature.com/wharton/innocence/1/

19. Michael Gross, *Rogues' Gallery: The Secret History of the Moguls and the Money that Made the Metropolitan Museum* (New York: Broadway Books, 2009), 55.

20. Tate Wilkinson, *Memoirs of His Own Life*. 4 vols. (London: Wilson, Spence, and Mawman, 1790), 111. Quoted in Judith W. Fisher,

"Audience Participation in the Eighteenth-Century London Theater," in *Audience Participation: Essays on Inclusion in Performance*, ed. Susan Kattwinkel (Westport, CT: Praeger, 2003).

21. Dennis Kennedy, *The Spectator and the Spectacle: Audiences in Modernity and Postmodernity* (Cambridge: Cambridge University Press, 2009), 15.

22. Ibid., 15–16.

23. Robert W. Wallace, "Poet, Public and Theocracy," in *Poet, Public, and Performance in Ancient Greece*, eds. Lowell Edmunds & Robert W. Wallace (Baltimore and London: The Johns Hopkins University Press), 97–99.

24. Arthur Pickard-Cambridge, *The Dramatic Festivals of Athens*, Second Edition. Rev. John Gould and D. M. Lewis (Oxford: Clarendon Press, 1988), 273.

25. Wallace, "Poet, Public and Theatocracy," 101.

26. Pickard-Cambridge, *The Dramatic Festivals of Athens*, 272–275.

27. Wallace asserts that both Plutarch's and Seneca's stories are almost certainly fictitious, but they nevertheless provide useful data about the climate of the Theater of Dionysus. See "Poet, Public and Theocracy," 102.

28. Pickard-Cambridge, *The Dramatic Festivals of Athens*, 275.

29. Ibid., 277.

30. Melveena McKendric, *Theatre in Spain, 1490–1700* (Cambridge: Cambridge University Press, 1992), 192.

31. Jeffrey Ravel, *The Contested Parterre: Public Theater and French Political Culture, 1680-1791* (Ithaca and London: Cornell University Press, 1999), 9.

32. Ibid., 6–7.

33. Ibid., 100.

34. Frederic William John Hemmings, *The Theatre Industry in Nineteenth-Century France* (Cambridge: Cambridge University Press, 1993), 123, 126.

35. Charles Dickens, *Great Expectations: A Norton Critical Edition*, ed. Edgar Rosenberg (New York: W.W. Norton & Company, 1999), 194.

36. Quoted in Lynne Conner, *Pittsburgh in Stages: Two Hundred Years of Theater* (Pittsburgh: University of Pittsburgh Press, 2007), 25.

37. Ibid., 25–26.

38. Lawrence Levine, *Highbrow/Lowbrow: The Emergence of Cultural Hierarchy in America* (Cambridge: Harvard University Press, 1990), 92.

39. Carlotta Sorba, "To Please the Public: Composers and Audiences in Nineteenth-Century Italy," *Journal of Interdisciplinary History* xxxvi, no. 4 (Spring 2006): 597.

40. John A. Davis, "Opera and Absolutism in Restoration Italy, 1815–1860," *Journal of Interdisciplinary History* xxxvi, no. 4 (Spring 2006): 582.

41. Hemmings, *The Theatre Industry in Nineteenth-Century France*, 105.
42. Quoted in Hughes, *The Drama's Patrons*, 71.
43. Hemmings, *The Theatre Industry in Nineteenth-Century France*, 113.
44. Thomas Forrest Kelly, *Five Nights: Five Musical Premieres* (New Haven, CT: Yale University Press, 2000), 299.
45. Ellen Barry, "Wild Applause, Secretly Choreographed," *New York Times*, August 19, 2013: AR1.
46. Ibid.
47. H. Barton Baker, "Famous Theatrical Riots," *Belgravia: An Illustrated London Magazine* 36 (July to October 1878), 482.
48. Peter Wilson, *The Athenian Institution of the Khoregia: The Chorus, the City and the Stage* (Cambridge: Cambridge University Press, 2000), 96.
49. Pickard-Cambridge, *The Dramatic Festivals of Athens*, 69.
50. "Demos: Classical Athenian Democracy" (www.stoa.org/demos)
51. Ravel, *The Contested Parterre*, 24–25.
52. Sorba, "To Please the Public," 599.
53. Ibid., 600.
54. Ravel, *The Contested Parterre*, 59–60.
55. Sorba, "To Please the Public," 602.
56. Wollenberg, *Concert Life in Eighteenth-Century Britain. London*, 82–83.
57. Conner, *Pittsburgh in Stages*, 6.
58. Wollenberg, *Concert Life in Eighteenth-Century Britain*, 14.
59. All quoted material from Drama League bulletins comes from a photocopy of an original Bulletin issued on January 30, 1914, by the Pittsburgh chapter and housed in the author's collection.
60. Interestingly, though The Drama League of America disbanded in the late 1930s, the similarly named Drama League, a nonprofit based in New York City, shares the same mission: "to increase awareness of quality professional theatre." See www.dramaleague.org
61. Pickard-Cambridge, *The Dramatic Festivals of Athens*, 97.
62. The phrase is associated with British cultural critic Matthew Arnold, whose definition of culture, "the best that has been thought and known in the world," was widely disseminated in the United States in the 1880s. See Arnold's treatise, Matthew Arnold, *Culture and Anarchy*, http://www.gutenberg.org/cache/epub/4212/pg4212.html.
63. Robert G. Allen, *Horrible Prettiness: Burlesque and American Culture* (Chapel Hill: The University of North Carolina Press, 1991), 183.
64. Levine, *Highbrow/Lowbrow*, 182.
65. Calvin Tompkins, *Merchants and Masterpieces: The Story of the Metropolitan Museum of Art* (New York: E.P. Dutton, 1970), 84–85.
66. Levine, *Highbrow/Lowbrow*, 132.
67. Ibid., 136.

68. Eliot Forbes, *Thayer's Life of Beethoven* (Princeton, NJ: Princeton University Press, 1964), 187 quoted in Kenneth Hamilton, *After the Golden Age: Romantic Pianism and Modern Performance* (Oxford: Oxford University Press, 2008), 86.

69. Hamilton, *After the Golden Age*, 85.

70. Ibid., 82.

71. Oliver Daniel, *Stokowski: A Counterpoint of View* (New York: Dodd, Mead & Co., 1982), 288-89 as quoted in "Greg Sandow on the Future of Classical Music," February 17, 2005. http://www.artsjournal.com/sandow/2005/02/applause.html

72. Matthew Riley, *Musical Listening in the German Enlightenment: Attention, Wonder and Astonishment* (London: Ashgate, 2004), 1–2.

73. Johnson, *Listening in Paris*, 3.

74. Levine, *Highbrow/Lowbrow*, 167. According to theater historians Jim Davis and Victor Emeljanow, rowdy audience behavior in England's commercial theaters lasted through the end of the nineteenth century, despite the persistence of a long-accepted narrative in cultural histories purporting a relationship between the rise of the respectable middle-class audience in Victorian England and the subsequent containment of low-brow audience behavior. In other words, the nineteenth century did not "cure" the theater audience by quieting it down, as many believe. Jim Davis and Victor Emeljanow, *Reflecting the Audience: London Theatre-going, 1840–1880* (Iowa City: University of Iowa Press, 2001), 98.

75. Paula M. Niedenthal, Lawrence W. Barsalou, Francois Ric, and Silvia Krauth-Gruber, "Embodiment in the Acquisition and Use of Emotion Knowledge," in *Emotion and Consciousness*, eds., Lisa Feldman Barrett, Paula M. Niedenthal, and Piotre Winkielman (New York: Guilford Press, 2005), 22; Quoted in Bruce McConachie, *Engaging Audiences: A Cognitive Approach to Spectating in the Theater* (Palgrave-Macmillan, 2008), 67.

76. Ibid., 97.

77. Carl R. Plantinga, *Moving Viewers: American Film and the Spectator's Experience* (Berkeley: University of California Press, 2009), 6.

78. William Webber, "Did People Listen in the 18th Century?," *Early Music* 25, no. 4 (Nov., 1997): 681.

79. Butsch, *The Citizen Audience*, 66.

80. Ibid.

81. See Lynne Conner, *Spreading the Gospel of the Modern Dance: Newspaper Dance Criticism in the United States, 1850–1923*, Chapter One (University of Pittsburgh Press, 1997) and Tice L. Miller, *Bohemians and Critics: American Theatre Criticism in the Nineteenth Century* (Metuchen, NJ: Scarecrow Press, 1981), 2–6.

82. The newspaper arts column first appeared in the antebellum period as an imitation of the European *feuilleton* and gradually evolved into a personality vehicle for the first generation of signed newspaper

critics. In the 1870s and 1880s, the columns tended to cover all
of the performing arts—the *New York Daily Tribune* published a
Sunday column called "Music and the Drama," while the *New York
Times*' umbrella page, "The Theatrical Week," was broken into
"Notes on Music," "Notes on the Stage," and "New Bills for the
Week." By the turn of the century, these columns and their authors
had become largely specialized according to discipline. See Lynne
Conner, *Spreading the Gospel of the Modern Dance*, 13–14.

83. Richard Butsch, *The Making of American Audiences: From Stage
to Television, 1750–1990* (Cambridge: Cambridge University Press,
2000), 9.

84. Quoted in Peter Smith, "Ecology of Picture Study," *Art Education*
38, no. 5 (September 1986): 48. The text in question is Oscar Neale's
Picture Study in the Grades, which was published in 1927 toward the
end of the Picture Study Movement.

85. Belief in the connection between childhood exposure to studio practice of the arts and lifelong participation (as audience members) is still
widely held among contemporary arts workers and is supported by
recent research conducted by the National Endowment for the Arts.
According to researchers Nick Rabkin and Eric Hedberg, "Long-term
declines in Americans' reported rates of arts learning align with a
period in which arts education has been widely acknowledged as deval-
ued in the public school system." Nick Rabkin and Eric Hedberg, *Arts
Education in America: What the Declines Mean for Arts Participation*
(Washington: National Endowment for the Arts, 2011), 9.

86. The text book, *Textbooks of Art Education: Book Two (Second Year)*,
was published by The Prang Educational Company (New York,
Boston, Chicago) and contains the following preface: "These books
were planned in a series of conferences and consultations with leading art theorists and educators."

87. The first pamphlets and books began appearing in the early 1830s,
beginning with the hopefully titled *Music Brought within Everyone's
Reach* (La Musique mise à la portée de tout la monde) by François-
Joseph Fétis.

88. Percy A. Scholes, *Music Appreciation: Its History and Technics* (New
York: J. J. Little and Ives Company, 1935), 14.

89. See Scholes, *Music Appreciation*, Chapter One for a thorough discussion of the history of the music appreciation movement in Europe
and the United States.

90. Public funding for the arts in the United States began in 1917 with
the introduction of the charitable tax code and was institutionalized beginning in 1957 when the Ford Foundation launched a new
model of foundational support by making arts program grants eli-
gible only to organizations with IRS nonprofit status. In 1965, the
first legislation designed to sustain direct government subsidy for
the arts was initiated through the implementation of the National

Endowment for the Arts, followed by a proliferation of state and municipal arts councils beginning in the late 1960s. The first foundation-issued reports on the health of the serious arts were issued by the Rockefeller Foundation in the mid-1960s and were focused on the need for a not-for-profit structure to support the supply side of the arts economy, a response to the poverty of imagination and aesthetic innovation within the commercial arena. See *The Performing Arts: Problems and Prospects, the Rockefeller Panel Report on the Future of Theatre, Dance, Music in America* (New York: McGraw-Hill, 1965) and William J. Baumol and William G. Bowen, *Performing Arts: The Economic Dilemma* (Cambridge: MIT Press, 1968).

91. Lynne Conner, "In and Out of the Dark," 113.

3   GEOGRAPHIES OF SOCIAL INTERPRETATION

1. Mark Rosewater, *Magic: The Gathering*, http://www.wizards.com/ Magic/Magazine/Article.aspx?x=mtg/daily/mm/157

2. Henry Jenkins with Katie Clinton, Ravi Purushotma, Alice J. Robison and Margaret Weigel, "Confronting the Challenges of Participatory Culture: Media Education for the 21st Century," http://www. macfound.org/media/article_pdfs/JENKINS_WHITE_PAPER.PDF

3. Ibid.

4. For more on the Citizen Science movement, see Alan Irwin, *Citizen Science: A Study of People, Expertise, and Sustainable Development* (London and New York: Routledge, 1995).

5. http://www.amazon.com/Avery-Durable-Binder-EZ-Turn-17032/ product-reviews/B001B0CTMU/ref=dp_top_cm_cr_acr_txt?ie= UTF8&showViewpoints=1&tag=vglnkc7321-20

6. See Charlene Li and Josh Bernoff, *Groundswell: Winning in a World Transformed by Social Technologies* (Cambridge, MA: Forrester Research, 2011).

7. Nicholas Abercrombie and Brian Longhurst, *Audiences: A Sociological Theory of Performance and Imagination* (London: SAGE Publications, 1998), 127.

8. Edward Hirt, Dolf Zillman, Grant A. Erickson, and Chris Kennedy, "The Costs and Benefits of Allegiance: Changes in Fans Self-ascribed Competencies after Team Victory versus Team Defeat" *Journal of Personality and Social Psychology 63* (1992): 725.

9. W. Spinrad, "The Function of Spectator Sports," in *Handbook of Social Science of Sport*, eds. Gunther Luschen and George H. Sage, 354 (Champagne, IL: Stipes, 1981).

10. Matt Hills, *Fan Cultures* (London and New York: Routledge, 2002), ix.

11. "Veena Versus the Superviewers" *New York Times*, March 14, 2012, MM48

12. Charles Leadbeater, *We Think: The Power of Mass Creativity* (Windsor: Profile Books, 2008), xxix.

13. Dennis Chong and James N. Druckman, "A Theory of Framing and Opinion Formation in Competitive Elite Environments." *Journal of Communication 57* (2007): 100.

14. Varda Burstyn, *The Rites of Men: Manhood, Politics and the Culture of Sport* (Toronto: University of Toronto Press, 1999), 109.

15. See Arie W. Kruglanski, Amiram Raviv, Daniel Bar-Tal, Alona Raviv, Keren Sharvit, Shmuel Ellis, Ruth Bar, Antonio Pierro, Lucia Mannetti, "Says Who?: Epistemic Authority Effects in Social Judgement" in *Advances in Experimental Social Psychology*, ed., Mark P. Zanna (New York: Academic Press, 2005): 345–392.

16. Ibid.

17. Paul J. Silvia, *Exploring the Psychology of Interest* (New York: Oxford University Press, 2006), 4.

18. David Bohm *On Dialogue*, ed., Lee Nichol (London and New York: Routledge, 1996), 9–10.

19. Lee Ross, David Greene, and Pamela House, "The 'False Consensus Effect': An Egocentric Bias in Social Perception and Attribution Processes." *Journal of Experimental Social Psychology 13*, no. 3 (1977): 2.

20. James E. Zull, *The Art of Changing the Brain: Enriching the Practice of Teaching by Exploring the Biology of Learning* (Sterling, Virginia: Stylus, 2002), 56–57.

21. See Gerard Genette, *Paratexts: The Thresholds of Interpretation*, trans. James E. Lewin (Cambridge: Cambridge University Press, 1997).

22. Jonathan Gray, *Show Sold Separately: Promos, Spoilers, and other Media Paratexts.* (New York: New York University Press, 2010) 1.

23. Ibid.

24. Ibid., 23.

25. "Rebuilding Student Supports into a Comprehensive System for Addressing Barriers to Learning and Teaching" (Center for Mental Health in Schools) http://smhp.psych.ucla.edu/summit2002/resourceaids.htm

26. See Nick Couldry, "Liveness, 'Reality', and the Mediated Habitus from Television to the Mobile Phone," *The Communication Review 7*, no. 4 (2004): 353–361.

27. Henry Jenkins, *Convergence Culture: Where Old and New Media Collide* (New York and London: New York University Press, 2006), 2.

28. Charles Leadbeater, *We Think: Mass Innovation, Not Mass Production* (London: Profile Books, 2009), xix–xx.

29. Kendal Blanchard, *The Anthropology of Sport: An Introduction.* Revised Edition (Westport, CT: Bergin & Garvey, 1995), 40.

30. Pierre Bourdieu, "How Can One Be a Sports Fan?," in *The Cultural Studies Reader*, ed., Simon During (New York: Routledge, 1994), 430-431.

31. "Sportification Process: Marx, Weber, Durkheim and Freud," *Sports and Modern Social Theorists*, ed. Richard Giulianotti (New York and London: Palgrave Macmillan, 2004), 16.

32. Kendall Blanchard, *The Anthropology of Sport: An Introduction*. Revised Edition (Westport, CT: Bergin & Garvey, 1995), 56–57.
33. Quoted in Dave Zirin, *A People's History of Sports in the United States: 250 Years of Politics, Protest, People, and Play* (New York and London: The New Press, 2008), 3.
34. Quoted in Conner, *Pittsburgh in Stages*, 53.
35. For more information on the role and history of statistical analysis in baseball spectatorship see Alan Schwarz, *The Numbers Game: Baseball's Lifelong Fascination with Statistics* (New York: Thomas Dunne Books, 2004).
36. John Horne, *Sport in Consumer Culture* (New York: Palgrave Macmillan, 2006), 41.
37. Grant Jarvie, *Sport, Culture and Society: An Introduction* (London: Routledge, 2006), 141.
38. https://play.google.com/store/apps/details?id=com.yinzcam.nfl.steelers&hl=en
39. http://builtforhockey.com/top-15-hockey-websites
40. Related material in this section was previously published in Lynne Conner, "e-Interpreting: The Audience as Cultural Repository," *Theatre Annual: A Journal of Performance Studies* 65 (2012): 23.
41. Ibid. For a review of the critical literature surrounding female sports fans, see Victoria K. Gosling, "Girls Allowed?: The Marginalization of Female Sports Fans," in *Fandom: Identities and Communities in a Mediated World*, eds., Jonathan Gray, Cornel Sandvoss, and C. Lee Harrington, , 250–260 (New York: New York University Press, 2007).
42. Quotes in Daniel McGinn, "Let's Talk Touchdowns" http://www.thedailybeast.com/newsweek/2008/11/20/let-s-talk-touchdowns.html
43. Jean M. McCormick, *Talk Sports like a Pro: 99 Secrets to Becoming a Sports Goddess* (New York: Penguin, 1999).
44. Penelope Trunk, "The Brazen Careerist," January 13, 2010, http://www.readthehook.com/86681/brazen-careerist-sports-talk-win-faking-it-pro
45. See http://www.forbes.com/sites/tomvanriper/2012/10/02/the-sports-women-watch-2 and www.womentalksports.com/index.php
46. Vin Crosbie, "Rebuilding Media," *Corante*: http://rebuildingmedia.corante.com/archives/2006/04/27/what_is_new_media.php
47. Ibid.
48. Mark Andrejevic, "Mediated Interactivity: Tools for Democracy or Tools for Control," *Communication Currents: Knowledge for Communicating Well* 2, no. 1 (February 2007): http://www.natcom.org/CommCurrentsArticle.aspx?id=840
49. http://www.facebook.com/help/search/?q=like.
50. Sherry Turkle, "The Flight from Conversation," *New York Times*, April 22, 2012, SR1.

51. Ibid.
52. Nick Couldry, *Media, Society, World: Social Theory and Digital Media Practice* (Cambridge: Polity Press, 2012), 15.
53. Gray, *Show Sold Separately*, 210.
54. http://blogs.amctv.com/mad-men/episodes/
55. http://www.sho.com/site/message/boards.do?groupid=1633
56. http://thechaselounge.net/showthread.php?t=2204
57. http://www.amctv.com/shows/talking-dead/about
58. http://theopenutopia.org/social-book
59. Jennifer Howard, "With 'Social Reading,' Books Become Places to Meet," *Chronicle of Higher Education*, November 26, 2012, http://chronicle.com/article/Social-Reading-Projects/135908
60. http://www.kobobooks.com/readinglife?utm_source=AffiliateNetwork&utm_medium=Affiliate&utm_campaign=Affiliate
61. http://www.wattpad.com/
62. "Why Wattpad Works," *The Guardian*, July 6, 2012, http://www.guardian.co.uk/books/2012/jul/06/margaret-atwood-wattpad-online-writing?newsfeed=true
63. Jesper Juul, *A Casual Revolution: Reinventing Video Games and Their Players* (Cambridge: MIT Press, 2009), 128.
64. Ibid., 121.
65. This is not to gloss over the problematic nature of the culture of talk in the gaming sphere, where homophobic, sexist, and racist language is known to be rampant. For further reading, see Betsy James DiSalvo, Kevin Crowley, and Roy Norwood, "Learning in Context: Digital Games and Young Black Men," *Games and Culture*, 3.2 (2008), 131–141 and Tanner Higgin, "Blackless Fantasy: The Disappearance of Race in Massively Multiplayer Online Role-Playing Games," *Games and Culture* 4.1 (2008), 3–26.
66. Garry Crawford and Jason Rutter, "Playing the Game: Performance in Digital Game Audiences," in *Fandom*, eds, Jonathan Gray, Cornel Sandvoss and C. Lee Harrington (New York and London: New York University Press, 2007), 279.

PART II   FACILITATING ARTS TALK

1. http://www.gutenberg.org/cache/epub/2891/pg2891.txt
2. William Cronon, "Only Connect," *The American Scholar 67*, no. 4 (Autumn 1998), www.williamcronon.net/writing/Cronon_Only_Connect.pdf
3. Christopher B. Nelson, "The Relevance of a Liberal Education in the 21st Century and…Beyond" (keynote address of president of St. John's College, Annapolis, Maryland, at a Colloquium at the University of Mary Washington on the Future of Liberal Education, November 5, 2007), http://www.stjohnscollege.edu/about/AN/archives.shtml

4. Marilla Svinicki, Anastasia Hagen, and Debra Meyer, "How Research on Learning Strengthens Instruction," in *Teaching on Solid Ground: Using Scholarship to Improve Practice*, eds., Robert Menges and Maryellen Weimer, 273 (San Francisco, CA: Jossey-Bass, 1996).
5. Joseph Margolis and David E. Cooper, eds., "Interpretation," *A Companion to Aesthetics* (Oxford: Blackwell, 1992), 237.

4   Building Audience Learning Communities

1. Jacque Rancière, *The Emancipated Spectator* (London and New York: Verso, 2009), 11.
2. John D. Bransford, Ann L. Brown, Rodney R. Cocking, eds. *How People Learn: Brain, Mind, Experience, and School* (Washington, DC: National Academy Press, 2000), 4.
3. James E. Zull, *The Art of Changing the Brain: Enriching Teaching by Exploring the Biology of Learning* (Sertling, VA: Stylus, 2002), 98.
4. Ibid., 104.
5. Bransford, Brown, Cocking, *How People Learn*, 116.
6. Ibid., 116–117.
7. Zull, *The Art of Changing the Brain*, 122.
8. Bransford, Brown, Cocking, *How People Learn*, 5.
9. Zull, *The Art of Changing the Brain*, 105.
10. Cited in Patricia Cranton, *Understanding and Promoting Transformative Learning: A Guide for Educators of Adults* (San Francisco, CA: Jossey-Bass, 1994), 9.
11. Thomas B. Sheridan, "Attention and Its Allocation: Fragments of a Model," in *Attention: From Theory to Practice*, eds. Arthur F. Kramer, Douglas A. Wiegmann, and Alex Kirlik, 16 (Oxford: Oxford University Press, 2007).
12. Ibid.
13. David Kahneman, *Thinking, Fast and Slow* (New York: Farrar, Straus and Giroux, 2011), ebook location 629.
14. Ibid., ebook location 196.
15. Ibid, ebook location 690.
16. Jeffrey Ravel, *The Contested Parterre: Public Theater and French Political Culture, 1680–1791* (Ithaca and London: Cornell University Press, 1999), 54.
17. Bruce McConachie, *Engaging Audiences: A Cognitive Approach to Spectating in the Theatre* (Palgrave-Macmillan, 2008), 28.
18. See John S. Noffsinger, *Correspondence Schools, Lyceums, Chautauquas* (New York: Macmillan Company, 1926).
19. For a thorough investigation of the field of adult learning, see Sharan B. Merriam, Rosemary S. Caffarella, and Lisa M. Baumgartner, *Learning in Adulthood: A Comprehensive Guide*, Third Edition (San Francisco, CA: John Wiley and Sons, 2007).

20. See Jane Vella, *Learning to Listen, Learning to Teach: The Power of Dialogue in Educating Adults*. Revised Edition (San Francisco, CA: Jossey-Bass, 2002).

21. Merriam, Caffarella, and Baumgartner, *Learning in Adulthood*, 29.

22. Ibid., 30–32.

23. Phillip Hall Coombes, *The World Crisis in Education: A View from the Eighties* (New York: Oxford University Press, 1985), 92.

24. Merriam, Caffarella, and Baumgartner, *Learning in Adulthood*, 36.

25. Ibid., 35.

26. Merriam, Caffarella, and Baumgartner, *Learning in Adulthood*, 59.

27. Ibid., 68.

28. Ibid., 88.

29. See, for example, Mary V. Alfred, "Philosophical Foundations of Andragogy and Self-directed Learning: A Critical Analysis from an Africentric Feminist Perspective," Michelle Glowacki-Dudka, ed., Proceedings of the 19th Annual Midwest Research to Practice Conference in Adult, Continuing, and Community Education (Madison: University of Wisconsin, 2000), 21. Cited in *Learning in Adulthood*, 89.

30. Bransford, Brown, Cocking, *How People Learn*, 26–7.

31. See *Pedagogy of the Oppressed*, trans. Myra Bergman Ramos (New York: Herder and Herder, 1970).

32. Vella, *Learning to Listen*, 14.

33. Bransford, Brown, Cocking, *How People Learn*, 153.

34. Rancière, *The Emancipated Spectator*, 17.

35. Bransford, Brown, Cocking, *How People Learn*, 16.

36. *arts inc.*, xvi.

37. http://bwog.com/2012/11/29/lecturehop-art-and-state/

38. Bransford, Brown, Cocking, *How People Learn*, 21.

39. Zull, *The Art of Changing the Brain*, 128.

40. *"Spoiler Alert: Stories Are Not Spoiled by 'Spoilers',"* http://ucsdnews. ucsd.edu/newsrel/soc/2011_08spoilers.asp

41. Ibid.

42. In Clayton Lord, ed., *Counting New Beans: Intrinsic Impact and the Value of Art* (San Francisco: Theatre Bay Area, 2012), 73.

43. Sali Ann Kriegsman, "Meeting Each Other Half Way," *Dance/USA* 15, no. 3 (Winter 1998): 12–15, 26.

44. Jennifer Dunning, "Gimmicks and Games to Create Dancegoers," *New York Times*, July 16, 2001, http://www.nytimes.com/2001/07/16/ arts/gimmicks-games-create-dancegoers-people-aren-t-born-loving-pas-de-deux-so-art.html?pagewanted=all&src=pm

45. Patricia Martin, "Tipping the Culture: How Engaging Millennials Will Change Things" (Chicago: Litlamp Communications, 2010), 11.

46. Quoted in Vella, *Learning to Listen*, 20.

47. See Peggy Thoits and Lauren Virshup, "Me's and We's: Forms and Functions of Social Identities," in *Self and Identity: Fundamental Issues*, eds., R. Ashmore and L. Jussim, 106–133 (Oxford: Oxford University Press, 1997).

48. http://www.lcinstitute.org/about-lci/imaginative-learning

5 Fundamentals of Productive Talk

1. Daniel Menaker, *A Good Talk: The Story and Skill of Conversation* (New York: Twelve, 2010), 9.

2. David Bohm, *Unfolding Meaning: A Weekend of Dialogue with David Bohm* (London: Routledge, 1996), 17.

3. Ronald Wardhaugh, *How Conversation Works* (Oxford: Blackwell, 1985), 30.

4. Ibid., 39.

5. David Bohm, *On Dialogue*, ed., Lee Nichol (London and New York: Routledge, 1996), 7.

6. See Sarah Michaels, Mary Catherine O'Connor, Megan Williams Hall, and Lauren B. Resnick, *Accountable Talk Sourcebook: For Classroom Conversation that Works*, version 3.1 (Pittsburgh: University of Pittsburgh, 2010).

7. Parker J. Palmer and Arthur Zajonc, *The Heart of Higher Education: A Call to Renewal/Transforming the Academy Through Collegial Conversations* (San Francisco: Jossey-Bass, 2010), 29.

8. Ibid., 30.

9. Thomas Szasz, *The Second Sin* (Garden City, New York: Anchor Press, 1973), 18.

10. Rob Reich, "The Socratic Method: What It Is and How to Use It in the Classroom" in *Speaking of Teaching* (Stanford University Center for Teaching and Learning Newsletter, Fall 2003, 13.1), 1.

11. "Friends General Conference Worship Sharing Guidelines" http://www.fgcquaker.org/resources/worship-sharing-guidelines

12. Bohm, *On Dialogue*, 3.

13. Judy Brown, "Dialogue: Capacities and Stories" in *Learning Organizations: Developing Cultures for Tomorrow's Workplace*, ed., Sarita Chawla and John Renesch, 158 (New York: Productivity Press, 1995).

14. Thijs Fassaert, Sandra van Dulmen, Francois Schellevis, and Jozien Bensing, "Active Listening in Medical Consultations: Development of the Active Listening Observation Scale (ALOS-global)," *Patient Education and Counseling* 68, no. 3 (2007): 260.

15. Ibid, 259.

16. Ken Bain, *What the Best College Teachers Do* (Cambridge, MA: Harvard University Press, 2004), 143.

17. William F. Eadie and Paul E. Nelson, "Conversation in America: Changing Rules, Hidden Dimensions" in *The Changing Conversation*

in America: Lectures from the Smithsonian, eds. William F. Eadie and Paul E. Nelson, 1 (Thousand Oaks, CA: Sage Publications, 2002).

18. Julia T. Wood, "Changing Relationships, Changing Conversations" in *The Changing Conversation in America*, 138–139.

19. See Deborah Tannen, *You Just Don't Understand* (New York: William Morrow, 2007).

20. See Bobbi J. Carothers and Harry T. Reis, "Men and Women Are from Earth: Examining the Latent Structure of Gender," *Journal of Personality and Social Psychology* 104, no. 2 (February 2013): 385–407.

21. Elaine Richardson, *Hiphop Literacies* (London and New York: Routledge, 2006), 11.

22. Wood, "Changing Relationships, Changing Conversations" in *The Changing Conversation in America*, 141.

23. Geneva Smitherman, *Talkin and Testifyin: The Language of Black America* (Detroit: Wayne State University Press, 1986), 108.

24. Ibid. For more information on the culture, aesthetics, and linguistic formations of African America rhetoric, see Marsha Houston and Julie T. Wood, "Difficult Dialogues: Communicating across Race and Class" in *Gendered Relationships*, ed., J. T. Wood (Mountain View, CA: Mayfield, 1996), Elaine Richardson, *Hiphop Literacies*; Ronald L. Jackson II and Elaine B. Richardson, *Understanding African American Rhetoric: Classical Origins to Contemporary Innovations* (New York: Routledge, 2003), and Barbara Hill Hudson, *African American Female Speech Communities: Varieties of Talk* (Westport, CT: Bergin & Garvey, 2001).

25. "How Can 'White' Theaters Attract Black Audiences? Bridge the Theater Etiquette Divide," Onstage/Backstage: Covering Chicago's Theater Scene: http://www.wbez.org/blog/onstagebackstage/2011–03–07/how-can-white-theaters-attract-black-audiences-bridge-theater-etiqu

26. http://www.artsjournal.com/sandow/2013/06/white-low-affect-respectful.html

27. See, for example, reader feedback to a *Huff Post* blog by Tamika Sayles titled "Black Audiences Should Feel Included Rather than Targeted: What Is the Theatre Industry Doing to Reach Them?," http://www.huffingtonpost.com/tamika-sayles/black-theatre-audiences_b_1739184.html; and readers debating Latino audience behavior on Broadway, http://broadwayworld.com/board/readmessage.php?page=3&thread=1042937&mobile=on.

28. Benjamin J. Broome, "Managing Differences in Conflict Resolution: The Role of Relational Empathy," in *Conflict Resolution Theory and Practice: Integration and Application*, eds., Dennis J. D. Sandole and Hugo van der Merwe, 98 (Manchester and New York: Manchester University Press, 1993).

29. Ibid., 99.

194 Notes

30. See Sarah Michaels et al., *Accountable Talk Sourcebook*.
31. Robert Boice, *First-Order Principles for College Teachers: Ten Basic Ways to Improve the Teaching Process* (Bolton, MA: Anker Pub Co, 1996), 38.
32. Ivan Boszormenyi-Nagy, J. Grunebaum, and D. Ulrich, "Contextual Therapy," in *Handbook of Family Therapy*, Vol. 2, eds. A. Gurman and D. Kniskern (New York: Brunner/Mazel, 1991); originally cited in Pam Korza, Andrea Assaf, and Barbara Schaffer Bacon "INROADS: The Intersection of Art & Civic Dialogue": http://animatingde-mocracy.org/publications/papers-essays-articles/arts-based-civic-dialogue
33. Ken Bain, *What the Best College Teachers Do*, 118.
34. Vella, *Learning to Listen*, 3.
35. Michael Hays, *The Public and Performance: Essays in the History of French and German Theatre 1871–1900* (Ann Arbor: UMI Research Press, 1981), 116.
36. See Chapter 2.

6 Arts Talk

1. Bertolt Brecht, "Emphasis on Sport" in *Brecht on Theatre: The Development of an Aesthetic*, ed. and trans. John Willett (New York: Hill and Wang, 1992), 7.
2. Alan S. Brown and Jennifer L. Novak-Leonard, in partnership with Selly Gilbride, PhD, *Getting in on the Act: How Arts Groups Are Creating Opportunities for Active Participation* (San Francisco, CA: James Irvine Foundation, 2011), 5.
3. Andrew Taylor, *Cultural Organizations and Changing Leisure Trends, A National Convening, Online Discussion and White Paper* (Alexandria, VA: National Arts Strategies and the Getty Leadership Institute, 2007), 4.
4. "Audience 2.0: How Technology Influences Arts Participation" (Washington, DC: National Endowment for the Arts, 2010), 7. Other useful reports that tackle participation as engagement include: Kevin F. McCarthy and Kimberly Jinnett, *A New Framework for Building Participation in the Arts* (RAND Corporation, 2001); Chris Walker, Stephanie Scott-Melnyk, and Kay Sherwood, *Reggae to Rachmaninoff: How and Why People Participate in Arts and Culture* (Washington, DC: The Urban Institute, 2002); The Curb Center for Art, Enterprise & Public Policy at Vanderbilt's *Happiness and a High Quality of Life: The Role of Art and Art Making* (2007); Mark J. Stern, "Age and Arts Participation: A Case Against Demographic Destiny," NEA Research Report #53 (National Endowment for the Arts, 2011); and Jennifer Novak-Leonard and Alan Brown, "Beyond Attendance: A Multi-Modal Understanding of Arts Participation" (NEA Research Report #54), 2011. Outside of the US context, see "'Not for the

Likes of You': Phase One and Two Final Reports for Arts Council England" (Edinburgh: Morton Smyth Limited, 2004) and Vanessa Martin, Catherine Bunting, and Anni Oskala, *Arts Engagement in England 2008/09: Findings from the Taking Part Survey* (London: Arts Council England, 2010).

5. Clayton Lord. ed., *Counting New Beans: Intrinsic Impact and the Value of Art* (San Francisco: Theatre Bay Area, 2012), 452.

6. Alan Brown and Rebecca Ratzkin, "Understanding the Intrinsic Impact of Live Theatre: Patterns of Audience Feedback across 18 Theatres and 58 Productions" in *Counting New Beans*, 73.

7. culturalpolicy.uchicago.edu/culturelab

8. In 1991, the Lila Wallace-Reader's Digest Fund launched Building Audiences, an initiative to "help 42 nonprofit theaters around the country expand and diversity their audiences." While this program was not devoted solely to enrichment programming (some monies were used to build marketing campaigns, for example), it did provide insight and guidance for later programs such as the Arts Experience Initiative. See "Building Audiences: Stories from America's Theaters" (New York: Lila Wallace-Reader's Digest Fund, 1996).

9. "Engaging Audiences: The Wallace Foundation Arts Grantee Conference Book" (New York: The Wallace Foundation, 2009), no page number available.

10. http://projectaudience.ning.com

11. http://www.tcg.org/fifty/revolution.cfm

12. At the time of writing, the Exploring Engagement Fund was undergoing a delay for "refining the guidelines." See http://irvine.org/grantmaking/our-programs/arts-program/exploring-engagement-funds/exploring-engagement-fund.

13. This is a very small sampling of the types of audience-centered programming and initiatives in operation at the time of publication. For other compilations of audience-centered programming, see Doug Borwick, *Building Communities, Not Audiences: The Future of the Arts in the United States* (Winston-Salem, NC: ArtsEngaged, 2012); Alan Brown, "Getting In on the Act"; Lynne Conner, *Project Brief: The Heinz Endowments' Arts Experience Initiative*; Nina Simon, *The Participatory Museum* (Santa Cruz: Museum 2.0, 2010); Jennifer Radbourne, Katya Johanson, and Hilary Glow, eds., *The Audience Experience: A Critical Analysis of Audiences in the Performing Arts* (Wilmington, NC: Intellect, 2013), and a description of the 54 Wallace Foundation Excellence Awards projects at http://www.artsjournal.com/leadorfollow/features-audience-engagement-projects. For ongoing descriptions and assessment of audience engagement projects, see (among others) Nina Simon's "Museum 2.0," http://museumtwo.blogspot.com; Ian David Moss's "Createquity," http://createquity.com; and a number of blogs published in ArtsJournal.com: Doug Borwick's "Engaging Matters,"

Doug McClellan's "Diacritical," Diane Ragsdale's "Jumper," Greg Sandow's "The Future of Classical Music," Matt Lehrman's "Audience Wanted," Clayton Lord's "New Beans," and Andrew Taylor's "Artful Manager."

14. http://www.streb.org/V2/space/index.html
15. http://www.theatreinchicago.com/newswire.php?newsID=506
16. http://beyondthescore.org/about/
17. Author conducted interview with Sarah Wilkes, On the Boards Managing Director, March 22, 2010.
18. http://www.lincolnbid.org/events/view/jazz-linclon-center-swing-university-education-adults
19. http://www.artprize.org/about/mission.
20. http://www.playhousesquare.org/buzzextra/next-to-normal/century.html
21. October 5, 2009, Issue 45–41; http://www.theonion.com/articles/struggling-museum-now-allowing-patrons-to-touch-pa,2821
22. "Getting in on the Act," 5.
23. For more on the culture and history of participatory theater see Susan Kattwinkel, ed., *Audience Participation: Essays on Inclusion in Performance* (Westport, CT and London: Praeger, 2003) and Gareth White, *Audience Participation in Theatre: Aesthetics of the Invitation* (Palgrave Macmillan, 2013).
24. "Tipping the Culture," 6.
25. *Inspiriting Influences: Tradition, Revision, and Afro-American Women's Novels* (New York and Oxford: Columbia University Press), 49.
26. Two interesting exceptions include the Barrington Stage Company's iCritic project and the Hirshhorn Museum's Interpretive Guide program. iCritic is a booth in the lobby of the theater where patrons are invited to record short video responses to the shows that can be shared via YouTube, e-mail, or other social media platforms. In its first season, more than "150 videos were recorded, with the total number of views exceeding 4,400." http://www.tcgcircle.org/2011/11/critical-power-to-the-people/ The Hirshhorn protocol features three types of interpretive programming for visitors to choose from: discussion, dialogue and conversation. Discussions are essentially lectures led by experts, dialogues are facilitated discussions that "may be redirected in response to questions and interests" from the audience, and conversations "avoid the hierarchy of leaders and listeners." Miriam Weisfeld, "Make It Hurt So Good," *Howlround* (December 7, 2011): http://howlround.com/make-it-hurt-so-good
27. See Arie W. Kruglanski, Amiram Raviv, Daniel Bar-Tal, Alona Raviv, Keren Sharvit, Shmuel Ellis, Ruth Bar, Antonio Pierro, Lucia Mannetti, "Says Who?: Epistemic Authority Effects in Social Judgement" in *Advances in Experimental Social Psychology*, ed., Mark P. Zanna (New York: Academic Press, 2005): 345–392.

28. Steven J. Tepper, *Not Here, Not Now, Not That! Protest Over Art and Media in America (Chicago:* University of Chicago Press, 2011), 269.
29. See http://www.pinkyshow.org/faqs. *The Pinky Show* was a project of Associated Animals Inc., a 501(c)(3) educational nonprofit organization based in Hawaii.
30. http://www.pinkyshow.org/videos/we-love-museums-do-museums-love-us-back
31. Paul DiMaggio, "The Nonprofit Instrument and the Influence of the Marketplace on Policies in the Arts," in *The Arts and Public Policy in the United States,* ed., W. M. Lowry, 58–59 (Englewood Cliffs, NJ: Prentice-Hall, 1984).
32. Tepper, *Not Here, Not Now, Not That!,* 271.
33. Richard Butsch, *The Citizen Audience: Crowds, Publics, and Individuals* (New York and London: Routledge, 2008), 103–104.
34. Bill Ivey, *arts, inc.* (London: University of California Press, 2008), 24.
35. Author conducted interview with Andrew Taylor, February 11, 2010.
36. *Slog* News & Arts, The Stranger.com, December 10, 2009: slog.thestranger.com/slog/archives/2009/12/10/the-award-show
37. December 15, 2009: www.thesunbreak.com/2009/12/15/the-award-show-a-discussion
38. Pierre Bourdieu, *Distinction: A Social Critique of the Judgment of Taste,* trans. Richard Nice (Cambridge, MA: Harvard University Press, 1984), 57.
39. http://www.huffingtonpost.com/michael-kaiser/the-death-of-criticism-or_b_1092125.html
40. http://www.culturebot.net/2011/11/11716/why-arent-audiences-stupid-andy-version
41. See, for example, Nicholas Carr, *The Shallows: What the Internet is Doing to Our Brains* (W. W. Norton & Company, 2011) and Andrew Keen, *The Cult of the Amateur: How Today's Internet is Killing Our Culture and Assaulting Our Economy* (London and Boston: Nicholas Brealey Publishing, 2007).
42. Kenneth A. Telford, *Aristotle's Poetics: Translation and Analysis* (Lanham, MD: University Press of America, 1961), 6–7.
43. John D. Bransford, Ann L. Brown, Rodney R. Cocking, eds. *How People Learn: Brain, Mind, Experience, and School* (Washington, D.C.: National Academy Press, 2000), 45–46.
44. http://hospitalityq.com/about-us
45. Robin Pogrebin, "Come for the Drinks, Stay for the Drama, at the Public," *The New York Times,* September 22, 2012, c1.
46. http://www.bsomusic.org/main.taf?p=11,3
47. Quoted in Greg Sandow, "The Future of Classical Music," December 19, 2012: http://www.artsjournal.com/sandow/2012/12/mavericks-continuing.html

48. http://www.youtube.com/watch?v=GBaHPND2QJg
49. This redistribution of traditional status markers resonates with the trend for "placemaking," a community development concept originally deployed by architects and urban planners in the 1970s as a way to create social life in public spaces (and to suppress the central city slum-razing strategies then in operation in most American cities). According to Lynda H. Schneekloth and Robert G. Shibley's *Placemaking: The Art and Practice of Building Communities,* "Placemaking is the way in which all human beings transform the places they find themselves into the places where they live" (New York: John Wiley and Sons, 1995, 1). As an urban development strategy, placemaking intuitively involves participation because it promotes the ideal of a "sense of place" characterized by the way that people use and participate in a community's varied infrastructures. The National Endowment for the Art's Creative Placemaking initiative argues, for example, that when public, private, nonprofit, and community sectors "strategically shape the physical and social character of a neighborhood, town, city, or region around arts and cultural activities," they bring an usual range of people together to "celebrate, inspire, and be inspired" (http://www.nea.gov/pub/CreativePlacemaking-Paper.pdf). Here arts participation is linked with sense of place by virtue of a shared environment that, in the ideal, exposes citizens, whether arts fans or not, to the values of art-making and art consumption. In this construct, sacred cultural spaces are no longer necessary components of cultural vitality.
50. Vella, *Learning to Listen*, 8–10.
51. Ibid., 6.
52. Zull, *The Art of Changing the Brain*, 52.
53. Ibid., 59.
54. W. K. Wimsatt and Monroe Beardsley, "The Intentional Fallacy" *Sewanee Review* 54 (1946): 468–488.
55. Jacques Rancière, *The Emancipated Spectator,* trans. Greg Elliott (London and New York: Verso, 2009), 14.
56. Diane Ragsdale, *The Excellence Barrier: To Attract and Retain New Audiences Arts Organizations May Need to Stop Selling Excellence and Start Brokering Relationships between People and Art(ists),* http://www.artsjournal.com/jumper/wp-content/uploads/2010/09/Ragsdale-The-Excellence-Barrier-WSAA-2010.pdf
57. David Dorfman Dance program for "Prophets of Funk" at the Bates Dance Festival, August, 2012. Author's collection.
58. Nina Simon, *The Participatory Museum* (Santa Cruz, CA: Museum 2.0, 2012), 187.
59. For further exploration of the value of community partnerships see Bill Adair, Benjamin Filene, and Laura Koloski, eds., *Letting Go? Sharing Authority in a User-generated World* (Philadelphia, PA: The Pew Center for Arts and Heritage, 2011).

60. At the Santa Cruz Museum of Art & History (directed by Nina Simon), for example, community collaboration is part of the core mission. Among the many useful strategies outlined in the Museum's online guide for establishing community partnerships is this critical reminder: "Collaboration Is Based upon Communication. Get Ready to Talk." See "Radical Collaboration: Tools for Partnering with Community Members," *Museum 2.0* (February 20, 2013): http://museumtwo.blogspot.com/2013/02/guest-post-radical-collaboration-tools.html

61. See Brian Cowan, *The Social Life of Coffee: The Emergence of the British Coffeehouse* (New Haven, CT: Yale University Press, 2005) and Markman Ellis, *The Coffee House: A Cultural History* (London: Weidenfeld & Nicolson, 2004).

62. See Ray Oldenburg, *The Great Good Place: Cafes, Coffee Shops, Community Centers, General Stores, Bars, Hangouts, and How They Get You Through the Day* (New York: Paragon Books, 1989).

CONCLUSION: THE PLEASURES OF INTERPRETATION IN THE LIVE | DIGITAL ERA

1. Dwight Garner, "A Critic's Case for Critics Who Are Actually Critical," *New York Times*, August 19, 2012, MM42.

2. Clay Shirky, *Here Comes Everybody: The Power of Organizing without Organizations* (New York: Penguin Group, 2008), 16.

INDEX

audience etiquette, 3, 9
audience gestures, 46
audience leagues, 56
audience learning communities, 137–8,
　　155–68
Audience Project (Mellon Foundation),
　　141
audience reaction, 154
Audience (R)Evolution, 141
Audiences (Abercrombie and
　　Longhurst), 71–2
audience sovereignty, 43, 57, 63, 86,
　　145
Auslander, Philip, 9–10
authentic listening, 129
Authority Effect, 148–9, 151, 152
A.W.A.R.D.S. (Artists With Audiences
　　Responding to Dance Show), 143,
　　153

Bain, Ken, 125, 132
Baltimore Symphony, 157
Barrington Stage Company (iCritic
　　booth), 196n. 26
Battle of Hernani, 50–1
Beadle's Dime Base-Ball Player, 85
Beethoven, 58, 59
Bennett, Susan, 19, 176n. 10
Bentham, Jeremy, 74
Ben-Tor, Tamy, 131–2
"Beyond the Score," 143
biology. See neurobiology/neuroscience
Black Arts, 146
Blanchard, Kendall, 83
Bloom, Paul, 15, 26, 34, 36
body language, 128
Bohm, David, 32, 75, 117–18, 119, 122
Boice, Robert, 130–1
Bolshoi, 51
Boszormeny-Nagy, Ivan, 132
Bourdieu, Pierre, 27–9, 83, 153
Breaking Bad, 92
Brecht, Bertolt, 36
Brooklyn Museum, 143, 157
Brooks, Van Wyck, 29
Brown, Alan S., 113, 140, 144

Building Audiences, 195n. 8
Butsch, Richard, 42, 43, 62–3, 151

Cage, John, 114
call-response pattern, 127, 146
"Capacities for Imaginative Learning"
　　program, 116
Casual Revolution, A (Juul), 94
Cesnola, Luigi Palma de, 58
chef de claque, 50
Chicago Symphony Orchestra, 143
Chitlin Circuit, 146
circular discourse, 127
citizen science movement, 70–1
citizenship, 82–3
City Dionysia, 40, 52–3, 56–7, 113
civic festivals, 40, 180n. 2
claques/claqueurs, 49–51
class, 29–30, 42, 61, 62–3
Classical Revolution, 157
Click! 143
co-creation, 144–5
coffee houses, 166–7
cognitive theory, 19–20
collaborative problem-solving, 70–1
Comédie Française, 41, 48, 50, 51, 54
commerce, 180n. 2
community partnerships, 166–8
competition
　　arts, 56–7
　　community-driven, 143
　　controversy over, 153–4
　　conversation and, 118
　　engagement and, 69
　　gaming and, 94
　　popular culture and, 68
　　reality shows and, 92
　　sports spectatorship and, 83
Concert Companion, 158
Concert Life in Eighteenth-Century
　　Britain (Wollenberg and
　　McVeigh), 44
conflict avoidance, 161
conflict resolution practices, 130
consumer culture, 74, 79–80, 86
consumption patterns, 28

orality, 146
organizations, audience-centered, 55–6

Palmer, Parker J., 120, 125–6
pamphlet wars, 54
paratexts
  arts and, 111, 171
  consumer-produced, 80
  fan-produced, 86–7
  incorporated, 90–1
  need for in the arts, 112
  role of, 76–8
  sports-related, 81–2, 85–7
  technology and, 79, 111
  television and, 90–2
Paris Opéra, 45, 50, 54
participation
  definitions of, 2, 70, 139–40
  direct, 144–6
  engagement and, 67–8, 69
  funding and, 150–1
  marketing and, 143–4
  motivation for, 159–60
  ownership and, 70
  popular culture and, 70–3
  rise in, 2
  support for, 140–1
  technology and, 196n. 26
participatory culture, 70
patron's blogs, 142
Paulus, Diane, 145
peer-to-peer processing, 105
perceptual encounter, meaning making
  and, 19
Performing Arts in a New Era, The
  (RAND), 2
Perry, Tyler, 146
Peterson, Richard, 28
petty producers, 72, 87, 152–3
physical environment, 132–5
Pickard-Cambridge, Arthur, 47
Picture Study (1927), 63
"Pinky Show, The," 149
Placemaking (Schneekloth and Shibley),
  198n. 49
Plantinga, Carl R., 60

Plato, 16, 28–9, 35, 46, 121
play, 82
pleasure, 15–16, 34–6, 173
Poetics (Aristotle), 35–6
Politics (Aristotle), 47
popular culture
  paratexts and, 76–7
  as source for comparisons, 68–9
  See also sports spectatorship;
  television
power, 165
power distribution (in arts industry),
  3, 5, 34, 55, 64–5, 134–5, 144,
  153–4, 165, 170–1
powerful questioning, 121–2, 124, 130
praxis, 110
proagon, 52–3, 113
productive talk
  defining, 118–23
  genesis of, 98
  physical environment and, 132–5
  values and strategies for, 125–32
public opinion, 74, 143, 151–2
Punch Drunk theater company, 145

Quakers, 122, 123, 124
Querelle des Bouffons, Le, 55
querelles, 55
questioning, powerful, 121–2, 124, 130

Rabkin, Nick, 185n. 85
Ragsdale, Diane, 163
Rancière, Jacques, 110, 162
Ratzkin, Rebecca, 113, 140
Ravel, Jeffrey, 47–8, 54, 105
reader-response critical tradition, 18
reality shows, 91–2. See also television
reception theory, 1, 52
recorded performance, live vs., 9–10
reflection, 98
Reich, Rob, 121–2
relational empathy, 130
religious dialogue, 122
respect, 125–6, 128
Rockefeller Foundation, 186n. 90
Rosewater, Mark, 94, 95

Lightning Source UK Ltd.
Milton Keynes UK
UKOW06n1359150515

251626UK00003B/48/P